A Western Horseman Book

# TEAM ROPING
## WITH JAKE AND CLAY

By Fran Devereux Smith

With

Jake Barnes and Clay O'Brien Cooper

Illustrations by Dwayne Brech

Photographs by Fran D. Smith, Gary Vorhes, Kathy Swan, Rick Swan, Brenda Allen, and Dan Hubbell

# TEAM ROPING
## WITH JAKE AND CLAY

*Published by*
**Western Horseman Inc.**
3850 North Nevada Ave.
Box 7980
Colorado Springs, CO 80933-7980

*Design, Typography, and Production*
**Western Horseman**
Colorado Springs, Colorado

*Cover photograph by*
**Dan Hubbell / PRCA Photo**

*Back cover photograph by*
**Kathy Swan**

*Printing*
**Publisher's Press**
Salt Lake City, Utah

*First Printing: September 1998*

ISBN 0-911647-47-3

# DEDICATION & ACKNOWLEDGEMENT

First, I thank God for giving me the talent and putting
the desire in my heart to be a great roper.

Next, I'd like to thank my family for giving me the opportunity to
get started by providing me with the livestock and financial
support and the encouragement to try to fulfill my dreams.

I'd also like to thank my friends for their support through the
years, particularly Allan Bach for inviting me to join the PRCA
my rookie year and Ricky Green for all of his support.
My thanks to Jan and K.R. "Popeye" Boltinghouse, Llano, Tex.,
for providing me with great horses at the beginning of my
professional career. Tom Cox, Cave Creek, Ariz., also has provided
me with practice horses during my career, and Ross Gosney,
Bayfield, Colo., has provided practice cattle.
My thanks, too, to all the drivers who have hauled my horses
around the country: Mike Calhoun, Jason Lutjen,
Billy Gillum, Keith Johanson, Scott Davis, and Jeff Johnson.

Thanks, Clay, for catching every steer I turned by two feet!

JAKE BARNES

# DEDICATION &
# ACKNOWLEDGEMENT

I'd like to thank God for giving me the talents, abilities,
and opportunities in my life. He made it all possible by
giving me my parents, my family, and my friends, who
have altogether made it possible for me to succeed.
I dedicate this book to them.

I'd like to acknowledge all the great ropers and
horsemen who have gone before me, who set the mark and
provided the inspiration for me to achieve my goals.

Thanks to Jake for dragging all those steers in my loop!

CLAY O'BRIEN COOPER

# INTRODUCTION

## Jake Barnes

ALTHOUGH Jake was born in Huntsville, Tex., both parents came from ranching families in New Mexico. The great uncle for whom he was named, Jake McClure, was a world champion calf roper, and his mother's brother was top calf roper Junior Vaughan. Jake's dad, a one-time agriculture teacher and extension agent, also team roped and put on jackpot ropings.

"Roping," said Jake, "has always been a part of my family. I was always intrigued with roping. I think I was born to rope."

The fascination held, from junior rodeos through high school and into college. But the lure of jackpot roping appealed most to Jake, who was soon making a good living pursuing the sport. By 1980, he had turned professional. Then he received a call from the 1979 world champion: "Hi, I'm Allen Bach, and I'm looking for a partner."

Jake's response was quick. "Yeah, right, who is this really?"

At the time he had been in college for 3 years. His friend, Tee Woolman, another top hand, suggested that Jake team up with Bach: "You'll always wonder if you could have made it or not."

Jake and Allen made it to the National Finals Rodeo that year and roped together for 3 years. And although Jake and Clay O'Brien Cooper roped together at times prior to 1985, Clay had partnered with Tee, and Jake also had competed with team roping legend Leo Camarillo.

But it was Allen's roping clinics that forced Jake into really studying his sport. "People began to come to my clinics with their problems and bad habits: 'Why do you do this? Why does a steer do this? Why does a horse do that?' That's what really got me to understand the funda-mentals. It's not a guessing game anymore why certain things work or don't."

Because of that, Jake seldom falls into a self-induced slump nowadays. If he misses, he knows why he did and what needs to be corrected. As a result, his consistency has improved.

"Now," Jake explained, "my slumps come from a lack of horse. As long as I have a great horse, I'm going to rope great. But when I don't have a good-enough horse and have to rely more on my ability, I start making mistakes, taking shortcuts, trying to reach, to do more things than I'm capable of doing. The older I get, the more I see how great horses make great ropers. Looking back, Clay and I both had great horses at the time."

Even with the good horses, Jake commented that the team's 100-head-a-day practice habit helped put the Barnes and Cooper team at the top of the game. "Clay and I were so versatile that if we had to make a 4-second run, we were able to do it. Or if we just needed to catch the steer, we could. Our fundamentals were that good. We had every base covered. Some guys can only rodeo-rope and try to make fast runs; some guys are more conservative and lean more toward the average side. We were able to go both ways. I credit a lot of it to our persistence in practicing.

"There were points in my roping where I knew I wasn't the best," Jake went on to say, "but my work ethic has always been great. I always knew that if I worked harder than anybody else, I could get to the top. I can remember, as a child, people would tell me I had natural ability, but I never really knew what that meant. I was working extremely hard on my roping—and everyone talked about natural ability. Roping comes easier for some than for others, but it never did come real easy for me. It was hard at times, but I stuck it out.

"I think Clay and I brought team roping to a different level at the time, a higher level. The guys saw how successful Clay and I had been, and they started trying to imitate our style, picking up on it."

## Clay O'Brien Cooper

Clay was raised in California, where his stepfather, Gene O'Brien, ran weekly Saturday and Sunday jackpots for 12 years. "I had chores, cleaning the corrals, feeding every morning and evening, and going to school. When I got home, if I did good in school, then I was able to rope all I wanted. So that was the environment I grew up in, and all I really knew from a young age."

Clay roped in junior rodeos in southern California for a few years, and when he later moved to Arizona, he competed in jackpot ropings and amateur rodeos. Then he attended junior college for a year and qualified for the College National Finals Rodeo.

However, it was his early years in California that had a major impact on Clay's roping. "It was as if my life was all set up for me to learn the things I needed to learn," he said, telling of the prestigious ropings in Chowchilla, Oakdale, and Las Vegas, where the winners were determined by the average time on eight or ten head. "The emphasis," Clay explained,

"was on being able to catch more in a row, not necessarily on speed, but consistency. The guys who were considered the elite in heeling were the guys who could catch every time.

"First on the list was Leo Camarillo. He was winning championships in the Professional Rodeo Cowboys Association, but he was also the king at the average ropings. Walt Woodard was another one, and Allen Bach, Ricky Greene, and Jerold Camarillo. They were the ones I was most impressed with and wanted most to pattern myself after. There were some local guys around, too, Gary Mouw and Don Beasley, who were really good and who primarily made their living going to jackpot ropings. Those are the guys I watched really carefully."

And from an early age, Clay closely studied what the top ropers were doing. By the time he was 8 or 9 years old, he said, "I knew the direction I wanted to go. I was, I guess, good at watching and mimicking what the good ropers did. So I started trying to develop my skills, and the dream started forming in my mind about what I wanted to be and what I wanted to do."

Because, at the time, the emphasis was on the average ropings more than anything else, Clay worked most at developing his fundamental skills, the "good basic techniques," he said, that are "what it takes to be consistent when you heel a steer."

"Whatever level you're on," he explained, "whether you're a novice or a top header or heeler, everybody has to do primarily the same basic maneuvers in order to ride the horse into position and catch a steer. Your roping level is based on how well you can perform those maneuvers time after time.

But everybody has to do the same thing, so you train your reaction and response."

Clay fine-tuned his reactions and responses, then partnered with his brother-in-law, Bret Beach, in the early 1980s, when he first joined the PRCA. At the time Jake was roping with Bach, but along the way, Jake and Clay occasionally hauled to ropings together and competed as a team. Said Clay, "Jake and I always did really well together and got to be good friends. We had the same goals, so we hooked up in '85."

When two of the best partner up, winning the roping at a rodeo sometimes is easy enough. But with the wins come the losses. "It's a mental game and a physical game," Clay said. "That's what makes rodeo a tough life. This is a winner's game. You can stay alive and keep things afloat only by winning."

And win they did. Jake and Clay brought their goals to fruition, winning more team roping championships than any other team. "To win a championship," Clay commented, "there are so many things to be considered, so many variables—the luck of the draw, how you draw up throughout the year, what you're mounted on, how the horses are working, whether they're sound or sore, how each guy has roped throughout the year.

"I think it takes that extra effort. You have to reach down inside, sometimes, and just not settle for anything less than what you're after because there are so many ups and downs."

## The Winning Combination

Jake Barnes and Clay O'Brien Cooper are the winningest team ropers in history—multiple PRCA world champions,

*Clay O'Brien Cooper (left) and Jake Barnes are the winningest team ropers in history.*

champions at every major rodeo in the country and the Bob Feist Invitational, winners of the Dodge National Circuit Finals, and the list goes on.

What makes these two men special among all the thousands of team ropers in the country? Is it chemistry, talent, athleticism, personality, persistence, and perseverance, or just plain magic? All these things and more, including good horses and supportive families, enter into their winning equation.

The most telling comments, however, came from Jake and Clay themselves while taping interviews for this book, Jake at his home in Arizona and Clay where he was living in Texas. At the time, neither was aware of what the other had said.

"Jake has the best ability," commented Clay, "more than anyone else in the game—the ability to be disciplined enough, to score right to the spot, to make sure that everything is in its right place as the run's happening. A lot of times that ultimately just comes down to catching the steer. Jake is the best as a header."

"Roping with Clay," said Jake, "I always felt that I had a big advantage over all the other ropers because he's the type who never misses. At times, it put pressure on me, knowing that all I had to do was catch, and the steer was going to be caught by two feet. It will be a long time before there's another roper like Clay. He can rope them fast and still catch two feet. He's a cut above the rest."

When each was asked about the best save his partner had made during their careers, again, their responses were similar.

"I think it was four of our world championships that came down to the last steer at the NFR," said Clay, "so probably a couple of those years during the finals. Each round, the leaders would switch back and forth, and we had to make up by winning three or four go-rounds right there at the end. Jake was just coming out, reaching to the end of his rope, and sticking it on every steer."

"I would say in 1995," commented Jake, "when we won our last championship. We averaged 5.9 seconds on 10 steers. We set the record then, we both had a clock, so to speak, and we were on the same page. Clay knew exactly what I was going to do when we were in trouble; he knew how to bail us out. When he was in trouble, I knew how to try and help him out. We complemented each other so well."

These almost sound like comments from card-carrying members of a mutual admiration society. But when two men have worked together as many years as these two have, each gets to know the other almost as well as he knows himself.

Work, however, is truly the operative word in this partnership. Jake and Clay first roped together in the early '80s as second partners, pairing up at jackpot events where a roper could enter with more than one partner. They became friends and discovered their goals were much the same.

"We wanted to win the PRCA championship," said Clay. "We both had gone to the NFR every year and were competing against that top group of guys, the top three or four who are just a little bit above the rest. When you're just underneath that level, you can see that with just a little more effort, a little more knowledge, a

# INTRODUCTION

little more compatible partnership—whatever it is—you can reach that next level. That was our common goal. Jake wanted to be on top, and I wanted to be on top also."

In the spring of 1985 Clay moved near Jake in Arizona. "We practiced nonstop," he explained. "That's all we did—eat, sleep, and rope. The shared goal was the start. We were compatible as a team, and we were willing to work at it. You can be blessed with your ability and talent, but if you aren't willing to go work harder than everybody else, it won't pay off.

"That, I think, was our motto more than anything: We were going to outlast the competition; we were going to out-practice them. If they beat us, they beat us; but it wasn't going to be from our lack of putting forth the effort."

Jake's comments reflected the same attitude. "I honestly think it was the desire to win," said Jake. "We're both really competitive. And I think Clay and I were like fruit that's getting ripe. At first, both of us lacked the experience, but the talent was there. The older and more mature you get, the more you lean toward the serious side. You decide, 'Okay, I'm going to give 110 percent 365 days a year.' I think we were both ready for that; the focus was there."

Somehow, it wasn't surprising that 110 percent was the figure Clay also had used during his interview. But just what does 110 percent translate into when a header and a heeler want to win the world in team roping?

"We bought 33 steers. We ran them through three times a day, every day, 100 head roughly, and it took 4 or 5 hours to do it," said Jake. "We each got to where we knew exactly what the other guy was going to do; it became second nature. We worked 24 hours a day at our roping, and it was something we really enjoyed and really wanted. It was clockwork; it was easy; it was fun."

Clay noted, "Jake and I both looked at things the same way and could go toward our goal in almost exactly the same frame of mind—how we saw it, what it would take to achieve it. And I talk about all the things it takes, but I believe it was by divine appointment that everything fell into place. We were in the right place at the right time."

Said Jake, "Clay and I were so blessed that things worked out. It could have gone either way two or three times at the NFR, for instance, but we were always able to pull it off. We had good times together, and fun times. But it was also business; we were so focused on wanting to win. It worked."

That much has become clearly obvious to anyone involved in the world of rodeo during the past decade. What is equally obvious is that both Jake and Clay are willing to share what they have learned about team roping along the way and spread their enthusiasm for the sport. Team roping will continue to benefit from their presence for years to come.

*Fran Devereux Smith, Associate Editor*
*Western Horseman Inc.*

# CONTENTS

   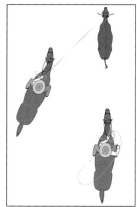

# 1 JAKE ON HEAD ROPES

MY ROPE is probably the most important tool for me besides my horse. For me to win, I have to have confidence, and there are two things I thrive on—my horse and my rope. If I have any doubt in either one, usually I won't rope very well. It's a funny game we play, and a lot of it is mental. If you get a certain feel for your rope, and it's not there, you doubt yourself.

## Feel

"Feel" is important to me in selecting the rope I use. Feel not only takes in the lay of a rope, which describes how stiff or soft a rope is, but also how well the rope works in my hand when I coil or swing it. The weight of a rope also enters into it, and that's affected by the size of the rope, which usually is determined by the size horns I'm roping.

A manufacturer's description of a rope doesn't mean much to me. I don't really go by the description on the tag—extra-soft, soft, medium-soft, medium; I go by feel—what feels good to me. I relate it to someone buying a pair of boots. No matter what size the boot, a person judges the fit by how good the boot feels on his foot.

A good roper knows what he wants to accomplish with his loop, and he can recognize if a particular rope makes his job easier or more difficult. For a novice roper, it takes time to develop such awareness, but eventually he, too, will develop a feel for the type rope that works best for him, making it easier for him to catch the steer.

*To me, the head rope I use is just as important as the horse I ride. Having confidence in both is important when I compete.*

# Lay and Size

Most ropes are marked in some way to indicate the lay, with the body or amount of stiffness in the rope ranging from extra-soft to hard. Each roper develops a feel or preference for the rope that has the right amount of body to suit him; the stiffness of that particular lay works best for his or her body type, strength, and style.

Too, a rope is sized according to its diameter. A ⅜ rope has a diameter of ⅜ inch. A ⅜-inch scant is just that—the diameter doesn't measure quite a full ⅜ of an inch. The same holds true, for instance, when you're talking about a ⁷⁄₁₆ or a ⁷⁄₁₆ scant.

Everybody's strengths are a little different. Women and young kids who start roping need a softer rope that is easier for them to swing. A big, strong man will probably use a full ⅜ or maybe even a ⁷⁄₁₆ because he has more strength. Put a light, soft rope in the hands of a man who weighs 250 pounds, and he's going to have a terrible feel for that rope. He needs more body to his rope because he has so much more strength. On the other hand, a youngster might lack the strength to swing such a stiff rope and probably would have difficulty handling it.

I see a lot of beginners choose a rope by the description on the tag, not by how the rope feels in hand. Whatever the rope is marked is what they use. But manufacturers and store clerks can make mistakes. Maybe the rope is just marked wrong, or maybe it was thrown in the wrong pile or just stored for a long period of time. When a rope has been stored for a long time, it tends to get stiffer with age and heat.

Personally, I don't like a rope that has much stiffness to it. A rope with a lot of body causes bounce. I want a fairly soft rope, but I don't want a little noodle either, because that causes the loop to collapse. I don't like a heavy rope; I use a ⅜ soft most of the time.

However, that depends somewhat on the type cattle I'm roping. If I'm roping smaller cattle with small horns, then I like a smaller, lighter rope. I would say, maybe, a ⅜-inch scant or maybe even a regular ⅜. I don't want a really heavy rope, but a softer one because I don't need as much body and don't need the loop to stay open as much with smaller-horned cattle. A rope with any bounce to it at all will bounce right off small horns a lot of times.

With big-horned cattle, I want a rope with a little more body, a little stiffer lay, so the loop stays open. When I draw older steers with bigger horns, then I want something with more weight, like a full ⅜, and anywhere from a soft to a medium, depending on the rope.

Something that can be a real problem is the length of your rope, and that's important to consider in comparison to your hand size. For instance, women and kids should use a ⅜-inch scant because it's a little less bulk in the hand, and they might also use a 30-foot rope. I normally use a 32-foot rope, but I like a little more tail than most ropers, and for rodeo roping, I like a little larger loop. For me to adjust my loop a little bigger with a 30-foot rope, I have to make my coils smaller to give me more length on the loop side and enough on the tail end. Then it feels awkward to me because of the short tail.

Usually I travel to 75 to 100 rodeos and maybe 30 ropings a year like the Bob Feist and the George Strait. I usually carry from five to ten ropes in my rope bag, just because every place I go, the cattle's horns and the size of the steers will be different.

I don't want to get to a competition and not have the right rope. I want to have the perfect rope with the perfect feel for every situation. When I have confidence in my rope and my horse, I have half the battle won.

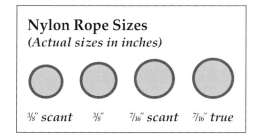

**Nylon Rope Sizes**
*(Actual sizes in inches)*

⅜" *scant*  ⅜"  ⁷⁄₁₆" *scant*  ⁷⁄₁₆" *true*

**Lay: The amount of twist in the strands of a rope, which affects how stiff or soft a rope feels.**

*"Feel" plays the major role in selecting which rope to use on any given day. The feel of a rope varies with its diameter, lay, and fiber content, and weather conditions also affect the feel.*

# Rope Fiber

Ropes are made of nylon or nylon-poly blends, and both have their strong points. Generally, a nylon rope seems to last a little longer than a blend, but the blend seems to have a faster feel to it. Most of the ropes I use are a nylon-poly blend.

It all goes back to feel. I don't know that much about how the ropes are made; but I can go on feel. I carry quite a few ropes around in my bag. When I get to an event, I pull them all out, and I go through every rope.

A rope doesn't feel the same from one day to the next. I can take a rope that feels great today, and tomorrow it may not feel as good—just because of the temperature, the way it was put in the bag, or the type head catch I had on the last run. All of this affects the rope.

So I go through all my ropes and pick one that has the feel I'm looking for. It's a process of elimination. When I run across the rope that has the perfect feel, that's the one I use for competition. Again, it's a process of elimination.

# Rope Storage

I prefer a rope bag because, for one thing, I can get more ropes in a bag than in a rope can. The rope can actually was designed for calf ropers, to control the stiffness of the rope. Because a can is smaller in diameter, I have to make my coils smaller so my ropes will fit; even then only a couple will fit in the can. I also prefer a rope bag because it was designed for nylon ropes.

But the temperature is what can make nylon feel good. Around 60 to 65 degrees is the perfect temperature for a nylon rope. The more heat it attracts, the stiffer it becomes. Whenever it gets into the 40s or 50s, the rope gets softer, so temperature is important.

Rope care is equally important with the ropes made of a poly-blend and nylon. In the winter, don't let those ropes get cold; keep them at room temperature so they have a consistent feel. If you don't, during cold weather, the rope gets really soft and has what we call backswing to it, which causes a figure eight in the loop as you swing it. I like to keep my ropes room temperature as much as possible; I don't let them get cold and soft.

In the summertime, it's the opposite. When you have the rope bag in your horse trailer, you have no climate control, and the heat in the trailer makes the ropes feel stiffer. Obviously, when it's hot, keep your ropes in the shade and try to keep your ropes cool. They'll have a better feel.

Weather really affects the feel of your rope. When the temperature or humidity changes, you have to try and compensate for the changes and maintain that good feel to your rope.

In the wintertime, I use a soft lay because, as it gets colder, the rope gets softer. So going to a stiffer lay helps compensate for the cooler temperature.

During the summer, I might do the reverse to compensate for the warmer temperatures. I use a softer lay because the rope will become a little stiffer. So I start out with an extra-soft rope, but as the heat affects it, the rope picks up some body.

In high humidity, ropes usually feel terrible; I hate it when a rope feels sticky. I use a cotton glove when I rope, and the sweat can go through the glove. If I don't wear a glove, I have moisture on my hands, so they feel sticky, and the rope doesn't feed as well.

There is one thing that helps when there is a lot of humidity and ropes tend to be sticky. Many ropers put baby powder in their rope bags and shake them up. The ropes get that slick feel to them, instead of feeling sticky.

# Breaking in a Rope

It's really important to me to break in a rope in the correct way before I go to a competition. I don't go out and immediately start roping with a new rope. What I fear most is that a new rope has a lot of bounce to it. If I don't throw a perfect loop, there's a good chance that I could pop it off the steer's horns. The second thing I worry about: The new rope won't hold on to the saddle horn.

In competition, when the rope hasn't been dallied with before, if the steer gets heavy, the rope is going to run around the saddle horn and won't grab onto the rubber as well when it is dallied. If the rope slides, it affects the handle you give your heeler because it affects his positioning on the steer.

New ropes have wax on them and run a lot in the summer. When it's really hot, they have a tendency to slip. If a steer wants to drag, the rope will run around the saddle horn. Because the rope is so hard and so slick, it won't bite into the rubber wrapped around the horn. But once a rope has been dallied three or four times and the rubber has penetrated into the rope, it grabs hold of the saddle horn better.

I don't particularly care for a really new

**Backswing:** A figure eight created by swinging a rope with the palm of the hand up as the rope rotates from 3 o'clock to 12 on the clock face. As the loop travels from 3 to 9 o'clock, the rope reverses, and the bottom of the loop becomes the top, which is what helps keep the loop open. Then from 9 until 3 o'clock, the rope reverts to its original position, with the top of the loop on top and the bottom of the loop on bottom, or at least level during that part of the rotation.

*I break in each new rope to help eliminate bounce and to keep the rope from running on the saddle horn when I dally. To help break a new rope's waxy finish, I often drag it around the arena, rotating the rope, to rough it up more equally all the way around.*

rope, just for the fact that a new rope has quite a bit of bounce to it. I don't like a rope that's completely worn out either because it has a really dead feel. I like a rope in between.

To break in a new rope, I drop all my coils and the tail of my rope and hold just the loop. Then, while I warm up my horse, I drag my rope around the arena for two or three laps. Dragging a new rope takes off the waxy finish, and then, when you dally, the rope bites into the horn and doesn't run so badly. While I'm walking or trotting, I keep rotating the loop. If I don't turn the rope over, it drags only on one side of the rope. It's kind of like using sandpaper; the rope gets just a little bit of fuzz on it. It's important to turn that rope over when dragging it so you get an even turn. If not, you only have one side that has fuzz on it, and the other side won't bite as well.

After that, I rope at least eight or ten steers with that new rope at home.

Although I've done it before, I don't think it's very smart to use a brand new rope in competition. But, perhaps, something happens. For example, suppose I was flying to a rodeo and my rope bag got lost. It's happened. Or I went to a roping, and my ropes all felt terrible. I had to crack out a brand new rope. Here's what I do.

I drag the rope around the arena a couple of times. Then I put the rope on a post and cinch up the saddle on my horse. I back my horse up and put tension on that rope to stretch it and try and take some of the bounce out of it. The stretching helps break the finish on the rope.

Also, I let the rope slide on the saddle horn, about where I dally from, to put

**Run: When a new rope being dallied doesn't bind on the horn rubber, but runs around the horn because of its hard, slick finish.**

some rubber on my rope. The rubber can penetrate the finish and help keep the rope from sliding, or running, when I do get the dally in competition.

By doing that, the rope is going to feel like it's had some steers roped with it before. Too, when those rope fibers are stretched, it takes the bounce out of the loop and coils. If you don't break that rope in and stretch it, then everything feels like it's in a coil.

# 2

# CLAY ON HEEL ROPES

*To me, working a rope helps maintain a good, balanced "feel" to it. How I form or shape a rope has a major impact on how it feels when I swing it.*

WHEN I SWING my rope, I am really in tune with the way it feels when it's going around my head. I can feel if it's just one tiny twist off; I can feel it in the bottom of the loop, the top of it, or the honda. The way I handle a rope, form it, and shape it all has to do with what that rope feels like in my swing.

Everybody develops his own feel. Some people like the back or the bottom part of the rope to curl under more—to have more backswing, as it's called. Some people like to have the rope flared more, or out the other way. It depends on your personal preference and feel. As for the individual feel in a rope, most people don't realize that you shape your rope to make it lay the way you want and to get the feel you want in it.

Probably the most common mistake I see ropers make when they come to clinics: They just pick up the rope, build the loop, swing it, throw it, pick it back up, build a loop, and they're ready to go again. A rope is made in a twist, and the rope always works toward the way it's twisted. People don't realize that. They don't know you have to work to keep a rope feeling good so that it is balanced and feels right. You shape the rope and maintain it. This is the other factor besides temperature that makes a difference on whether your rope will have a good feel or not.

## Lay and Size

A heel rope is a harder lay, or stiffer, and longer than a head rope. A head rope is from 30 to 32 feet, and a heel rope is 35 feet.

It's several lays stiffer than a head rope.

People starting out need to go with a softer lay, a medium or medium-soft. It's more manageable and easier to control when you're learning your swing and delivery techniques. A softer lay is easier to handle, easier to turn over in your swing, and easier to learn to dally with.

I don't like a really hard lay; I like a hard-medium, which is on the harder side of the medium lay. Lots of heelers use a medium-hard, which is the medium end of the hard-lay rope, but I don't like my rope to be too hard. There's a certain point when it's just too much, and you have to swing the rope too hard to make it do what you want. A too-hard rope is harder to dally with, too, and it doesn't bend around the steer's feet as well either, to stay on. That's just a personal preference.

## Rope Fiber

The fibers in heel ropes are either all nylon or a blend with some poly in it. The all-nylon rope is probably a little more tightly twisted, a little firmer feeling, and contains a little more body than the blended rope. The poly-blend is a little heavier rope, but has a little more deadness to it. It's not as lively, or coily, or springy as a nylon.

A rope, because of the fiber in it, reacts differently in different temperatures. The all-nylon rope reacts less to colder temperatures than the poly-blended because the poly in a blended rope typically reacts faster to the cold than does nylon. So I use an all-nylon rope more in cooler to colder temperatures and a poly-blended rope in the warmer to hotter temperatures.

In hotter temperatures, the poly in a rope tends to stabilize the nylon a little better. Nylon doesn't take heat very well, but it does handle the cold better. If your rope is all nylon and you're not up anytime soon at the roping, stick the rope under the truck or in a shaded, cool place. When the temperature rises in a nylon rope, it's going all over the place. That's how the fiber or the content of the rope reacts to the element of heat. The

nylon gets all squirmy, and the wax runs out of it then.

## Rope Storage

Years ago, before the machine-made ropes of nowadays, they had New England and Plymouth nylon rope, which was cut into big coils. All the rope companies would buy from those two companies, then age the rope for a year or so.

Everybody maintained their ropes back then by making a rope bag out of a gunny sack. You wet the gunny sack with water, wrung it out, and stuck your ropes in there to keep them cool. That made the all-nylon ropes feel good.

Now I prefer to store my ropes in a bag. Primarily, I'm conscious of the temperature I put any rope in. A rope is made with a twist, which will expand or get tighter as the temperature changes. The main thing to understand: Temperature makes a rope vary in what it does.

I put my ropes in a temperature that I think is going to be best—no matter where I am. If it is really cold, I put my ropes in the truck and turn on the heater. Or I take my rope bag into the motel or into the camper, where the temperature is more consistent. When you leave ropes in the trailer and it gets really cold, for example, your ropes will feel bad if you have to rope the next day. On the other hand, if it's really, really hot, I try to keep my ropes cool.

Sometimes people pick up a rope, and it doesn't lay just the way they think a rope ought to lay or have the right feel. Nine times out of ten, it's not the rope; it's just the environment. Maybe it was hot, or maybe they were in extreme cold.

I'm not as familiar with how humidity affects a rope because I haven't roped a whole lot in really humid areas. I do know that humidity makes you sweat, and it makes your ropes feel like they're sweating.

**Backswing:** Occurs when the bottom of the loop goes to the left although the loop is hanging vertically. With a backswing, a loop tends to curl under a steer's feet.

*Because temperature affects ropes so much, I'm always conscious of where I keep my rope bags. I might, for instance, put my ropes in the shade on a hot day or, during colder weather, put my bags in the truck cab and turn on the heater.*

*I usually keep several ropes in bags in my trailer so I can select the one that has the right feel, given the temperature and humidity wherever I'm roping that day.*

# Shaping a Rope

A brand new rope has to be shaped. If you pick up a brand-new rope, very seldom, when you swing it, will it feel just right. You have to work the loop, stretch the rope, twist it—basically form the rope.

I stretch my rope between my hands, working the rope by sliding it back and forth and pulling it against itself. If I make a coil or build a loop, I do it in a way to make the rope feel better to me. I'm trying to develop a feel to that rope. As I said, everybody develops their own feel when it comes to a rope, to have more back-swing or flare or whatever is their preference. That's where twisting and shaping a rope comes into play.

I'm basically shaping a rope by feel. I swing a new rope, and pull it against itself to shape it, and then I swing it again. And I do that until I get that rope to feel the way I want it to.

A lot of people don't know what to look for when shaping a rope. For heeling, the bottom of the rope in a heel loop has to be controlled; that's what's going to make your catch. That's the most important part of the loop to control, and that's basically the part of the rope that I'm forming and shaping so that in my swing and my delivery, I can be accurate. That part of my rope is controlled in my loop. If don't know where it is, or if it's jumping or curling out of place, then I'm not going to be accurate in where I put my loop.

As I said, some people like the bottom of the rope to have more backswing, and some like more flare. I like the bottom part of my heel loop right in the middle, so that with one swing, I can make it pull under a little bit or make it flare out a little bit. Depending on how I handle my hand, I can make the rope do what I want it to do.

*Each time I make a coil or build a loop, I want the rope to work—and feel—better in hand. I sometimes work a new rope by sliding it back and forth between my hands and then pulling the rope against itself.*

**Flare: Occurs when the bottom of the loop goes to the right even though the loop is hanging vertically. With flare, a loop tends to stay out in front of the steer's feet or to the side.**

# 3 JAKE ON HANDLING THE HEAD ROPE

*The more you handle your rope, the better feel you have for it.*

## Coiling the Rope

TO COIL A ROPE, start from the tail. Put the coils in your left hand and end with the honda in your right hand. Then build your loop.

To begin, hold the end of the rope with about 2½ feet of tail hanging from your left hand. Grasp the rope with your right hand and run your hand down the rope about another 3 feet. Then you shape the coil, bringing your right hand from the front, down, and to the rear. Put the top of that coil in your left hand. That's one coil.

Do exactly the same thing again—run your hand down about 3 feet and make another coil. Always try to make your coils even and have them lay flat in your left hand.

While you're making the coils, you turn the rope over counterclockwise, or roll or rotate it, to lay your coils in smoothly, just as you might wind up a garden hose. You must turn the rope over to get the twist in the coil, which makes the coils stack easily in your left hand. You have to turn the loop over every time you make a coil.

The coils in the left hand are kept flat. You don't want to stack the coils in your hand or cross them over one another. This is a real problem with beginner ropers. I have a large hand, so I can have a longer rope and still keep everything flat in my left hand. But when someone with a smaller hand has to stack the coils, the coils can get crossed over one another and create a kink or half-hitch in the rope. Then you can't let go of it easily, and that's not good.

*A sequence of three.*

1/ When coiling a rope, run your right hand about 3 feet down the rope and then shape your coil. Bring your right hand from the front, down, and to the rear before bringing the rope over to form the top of your coil, which you hold in your left hand.

2/ While holding the first coil in your left hand, run your right hand down the rope again to begin shaping the second coil.

*Do hold the coils of the rope flat in your left hand.*

*3/ Continue doing the same thing as you shape each new coil. Remember: Your coils should be even in size.*

Honda:
The eye at the end of a rope through which the tail runs to form a loop.

*Don't cross the coils over in your left hand. When the coils are smaller than average, there are more of them to hold and that increases the possibility that the coils won't lie flat and smooth in your hand.*

# Building the Loop

I build a loop by flipping the small loop backward over my thumb, catching it as it comes around under my hand, and letting the slack slide into the loop to make it larger. (See photographs.) Or you can catch the rope in front of the eye, pull the eye back toward your body, and let slack slide into the loop. Repeat this until you have the size loop you want.

The size of my loop is determined by the type of run I'm planning to make and the size of the steer's horns. If I'm making a rodeo run, for example, there's a good chance that I'll need some extension; my distance won't be as close because I'm reaching for the steer and trying to be fast. So I start with my loop slightly larger.

Also, the loop size depends on the steer. If I draw a steer I know doesn't run as hard, and I can get closer to him, I shorten everything because I want to make sure I get the rope tight on the steer's horns. That determines the type of handle I get and can give my heeler.

If I draw a steer I don't know, or one I think is going to run, I adjust to a bigger loop with more spoke between the honda and my handhold. This gives me more distance to reach with.

The average length of my spoke is about an arm's length. Some people choke up on the spoke, and some get too far back. If you catch up too short on the spoke, or too far back, either way, it throws your loop out of balance. Generally, hold the honda with your left hand and slide your right hand holding the spoke (the loop and the slack) toward your left shoulder, about to the collar bone. That's a rule of thumb, regardless of the roper's size.

The way you hold the loop and spoke in your hand is really important for heading. About 70 to 80 percent of the people do this correctly, but that means 20 to 30 percent are doing it incorrectly. The slack, the part that you dally with, coming through the eye, has to go on top. Compare holding the slack on top with holding the loop and the slack side by side.

What happens? Although this is just my theory, if you hold the rope with the loop and slack side by side, it's more awkward (to hold in your hand). Use your thumb to hold the rope these two ways—

**Handle: How well the header can maneuver a steer to best set him up to give the heeler a good throw.**

*A sequence of three.*
*1/ When your coils are complete, bring the loop around, shaping it in much the same way you did the coils.*

*2/ After you place the top of the loop in your left hand, use your right hand to slide the honda down the rope, to make the loop slightly larger.*

level and side by side. You can see that it's wider than having the slack on top of the loop.

The main reason for the way I hold the rope: I want to be able to release the loop only and still hold onto my slack. If I hold the two, the loop and the slack, side by side, there's no way I can do that. At some point, I have to release both the loop and the slack and then try to pick the one back up. This really affects the delivery in your throw. Most of the time, if someone lets go of the loop, the hand automatically goes down to pick up the slack.

Having one on top of the other lets me control my loop. I don't really feel I make a throw; all I do is let go of the loop part of

*3/ Notice how flat and smooth both the coils and the loop now are in my left hand.*

**Spoke:**
The distance between the honda and your hand holding the loop, made up of both the loop and the slack.

the rope. Most guys throw the whole rope and then try to pick the slack back up. But I try to get the rope out on the end of my fingertips, and when I release, I let go of just the loop. I use the loop to catch the horns, and I use the slack to get the rope tight around the steer's horns before I take it to the horn to dally.

Everybody sees this a little bit differently. In the two-step, another roper throws a loop and then picks up his slack; I drop my loop and don't have to make a second move; I already have the slack in my hand. There is a fine line there, though, when I release it. And, yes, I do lose contact somewhat, but not like most guys who throw and try to pick the slack back up. And the odds are less that I will miss my slack after I release my loop.

A sequence of four.

1/ To build an even larger loop without getting a kink in it, begin with your coils in your left hand and your loop in the right.

2/ Use your fingers to help roll the loop backward, over the top of your right thumb.

3/ *With the loop draped over your right forearm, let the slack slide into your loop. The honda will move up the slack, toward your left hand, as you create a larger loop.*

4/ *Now hold the loop with the coils in your left hand as you reposition your right hand on the loop, just as you held it at the start. You can roll the loop over your right hand as many times as necessary to create the size loop you want.*

Don't choke up too short on your spoke; it will throw your loop out of balance.

Do set the length of your spoke—the distance between your right hand and the honda—at about arm's length.

Do keep the slack coming through the honda on top of the loop as you hold the two strands in your hand. By doing so you can release only the loop as you throw and maintain your hold on the slack.

Don't hold your slack and your loop side by side in your right hand, which makes it seem as if you have more bulk in your hand.

# Swinging the Rope

The most common error I see at clinics when a beginner starts swinging a rope is that he swings it too high above his head. It's a natural reaction for him to think he has to do this to keep the rope from hitting him in the head. But when you do that, you're swinging with your wrist and the heel of your palm up, and that creates a figure eight in the loop and builds in problems.

A beginner usually swings with the rope above his head rather than leading or guiding the front part of his rope into the swing with his index finger. You lead with the front part, or top, of the loop. As you rotate the rope from 3 o'clock to 12 o'clock, the bottom part of the rope turns over.

It's like you're wearing a watch and want to see what time it is. When you rotate the top part of you hand over and down, that movement brings the top strand down and the bottom strand of the rope over your head. When you get to that point, where you're looking at the watch face, you pull the rope back toward your head and lift the bottom part of the rope over your head; then you lift the front part again. When you start rotating your hand over, the loop levels out and stays open, and you get the nice flat loop you want, which means you can have better control over where the tip is going and the angle of your delivery.

There's a rhythm to swinging a loop. It's like the rhythm of a hula hoop around the waist. That basically describes the rhythm that you learn in swinging your loop.

A lot of people perceive swinging a loop from front to back as kind of like fly-fishing. I don't see that at all. To me, it's natural that the rope swings in a circular motion. I stay in the center of the circle, rather than moving the circle forward and back around me. The wedding ring loop that trick ropers use is basically the same thing, but now, when you're roping, you have both strands in your hand and are swinging them both around and around.

In swinging a rope, I keep my shoulders parallel to the steer or dummy and my body posture forward. At clinics, I see a lot of people swing a rope with the hand really high; that puts the rope that much farther away from the steer's horns.

*Don't swing a rope with the heel of your hand up. That creates a figure eight in your loop.*

I also see guys who get their arms too far forward with their shoulders too square. Then you lose power because you swing more with the wrist, and don't use the strength in the arm and shoulder. The wrist, elbow, and shoulder all have to rotate at the same time to get maximum power in your swing. Imagine having a rock tied on the end of the rope so you can swing it. You put your shoulder and arm into your swing, pointing your left shoulder forward and cocking your right shoulder back. That's where you get the most power.

Some people don't understand the feel of the weight on the end of the loop—the tip. That weight is where you get the momentum of your swing and that's also what's going to make the rope feed into your loop to make it larger. If your swing is at the end of your wrist, but doesn't use the whole arm, you can get up some momentum to feed the rope, but it will be a lot harder, and you won't get up to full power.

31

*A sequence of four.*
*1/ Lead or guide the loop into the swing with your index finger.*

*2/ As your loop moves through the rotation of the swing, the bottom part of the loop will turn over as the heel of your hand rotates up. This is the point where you pull the rope back and lift it to clear your head.*

3/ *As the rotation continues, the front of the loop, where your honda is, moves to the top and takes the lead to complete the rotation.*

4/ *At the end of the swing, your index finger is still in proper position to again guide the rope through the next rotation.*

*Don't extend your arm and your elbow too much in your swing. That forces you into swinging more with your wrist, and you lose power in your swing.*

*Don't hold your shoulder too far back as you swing. Keep your shoulders square and perpendicular to the roping dummy or steer and your body position forward to maximize the power in your swing.*

# Feeding the Loop

It's a big advantage to feed a rope, to make the loop larger. If you start out with a predetermined loop size—one that is balanced and ready to rope with—it's extremely big. When you start out in the box with a big loop like that, you have a tendency to hook it under your foot, or you're going to hook it under your horse's tail.

I feel that starting out with a smaller loop is better. In one or two swings, I can have the loop balanced, fed out, and ready to rope. And if I get out a little bit late, I can use my loop as a tool to make my horse run faster. But if I have a big loop already fed out and balanced, when I leave the box, I could hook it under my stirrup or hang it under my horse's tail, or hit the chute or barrier with it.

It's a lot harder to start with a big loop compared to a small loop. When you get the smaller loop fed out and are ready to rope, the loop will end up being fairly large when it's balanced.

Feeding your loop is not a forceful motion; feeding your loop is just relaxing your grip on the top strand, which is your slack. A lot of people have problems with this. You want to hold the bottom strand tight, where the eye is, and the momentum of the swing pulls the slack into the loop as you relax your grip. Again, think of the rope's rotation, which is counterclockwise, as the face of a clock. The ideal time to feed the rope is from 3 o'clock to noon, as your hand comes around in the swing. The momentum of the swing, with the weight out on the tip of the loop, pulls more rope into your loop.

A lot of guys try to force this. You have to just let it flow. Use the momentum of the swing when it comes around; try and relax your grip as your hand rotates from 3 to 12. A lot of people try to feed from about 6 to 3, from behind the head, which creates a figure eight or backswing in the loop. The guys who do that are the ones who swing underhanded, palm up. But, done correctly, just the momentum of the swing will pull the slack into the loop.

You just open your hand a little, or loosen your grip, and it naturally feeds more rope through your hand. But it won't feed if you're holding on to the rope too tightly. You might have trouble feeding the

*A sequence of three.*
*1/ Begin with a small loop and practice feeding your loop to make it larger.*

loop if you're using a worn, fuzzy rope or if your hand is sweaty. I prefer using a cotton glove to eliminate a sweaty palm.

I hear guys all the time say, 'I can't feed a rope.' My comment on that: You have never spent enough time handling a rope. I promise you: I can take anybody and teach them how to feed a rope in 30 minutes or less.

Think about it. Everybody sits around and watches TV. So get one of those little kid ropes and, while you're sitting and watching TV, learn to handle a rope. The kid rope makes it a lot easier. Or when you go out in the morning to feed your horse, take your rope. Learn to handle your rope. It will enhance your roping so much— learning how to move your hands and

**Feed: When the slack between your coils and the loop slides into the loop to increase its size.**

2/ Do relax your grip on the slack and feed the loop as it moves from 3 o'clock to 12 in the rotation.

3/ When fed correctly, your loop stays open and flat. If you feed the loop incorrectly, it can create a figure eight or back-swing in the loop.

Lead: The amount of rope carried between your two hands, also called the slack between your hands.

improving your hand-eye coordination. Some people never move their hands enough, never do things with their hands, or learn to be creative with their hands.

You would think that brute strength is what you need for roping, but it requires so much finesse, so much fingertip control, like playing basketball. Once I get a rope fed out, everything goes to the fingertips. Then it's fingertip control. I don't feel I throw a rope; I just release the rope off my fingertips.

## The Lead

The lead is the amount of rope carried between your two hands, a little more than a coil in length. The lead is basically a coil hanging free between your hands, with the coils in your left hand and the loop in your right.

But the amount you end up with as a lead is determined by your distance from the steer and by how much rope you have

fed into your loop. If you get close to a steer, then you feed or position your hands closer together. You don't need as much lead because your position is closer to the steer, and then your shot becomes a delivery, rotating the loop off your fingertips to catch the horns.

If your position is farther back, you need your loop slightly larger. Now it becomes a throw or a reach, so you need more lead or slack between your hands. If your hands are too close together, your loop won't reach the steer's horns unless you drop a coil from your left hand. The closer your hands, the more it restricts your swing.

## Left-Handed Ropers

I have never seen a left-handed header. They just don't exist because everything about team roping is set up for a right-hander. A left-handed header couldn't rope the steer because his horse's head would be in the way if he was in position on the left side of the steer. He'd have to move over, rope the steer, flip the rope

36

*Do keep the correct amount of rope, or lead, between your two hands.*

*Don't drop a coil and create too much lead between your hands. Pick the coil back up before continuing to rope.*

over his horse's head, and grab the rope to dally with his right hand as he goes to lead the steer off. It's just not going to work effectively.

There are a lot of left-handed people who convert over to the right. When I was a kid, I was left-handed, and my dad taped my arm behind my back so I would learn how to do everything with my right hand. Now I can't do anything left-handed.

I don't particularly handle a steer any differently for a left-handed heeler than I do for a right-handed one. But it seems as though they like cattle to go straight across the arena. That's because usually a steer has a tendency, when you turn him, to wing to the outside, and that puts the steer up underneath the heeler's horse so he can't get a shot.

There are only one or two left-handers I have seen who heel the correct way. Most of them try to swing with the arm down and try to rope under the horse's neck. Button Shugart is the best left-handed heeler I've ever seen. He crosses over to

the opposite side of the steer, on the left hip. Then he has the same shot as a right-handed heeler although he's roping from the left side of the steer.

If a header turns the steer and comes across and keeps the steer on the end of the rope, it is easier for a left-handed heeler to cross over. But if the header goes straight up the arena, then the steer has a tendency to turn left; they always want to drift anyway. That's all right for a right-handed heeler, because everything stays to the outside, but not for the left-handed one.

A left-handed heeler does have an advantage over a right-handed heeler when he's roping in a small arena or when the cattle run hard and get against the left fence. Then it's easier for a left-handed heeler to get his position to rope the steer. A right-hander must ride farther down the arena to get his position, but the left-handed heeler can cut the corner and use the fence to block the steer.

# 4 CLAY ON HANDLING THE HEEL ROPE

I use the same basic procedures for handling a rope that most ropers use. For anyone, the important thing is to build a consistent pattern in how you handle a rope.

## Coiling the Rope

THERE ARE basic procedures—how you hold your rope and build it—that I do and that everybody who has roped quite a bit does. The main thing is to build a pattern in how you hold your coils and how you hold your loop so that your rope lays right and the coils lay right. They should be in order and the same size. Then when they come out of your hand, they should come out one at the time and in a succession.

To coil your rope, throw the whole rope down, and pick up the tail. You leave probably 3 or 4 feet of the tail hanging down, out of your left hand. Then you start building your coils. As you build the first one, you shape it, and then you put each coil in your left hand, making it the same size as the first one. The size of the coils in my left hand are probably about a foot, foot-and-a-half in diameter.

You hold the coils in your left hand in the order you built them. Then, they come out of your hand, one at the time and in order, so you can feed your rope out and into your loop as you need to.

You have three coils and the loop. That's standard procedure. Every good roper I've ever seen heeling uses three coils. Count the bottom of the coils, not the top. The top has four strands that you're holding, but on the bottom, you actually have three coils, then your loop, with about 3 or 4 feet of tail hanging down.

A sequence of three.

1/ When I shape a coil in my rope, I first slide my right hand down the rope and grasp it, then form a coil by using a forward, overhand motion.

2/ As I bring the top of the newly formed coil down toward my left hand, I make sure that it's the same size as my other coils. I then transfer the new coil to my left hand.

3/ I continue shaping and sizing each coil consistently. In my left hand, I hold the coils in the order I made them.

*Do make sure the coils lay smoothly in your left hand and in successive order.*

*Don't allow coils to cross over one another or tangle together.*

*Because my coils were held smoothly in my left hand, when I opened it, the coils fell to the ground in succession, just as they should leave my hand in succession when I'm actually roping.*

## Building the Loop

When it comes to building the loop, that's something you almost have to see to really understand. I'd have to measure a loop to tell you what size I use because I build it by feel and can't really tell you the dimensions.

With little cattle, I use a smaller loop. With small, fresh steers, who are kind of "waspy" and move a little faster, you want a smaller loop because you can swing it quicker. Plus, you don't need as much

*Ropers use three coils, counting the bottom of the coils, and a loop. I like to have 3 to 4 feet of tail hanging down when I build a loop.*

*A sequence of four.*
*1/ Here's one way to build a bigger loop. Start with your rope coiled and with a small loop in hand.*

*2/ Flip the loop back, over your right hand.*

loop to cover the feet because they aren't as wide as those on a big steer.

A big steer, obviously, will be a little slower moving, and cattle that have been roped out are too. Because those steers are slower in their movement, I tend to use a bigger loop to get more coverage, and I have a little more time and opportunity to use a bigger loop with slow cattle.

When I build a loop and hold it in my hand, the honda is probably a few inches above center on the loop. That's probably

*3/ As the loop rotates around from back to front, catch the loop with your forearm and across the heel of your hand. Now you can slide the slack into the loop, making it larger without creating a kink or twist.*

*4/ Then reposition your right hand around the loop and slack. The loop is not only larger, but also remains open.*

2½ to 3 feet from my hand, but that's not so great a distance when compared to the size of the loop.

When you hold the spoke in your right hand, you want the part that feeds through the honda, the slack actually, to be on top of or over to the right of the other strand of rope. Some people learn to hold this backwards, and then they have to release both when they release the loop.

*Do place your right hand far enough back from the honda. Mine is usually 2½ to 3 feet from the honda when I rope.*

*Do remember, when you build a loop, that the slack feeds through the honda and over the loop. Your right hand must be flexible so that you not only maintain your grip, but also can feed slack into the loop to make it larger.*

You should be able to hold one strand, the slack, and release the loop, which slides off your fingertips. But if you hold these backwards and let the one strand go, it's the slack. You still have the loop in your hand. So you have to turn them both loose and then regrab the rope before you can pull the slack tight.

If there's a kink in the loop, sometimes it's a good idea to flip it over your hand to keep the loop from having too much back-swing. That puts the twist the other way

*Don't choke up too closely on the honda when you build a loop, a problem novice ropers often have.*

*A sequence of four.*
*1/ Sometimes you have a kink, or twist, in your loop.
Here's one way to open it back out.*

*2/ With your right hand, grasp the loop a short distance
from the honda.*

so there isn't so much backswing.

Looking at the photographs will help
here because the photos are pretty much
self-explanatory and help clear up things
for many people.

# Swinging the Rope

The best thing in learning to swing a
rope is to have somebody show you how
to turn the rope over properly. The
swing—if learned improperly—can really

*3/ The slack feeds from your coils through the honda. Rotate the honda around the slack to take out the kink.*

*4/ Now realign your slack with the loop in your right hand. The loop is again fully open, and you're ready to rope.*

mess you up. Then it takes a while to fix—if you ever do get it corrected.

First, learn how to get the rope to travel—to come up and into the swing, go around in front, and then over your head, without having to raise your hand over your head to do it. That means if you turn the rope over correctly—turn it upside down at the right time in the rota-tion—the rope comes over your head correctly. It rotates and goes 'round, and comes back into the position again on the front side. The loop is rolling; it has a top and a bottom, so to speak, and comes around and turns over. One portion of the loop, for example, will come over your head, rotate completely around, and then roll right back into the same position where it started.

Being correct in your swing is like putting "English" on your loop, being able to put it where you need it—especially for heading. In heeling, the rope has a little less roll because you're trying to get the bottom down in your delivery. But for heading, you're trying to turn the rope over the horns, which makes the rope figure-eight after it goes on and close itself on the horns. The only way to get a lot of roll in turning that rope under, or upside down, is by learning how to use it over your head in the swing.

If you look at pictures taken at the right time in the rotation and look at proficient ropers—the guys who rope really well—at this point of their swings, their ropes are turned upside down over their heads. When you come out of that position, you can roll the rope right into the delivery.

If you don't learn to do that, then you have to swing your rope with your hand above your head in order to clear the top of it. You also have to make both pieces of the rope travel in the swing over your head. And the loop is more stationary and isn't turning over.

Find somebody who can help you learn properly how to turn the rope over. What you're trying to do is to develop correct muscle memory right from the start. If you don't get help and swing incorrectly, you can go for weeks, months, or years training your muscle memory to do things the wrong way; then it is so hard to change. If you're starting from scratch, it's well worth finding somebody knowledgeable to teach you how to turn the rope over, or roll your hand over, in your swing.

In an ideal swing, your hand doesn't come over the top of your head; it stays pretty much in the same position, but you're using a lot of wrist and elbow in the swing.

The most common mistake I see at clinics, when someone's learning to swing: They swing the rope with the palm up, instead of palm down, and they're not turning the palm over, which produces the roll of the swing. They should bring the palm back down as they come forward with the rope in rotation. My hand always stays in position, with the palm more down, pointed toward the ground or the right side and out. The worst problem is the complete opposite—palm up. Then you're just swinging two pieces of rope in a circle, and there is no rotation of the rope and, therefore, no control.

*A sequence of four.*
*1/ Learn to turn your rope over in the swing properly from the start so that you don't have to correct any bad habits later. Your index finger guides your loop through the rotation.*

*2/ As it rotates around your head, the loop will roll, or turn over. Here, the spoke side of the loop begins to turn down as the far side of the loop starts to rise.*

3/ *The far side of the loop, which continued to rise, has now turned over and is behind your head at this point in the swing. The spoke is more directly overhead.*

4/ *Continue to roll the rope as you swing, bringing it back to the original position with your index finger still leading the way.*

*Do use your wrist and elbow more, rather than extending your entire arm, when you swing your loop.*

*Don't swing with your hand too high overhead. Also resist rotating your hand and turning your palm up as you swing.*

*A sequence of three.*
*1/ Practice swinging your loop, making it first larger, then smaller, to gain better control of your rope. As you swing and the loop rotates around your right side, loosen your grip on only the slack to feed the loop. The momentum of the swing will push the slack into the loop, making it larger.*

# Feeding the Loop

After a novice gets a feel for how to turn the rope over his head, and he can make that movement and knows what has to happen, then he can start learning about feeding his loop.

You bring up the loop, and on the second swing around and in subsequent swings, you feed slack into the loop to increase its size. How much you feed into it depends on the amount of rope, the lead, between your hands. I'd say 6 to 8 inches at least.

Feeding the loop can be a little scary to someone just learning to handle rope; he has to turn the rope loose somewhat and let it slide. But feeding the loop gives you more control of the delivery of the loop and gives you a little better ability to do what's necessary with the rope in the delivery. Feeding balances the rope and gets it proportioned correctly, as far as the loop size and what's between your hands is concerned.

Feeding slack into the loop is not hard if it's done properly. You feed the slack with the power of your swing as it goes from behind you, around the right side, and toward the front. If your hand's in the correct position when you feed the loop, you can loosen up on that one strand, the slack, and the force of your swing will slide more of the slack into the loop.

Practice feeding and swinging your rope. Swing your loop and let the slack slide into the loop as you bring the rope up like you're going to deliver. Then as you bring the rope down and out of your swing, bring the loop to a stop, spread your hands apart, and pull the slack back out of the loop. This is just one procedure in rope handling.

It's something that takes a little thought at the start. But once you start handling the rope, pretty soon you don't even think about it; feeding the slack becomes natural. Watch other people do it; everybody brings up the rope, slides slack into it, brings it down, and slides the slack back out. But feeding the slack needs to be consciously done at the start as you are learning.

You can't have a death grip on the loop. The right hand has to be flexible. Learn how to hold the loop part with your thumb over the top of the other strand, the slack, and as the swing comes around, with your thumb over both strands. You learn to hold the one firmly, to keep it controlled, and loosen up on the slack so that, at the right time, you can let it slide.

Being flexible with your hands also allows you to better control the lead, the amount of rope between your hands, when you rope. When I start out, my

*2/ To pull the slack back out of the loop, as it again comes around your right side, begin to bring the rope down and out of the rotation of the swing.*

*3/ Spread your hands apart to bring the loop to a stop. This pulls the slack back out of your loop. You will end up with too much lead, or rope between your hands, and need to pick up a coil before starting the drill again.*

hands are extended. Then, as I feed the lead into my loop, I might end up with only about a foot or foot and a half between my hands right before I deliver my loop.

# Left-Handed Ropers

You can heel left-handed, but it's really difficult because the direction of things makes the angles totally opposite. Left-handed ropers have to compensate by turning the body more and in the way they position the horse. A left-handed roper pinpoints his focus on the left side. So it's more difficult, but he can apply the same rules the right-handed heeler uses. The thing he really has to compensate for is the horse's position.

You know the pattern. The steer goes out and then in one of three directions; it just depends on how the header leaves after his catch and where he takes the steer. But he will turn and change direction. A right-handed heeler always stays toward the inside of the turn; or if he's

more to the outside, he turns to the inside, and the steer ends up on his right. Or if the steer is on his left going down the arena, for instance, he turns, and the steer ends up on his right. On these basic positions, the right-handed heeler will be inside, to the left of his steer.

Another thing is the heeler's body position on the horse. His shoulders and hips are square and then, as he turns, he compensates with the angle of his swing. That's because he's trying to angle his rope to meet the angle of a steer primarily headed in this given direction.

The heeler can set up his angle to rope the steer because he will ultimately end up pretty much in the same position, no matter if the steer's body is a little bit this way or that way. The right-handed heeler sets up his angle of delivery in that 180-degree area behind the steer.

Left-handed, you have the same thing, but you're working off a different hand now. So your position or angle off the steer is totally against your body; you're

51

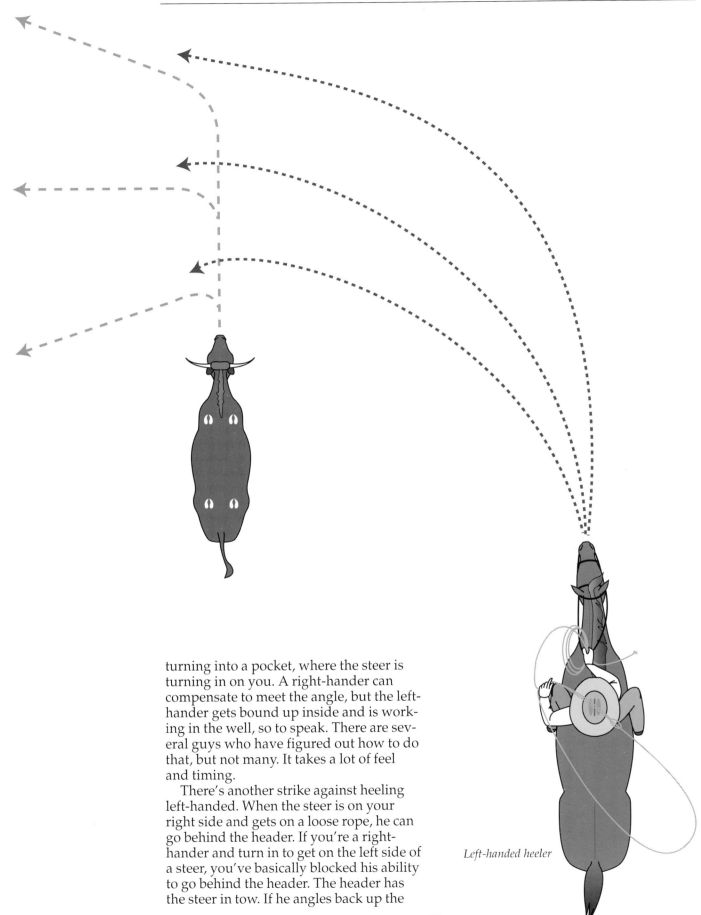

*Left-handed heeler*

turning into a pocket, where the steer is turning in on you. A right-hander can compensate to meet the angle, but the left-hander gets bound up inside and is working in the well, so to speak. There are several guys who have figured out how to do that, but not many. It takes a lot of feel and timing.

There's another strike against heeling left-handed. When the steer is on your right side and gets on a loose rope, he can go behind the header. If you're a right-hander and turn in to get on the left side of a steer, you've basically blocked his ability to go behind the header. The header has the steer in tow. If he angles back up the

52

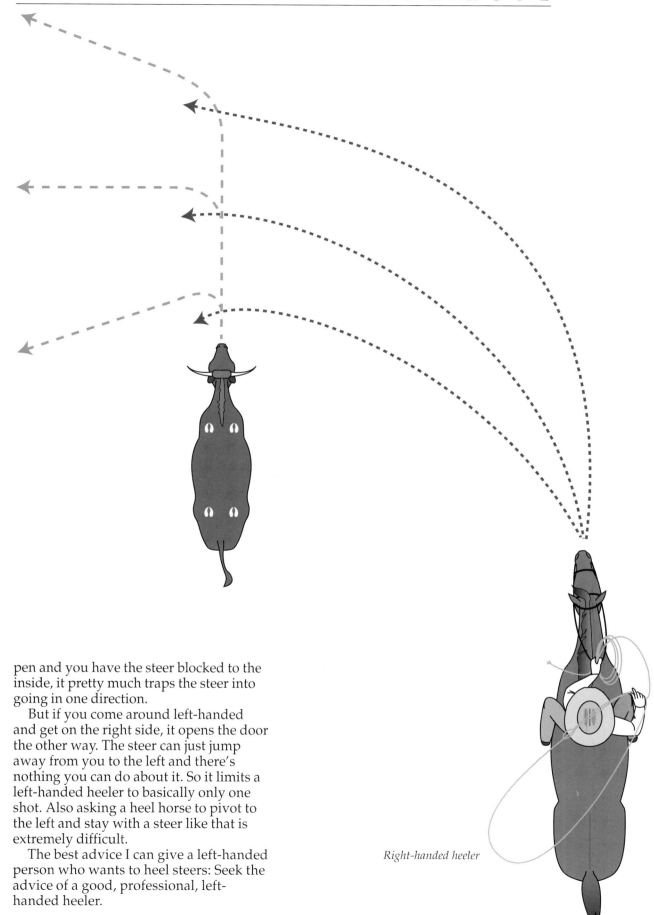

pen and you have the steer blocked to the inside, it pretty much traps the steer into going in one direction.

But if you come around left-handed and get on the right side, it opens the door the other way. The steer can just jump away from you to the left and there's nothing you can do about it. So it limits a left-handed heeler to basically only one shot. Also asking a heel horse to pivot to the left and stay with a steer like that is extremely difficult.

The best advice I can give a left-handed person who wants to heel steers: Seek the advice of a good, professional, left-handed heeler.

*Right-handed heeler*

53

# 5 JAKE ON ROPING THE HEAD DUMMY

WHEN YOU ARE comfortable handling your rope and building a loop, then it's time for you to practice on the heading dummy. A novice should have a lot of time on the roping dummy at first, maybe 2 or 3 months, to really understand and learn the fundamentals of roping a dummy.

It reminds me of playing pool. At first you tap the balls in, but you're not very good. But the more you shoot pool, the more you get into ball control, and the better you can hit and position the ball. You can actually play for the next shot. It all has a domino effect. The more you understand

and learn, the more control you have. It's the same with roping a dummy.

When I practice on the ground, I want to simulate and make it as close as possible to roping a real steer. But you do need lots of practice to learn to handle your rope and how to throw the perfect loop. It's similar to being a golfer. He won't learn to play his game during a tournament. He must go to the driving range and putting green.

The whole purpose of roping a dummy is to learn how to get the correct angle on your loop so that the curl in your rope will

*It takes lots of practice to really understand and learn the fundamentals of roping.*

come around and over the steer's shoulder without hitting it. At this point, I'm not really concerned so much about my slack or anything else. The thing I am concerned about is what I'm trying to accomplish with my loop—the reason why I rope the dummy.

I want the correct swing in my loop, so that the curl comes over the top of the bale or over the steer's back. To me that's the perfect loop, and that's all I'm trying to do when I rope the dummy. I've roped hours and hours at a time so I can perfect this loop, to make sure the tip of that rope comes over the top of the bale.

Granted, roping the dummy is different from roping live steers, but it teaches you rope control and how to focus. You begin to get the loop on the dummy, to understand the curl, and the mechanics. Also, by roping the dummy you can mentally strengthen yourself for competition by picturing a good run with all the right fundamentals.

As a kid, for example, when I was beginning to catch the dummy, I would try to catch 50 times in a row. If I missed, I had to start over. If I hit 49 and missed, I would start again and might be there all night. But that mentally prepared me and strengthened me for pressure. Competition boils down to pressure. People tense up and get a mental block.

What's the difference between the first steer and the last steer? They're all the same, but the money's won on the last steer.

# The Heading Dummy

For a heading dummy I like to use a natural set of horns with a horn wrap. I put the prongs for the horns in the end of a three-wire bale of hay, which I like better because it has enough height to it, but three-wire bales aren't easy to find in some parts of the country. I also use a canvas bale cover for the hay because an uncovered bale can be so messy.

A lot of novice ropers rope plastic, rubber, or fiberglass dummies mounted on either a sawhorse or a pipe stand. To me, that's like a golfer trying to learn to putt on cement. It's just an awkward feel. However, for some of the beginning drills that follow, I do recommend that a novice start by roping a 55-gallon barrel and a tire rim so he can learn to deliver his loop from right

to left, rather than making a forward throw.

Something I also suggest is that people start by roping a small set of horns. A big set is really intimidating and hard to rope at first. You can get frustrated pretty easily then because you will have a hard time figuring out the correct angle and delivery to get the loop on the horns. It's easier to learn by roping a small set first, then moving to larger horns.

# Focus and Concentration

Students always ask, "Where do you look? Where do you focus when you're roping?"

I don't focus on the right horn, and I don't focus on the left horn. A lot of guys have tunnel vision when they rope the dummy. They tunnel-vision to the right horn, to the left horn, or to the middle of the head. Basically, I look at both horns, but I see more to the right than I do to the left with my peripheral vision. Have you ever seen a funnel that's longer on one side? That's the way I see the steer.

I see more to the right although my concentration is fixed on the steer's horns. I can see that my heeler is in position as I go down the arena. The closer I get to my steer, my vision starts to tighten and focus on the steer's horns only.

*My focus is on both horns, but my concentration is on the left horn—the money horn.*

**Pitch:** The angle at which the loop is swung.

**Curl:** The tip of the loop that catches the left horn and continues on to go over the dummy's or steer's back to lock the loop securely around the horns.

*The bottom of the loop should go under the right horn and the tip of the rope should go around the left horn.*

*With the correct delivery, the tip of the loop continues to travel up and around to create a curl on top of the steer's back.*

To me, there's a difference between focus and concentration. Focus is what I'm seeing, but my concentration is on what I'm trying to accomplish with my loop. My focus is on both horns, but my concentration tells me not to miss the left horn because that's where I have to finish my throw. I catch that right horn 99.9 percent of the time. That tells me that when I do miss, I miss the left horn. So it makes sense for me to concentrate more on the left horn—not focus or look at it, but concentrate on it.

I know, mechanically, that the tip of the rope misses the left horn. The miss is caused by dropping the arm and trying to throw too hard on the last swing. So I concentrate more on the left horn, making sure that I get the tip of the rope over that horn—the money horn.

Although I focus on both horns, I don't want to tunnel-vision to one horn or the other horn. With tunnel vision—for example, to the right horn—that's all you're going to catch. When you focus too much on the left horn, then you start missing the right horn. So I must focus on both horns, but put my concentration on the left horn and make sure I have a smooth delivery and lots of follow-through.

## Positioning the Loop

When you rope the dummy, you also have to think about where you want the loop to strike the dummy. The bottom of your loop should go under the right horn and above the top of the right eye. That's a rule of thumb.

There is an area between the steer's horns and his ears. You place the bottom strand of your loop right in that wedge. Right above your handhold on the rope, maybe a foot and a half back from the honda, is the part of your rope that will go under the right horn. That part of the rope catches the right horn every time if it strikes the steer's head under the right

horn. And that's just the first thing to happen when you release the loop.

The tip of the rope should go around the left horn and create a curl on top of the steer's back, in the area between his horns. This locks the loop securely on the horns. This curl should hit the back of the dummy in the same spot every trip.

## Angle of Delivery

There's a certain way a correct loop must go on the steer—the bottom part must go under the right horn. In order to do that, you must pay attention to your angle of delivery, the pitch of your rope as it travels toward the dummy.

If a loop is too flat, it can sail right over the top of the steer's head, which is called frisbeeing the horns. As you rotate the loop forward to release it, the bottom part of your loop, the side farthest from you, has to be a little lower so you can place it around the right horn. It's like closing a door around the horns. Picture the loop as a door that shuts from the right horn to left.

With the correct delivery, the tip of the rope comes around the left horn and on top of the dummy with a curl, or figure

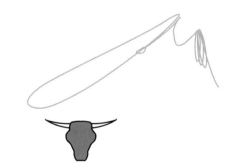

*When roping a small set of horns, you need more dip or angle on your loop.*

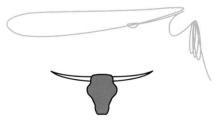

*For roping larger horns, position yourself farther back and flatten the loop out slightly in the delivery.*

eight. To me that's the perfect loop. If the curl goes too far over to the right side, then the curl could get over the horn again and create a hickey on the right horn, which is an illegal head catch.

With a loop that's too flat, the tip of the rope hits the dummy's shoulder, rather than going up and over the back. When a rope hits something solid like the bale of hay or a steer's shoulder, it kills the momentum of the loop. The rope reverses its direction, and the loop will pop off the steer's horns when you pull the slack.

The angle of delivery, with the tip down, is what makes the loop curl back and up on top. That's the key. What's tricky about roping: If you use an extreme angle to get the tip to come up and over the shoulder, then you can also set yourself up to split the horns. So you must be really focused and learn the right kind of control in your delivery.

The pitch of the rope also becomes important. The tip is down to ensure that when the loop goes on, the tip will continue to come around and go up and over the steer's back.

The smaller the horns, the softer the rope you can use and the tighter the swing, because you don't need as much follow-through; you're not covering as big a spread, or area. It's really important that you learn to swing the tip of your loop at the correct angle so the tip will go over the top of the back on the dummy, which allows the curl to lock the loop around the horns. Later, when you ride to a small-horned steer, you want to get in that same close position and make sure to use a lot of dip in your rope. Even if you have too much dip or angle on your loop, the worst that can happen is that you will rope the steer around the neck, which is better than waving your loop off and missing altogether.

Once you can rope the little set of horns, then graduate to a bigger set. That will require a completely different swing, position, and delivery. Remember: You're still trying to get the loop to go around both horns and your curl to go over the dummy's back.

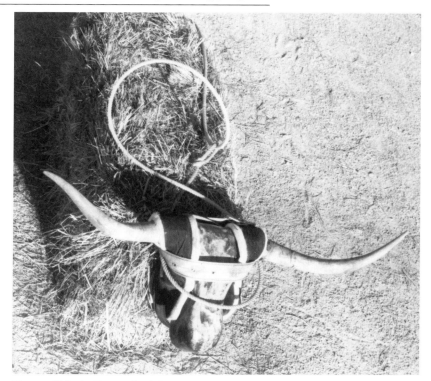

*To me, this is the perfect loop.*

*When the curl goes too far to the right side, the loop can create a hickey on the right horn.*

Hickey: An illegal head catch that happens when the tip of the loop curling over the steer's back comes too far to the right and catches the right horn again.

Frisbee the Horns: Throwing a too-flat loop that sails right over the top of the steer's head.

*A sequence of two.*
*1/ When the angle of delivery is too flat, the tip of the loop usually hits the side of the dummy, rather than curling up and over the back.*

*2/ Then the loop loses momentum and the rope reverses its direction, which makes it really easy to pop the loop off the horns when you pull the slack.*

*When you're too close to a big set of horns and the angle of delivery is steep, you'll probably split the horns.*

**Split the Horns: Catching the right horn, but having the top of the rope come in front of or underneath the left horn, rather than around it.**

If you get too close to big horns and use a lot of pitch in your swing, angling down too much, you're setting yourself up to split the horns. In other words, you'll rope the right horn and the tip of the rope will come in front of or underneath the left horn. That's because your position is too close and your delivery too steep, which also results in you dropping your shoulder and throwing too hard. When that happens, the chances are greater that you will split the horns.

When you rope bigger horns, you want a rope that has more body, a little more stiffness to it, so that it stays more open. You take a wider swing because you're covering a wider spread, and you're going to need a more precise delivery, allowing you more follow-through, to rope big-horned cattle. But don't try to throw hard on the last swing; that's a bad habit.

Instead, make sure to position yourself back far enough that you can extend your swing for a smooth delivery and flatten the loop out slightly in the delivery. You come across from right to left with your loop rather than throwing down, which is what you must do if you're too close to the dummy or steer.

Too, when you're actually roping horseback, if your horse gets too close to the steer and you try to pull him away, that motion will restrict your swing. Staying back in position from a big-horned steer allows you to make a wider swing to cover the wider set of horns and a nice smooth delivery with good follow-through.

The closer you are to a steer, the more angle you have in your delivery, so if you're farther back, naturally, your swing will be more level. However, when you deliver the loop, the tip still continues to come around and figure-eight over the steer's back. That's what you're trying to accomplish with your loop.

The curl over the back, which helps lock the loop around the horns, is not as important when roping bigger horns as it is with smaller horns. You just don't see many loops being waved off big-horned cattle, but it does happen.

Too, the angle of delivery is not quite as important when you rope big horns. Remember: If you have a lot of pitch in your rope and get too close to big horns, you're setting yourself up to split the horns.

When you rope bigger horns, make sure your position is farther back, use a bigger loop, and flatten the loop out so that you come across from right to left, rather than down, and have lots of follow-through in your delivery.

Once the rope makes the curl, then you take out all the slack. When the loop is tight on the horns, I want the slack in like an L or a backwards 7. Then, when I dally, my left hand will cross over on top, and the right hand comes underneath to the horn to make the dally counterclockwise.

However, when practicing on the dummy I'm not really concerned so much about my slack. What I am concerned about is what I'm trying to accomplish with my loop. The reason I rope the dummy is to get my angle right so the loop comes over the steer's back. To me that's the perfect loop. I've stood at the dummy for hours mastering the perfect loop with the tip coming around the left horn, going over the top of the bale, creating the curl right in the middle of the head behind the horns.

# The Perfect Loop and the Slack

To me, there are basically two misses when you're heading—popping the rope off the horns or splitting the horns.

If you pop the loop off the horns, it means the loop hit the steer's shoulder and bounced off. But everybody thinks it's the way you pull the slack that pops off the loop. To me, that has nothing to do with it, but that's been taught for years and years. Most ropers have been taught to pull the slack down by their hip, to keep from popping the loop off the horns.

I don't believe that at all. I believe that it's in the way the loop is swung and the type of delivery made when the loop goes on the horns. If you throw a perfect loop, to me, you don't even have to pull any slack.

If you have enough pitch in your swing, when the loop goes on, the tip will come back up and clear the steer's shoulder.

*Even though I was demonstrating Drill 3 here and didn't have any coils in my left hand, the photo shows the loop just as it made the curl over the dummy's back. That correct delivery, not the way the slack is pulled, helps lock the loop around the horns.*

*A sequence of two.*
*1/ Most ropers have been taught to pull the slack down by the hip to keep from popping the rope off the horns.*

*2/ With the correct delivery of your loop, the direction you pull the slack isn't a consideration. I pull mine straight out because that provides the best follow-through for my delivery.*

Then you can pull the slack. But if the loop goes on flat, when the tip comes around the left horn, the loop will hit the steer's side or shoulder.

If you can keep that tip from hitting the steer's shoulder and get the angle of your delivery steep enough, see what happens? The loop continues to come up. You can pull your slack straight up in the air, down by your hip, or straight out; it doesn't matter. I pull my slack straight out because it increases the chance for the rope to continue around and upward, kind of like the follow-through in a golf swing. A golfer's club, when he swings, goes all the way back over to the left; that's basically the way the loop goes on.

## Roping Drills

Here's how most people learn to rope: They get a rope, step up, and start trying to throw. They never put any thought into how they can make that rope go on easily. Roping a dummy is not like basketball, with a 12-inch hoop and a 10-inch basketball—now that's hard. But you can make your loop as big as you want, and you simply put the loop around the horns. It's all in how you approach your practice.

*Do make the same delivery and release from right to left when you switch from the barrel to the horns.*

*Roping a barrel helps you learn how to deliver the loop from right to left.*

**Drill 1:** Learn to rope the top of a 55-gallon barrel first. This teaches you to release your rope from right to left. You can rope from any position around the barrel, but you must mentally visualize the barrel as a dummy. The main thing is that you aren't just throwing a rope at a barrel, but are learning to rope it from the right to the left. Roping the barrel breaks you from developing the habit of making a forward throw. Instead, your delivery comes from right to left. Roping the barrel is also where you can learn how to release the loop without letting go of the slack.

**Drill 2:** Once you're able to catch the barrel confidently every time you throw, transfer to the dummy. Use the same technique and the same delivery from right to left when roping the dummy that you used on the barrel. When you rope the set of

*Don't make a forward throw down to the dummy.*

*A sequence of three.*
*1/ Drop the coils from your left hand and swing your loop.*

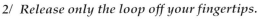

*2/ Release only the loop off your fingertips.*

*3/ Maintain your grasp on the slack. Don't release both the loop and the slack in your delivery.*

*Try putting your little finger between the slack and the loop if you have trouble releasing only the loop.*

*1/ With the coils back in your left hand, deliver the loop just as you did in Drill 3, releasing only the loop.*

horns, try to visualize them as the barrel. If you start splitting the horns when you rope the dummy, go back to the barrel until you have created the correct muscle memory for the angle and the delivery.

**Drill 3:** Most people learn to rope a dummy by using a forward throw and releasing both loop and slack from the hand at the same time, and then try to pick the slack back up. This makes you tend to not follow through in your delivery. It just doesn't make sense to me for a roper to let go of his slack and then have to pick it back up. If you do, as you let go of the loop, the slack falls, and your hand tends to drop to pick it up. That often causes you to split the horns.

This drill teaches you to get the loop on your fingertips and rotate the loop out of your hand in the delivery, allowing you to keep the slack in your hand. Try dropping the coils from your left hand and using only the loop to swing. Learn to release only the loop off your fingertips by roping the horns as if you were roping the barrel. Don't

worry about your slack yet. If you have trouble and let go of both the loop and the slack, try putting your little finger between your slack and the loop to separate them. Get used to releasing the loop only.

**Drill 4:** Once you have mastered catching the horns without releasing the slack from your right hand, put the coils back into your left hand, but continue to use the same technique. Teach yourself how to catch the horns first, and once you have made the catch and can see the tip of the rope go around the left horn, rotate your right hand over to get your slack and pull the rope tight around the dummy's horns. Using this drill, you can rotate the loop out of your hand and continue to follow through until the loop is around the horn, and then, in a continuous motion, you pull your slack. To me that's what follow-through is: being able to continue to send the loop around the horn until you know you've made the catch.

**Drill 5:** This is my newest invention . . . I'm always trying to come up with ways to help people correct their bad habits. Instead of using a set of horns, get a car tire rim and use some prongs through the holes in the rim to fasten it to the bale. A truck tire rim is

2/ *In a continuous motion, rotate your right hand over and grasp the slack.*

3/ *Using this drill, you can learn to release the loop, continue the follow-through to ensure that you've made the catch, and then pull your slack with no break in the motion.*

*Roping a tire rim helps train your muscle memory to make the correct release from right to left.*

*Even though you're roping the rim instead of horns, the loop should continue to curl in a figure eight.*

best because it's bigger. Mount the rim on a bale of hay, just as if it were a set of horns. Don't mount the rim flat and level on the bale; place it at an angle, perhaps 45 degrees, on the bale.

If you learn to rope this rim correctly from the start and train your muscle memory properly, you can train yourself not to split the horns with your loop. Again, do this by roping from right to left around the rim, not down to it. The tip of your loop can still come up and over the back of the dummy.

## Practicing Out of Position

When roping the dummy, you should start by standing in the ideal position. But you seldom get the same shot twice when you're actually roping horseback. However, you always should strive for that correct position. Position is everything in team roping. That should be your main focus no matter if you're roping afoot at the dummy or riding your horse and roping a steer— position yourself for the best shot.

But good position doesn't happen every time. So go one step at a time. Get the sweet spot down first—the most consistent and easiest shot. Then start working on the difficult shots so that you know how to catch when you find yourself in a bad position. When you change position, everything changes on the angles of delivery, and at first a beginner can't rope out of position. It's like someone handing you the keys to an Indy car and saying, "Go run a race." First you have to learn to drive it.

So practice roping the dummy first from the ideal position off the steer's left hip. Then begin to move around and learn how to rope it when you're out of position.

For example, if you move farther back from the dummy, it flattens things out. There's less down-pitch to the loop; the closer you approach the dummy or a steer, the more pitch you need in your loop. And for a reach, farther back from the dummy, you need more follow-through to really make sure you go across and complete the swing in your delivery.

If you move out of position farther to the left, for example, your elbow goes up more, and you will have a tendency to rope the steer's front feet. When you are farther to the left, the angle will pitch

*When you move farther back from the dummy, there's less down-pitch to the loop and you need more follow-through in your delivery.*

*When your position is farther to the left, your elbow goes up more as you swing to change the angle of delivery.*

*When you're out of position, in behind the steer, your elbow will drop, and you can't see the right horn.*

more to the left, like a heel loop. When your right elbow rises, the tip of your rope drops. When you release the loop, the angle forces the tip down even more and you can catch a front leg. Or, you might miss the right horn and snag the left because you don't get the bottom of the loop to strike the steer where it needs to.

When you're close to the steer, though, you can swing low on the right side—low with pitch. That ensures that you're going to catch the right horn. But when you start stepping back and going wide, you will have a hard time getting the rope to go underneath the right horn. Your whole arm gets higher the farther back and the more out of position you are.

# Horseback Dummy Roping

I've never done a lot of roping on a dummy when horseback, but I think it's a great idea. However, your angles for delivery will be different than when you're afoot.

Make the dummy two bales high. That's with the three-wire bales. They have a little more height than a two-wire bale and will give you the same height as the steer. You need the back of your dummy to be anywhere from 4 to 4½ feet high.

Another great idea is to build a riding dummy about the same height as your horse. Build a dummy horse, put your saddle on it, and then set it up with your dummy steer. You can work on the right body posture and rope the dummy.

I also have a dummy steer the same size as a live steer that can be dragged from a pickup or another horse. You can really work on your position while you rope it. But first you need to master roping the dummy while you're afoot.

# Practice and Attitude

When people practice roping the dummy, the most common problem I see is a lack of concentration. They don't really make the most of their practice time.

When I rope the dummy I'm trying to master my swing and delivery. Roping the dummy teaches me angles, how to judge my distances, and rope control.

I prefer roping alone for better concentration because, to me, the dummy is also an experimental lab. I try to figure out how to eliminate steps and rope more quickly, but end up with the same results. Roping has become so competitive that anyone who can eliminate steps and take shortcuts has the edge in competition. But these things have to be methodically thought out first when roping the dummy. The dummy is my drawing board to try different methods and techniques.

I watch every loop when I practice to see what it's doing. If my loop isn't doing the right thing, I want to change it. People always ask me how I do this or that. It's the pitch in your delivery, but you have to experience that. And you have to work on your angle. I'm a different height than you are; my arms are longer. You might have to use a little different technique to accomplish the same thing. The one thing I do know: You're going to spend a lot of hours learning how to get the loop to come up and on top of the steer's back, to clear the shoulder.

Think! A good delivery isn't something that happens when you pick up the rope. There is a reason a delivery happens the way it does—the angle on the loop. But most people just rope without considering that.

I did the same thing until I started to really study my loop, trying to figure out the mechanics of it. What causes my rope to do that? How can I make it do something different? You have control of your loop so you ought to be able to make it do whatever you want.

Many people who rope don't try to achieve a higher level of expertise. I've seen guys who rope the same today as they did 15 years ago; they're not any better now than they were 15 years ago. It amazes me that anyone can do that.

Here I am, and I just barely made it through high school, and didn't even apply myself at all when I went to college. I don't feel that I'm that educated at all. How in the world can I figure out something like this? Because I've spent a lot of hours studying roping. The more I got into roping and dissected it, the more the light came on.

Now, the further I get into my career, the more intrigued and interested I am in the horsemanship, for example. There are mechanics to a horse too—why he does certain things. It's really interesting to see what you can get out of this, or anything, if you put some thought into it.

We get a small percentage of people at clinics who actually want to raise their level of roping and horsemanship. Everybody says they want to be Jake Barnes or Clay O'Brien Cooper. Everybody has the desire, but how many have the want-to? Who wants to go out and physically rope a hundred steers a day or rope the dummy all night?

Most people turn on the television or get a book when they can't sleep. I used to drag my dummy out at 2 a.m. under a streetlight and rope for an hour. That's not for everybody, and everybody sees this through different eyes. But there is a very select handful of people who will actually pay the price it takes, and that's why, I think, there are only a handful of great ropers.

There's nothing wrong with someone who doesn't take it too seriously and wants to enjoy himself or use roping for stress relief from his job. It is mentally frustrating and physically hard to discipline yourself to study roping. If you worked all week, you don't want to work all weekend.

But for somebody who really enjoys his job, it's not work. This is not work to me; I do it every single day. I'd probably do it for free—I enjoy roping that much. Everybody else enjoys it too, sometimes just not as much as I do. Some don't have the time, or the ability, or the financial means; there are so many things involved. You need to have a perfect situation to be a great roper, and it isn't for everybody.

I do know this: You get out of roping just what you put into it. It's all discipline. I've been roping all my life, and I've won I don't know how much—over a million dollars now. When people come to my clinics I tell them, "I'm giving you a million dollars' worth of advice and techniques for the money you're paying. There are no secrets I'm holding back from you. You ought to be able to take these mechanics and fundamentals and turn them into anywhere from zero to a million dollars. It's whatever you want out of it."

# 6 CLAY ON ROPING THE HEELING DUMMY

## Different Perspectives

A LOT OF HEADERS change over to heeling and a large percentage of my students have roped calves and are familiar with riding and swinging a loop. Now they want to learn how to heel. Although they are familiar with handling the rope, the delivery of the heel loop is still difficult to learn.

It takes some natural ability to throw a good heel loop and a lot of hard work in figuring the angles and what has to take place in the delivery. The rope must go around the steer's back legs and the

bottom of the loop has to be controlled just right to go underneath the heels and catch.

A lot of people are taught roping from only one perspective. A beginner, for example, gets a horse and a rope and joins the local roping club. He starts throwing loops. Somebody always says, "This is how you do it," or "This is what so-and-so said works. You need to do it this way."

But there are many different ways to throw a heel loop. It all has to do with angles in different situations—the angle of entry and the angle of the loop.

So at first develop a good understand-

*There are many ways to throw a heel loop, but a lot of ropers learn from only one perspective.*

70

ing of those things, then apply them to your roping style and your swing. The individual roper has to work those things out for himself.

# Heeling Dummies

I would say the best thing for a stationary heeling dummy is a sawhorse with the legs set 2 to 3 feet wide. Don't make it very tall, ideally maybe 2½ to 3 feet high. But do make sure there's enough clearance so your heel loop can go through, underneath the dummy.

In a standing position, you can swing with the tip of your rope down toward the dummy. Remember that on a horse you're in an elevated position, and the simulation of your swing horseback should have more down-pitch. So you train your muscle memory for when you're on your horse—where it counts. If a dummy is too high, you'll be making thousands of simulated runs, thinking that this practice will help when you get horseback. But it really won't because the maneuver isn't simulated like it would be on a horse.

In one of our videos I also use a dummy without any front legs tied to a fence. You can tie it to suspend the hind legs at any height off the ground.

There are several commercial dummies available, but they don't seem to have any great advantages over a wooden sawhorse —not when it comes to basic procedure. Although there are commercial dummies and homemade dummies, you can train yourself on any dummy.

I don't think the dummies with swinging legs are good for practice. With them and with a lot of other dummies, it takes a little bit of a trick to catch, so you might be practicing a trick versus good procedure, good mechanical moves. That's what you have to watch out for with dummies.

When I rope, I see the hind end of the steer going up and down. The steer's legs are either going up, or they're going down. It's up-and-down timing, which you can get somewhat by adjusting the sawhorse up or down. But the movement of the steer's legs isn't back and forth.

There are some dummies that have a kind of loping action, and I like that. But to stand behind a dummy and have the legs just swing, I think, makes for bad practice. It makes no difference on the delivery of your loop, but it does concern timing. Ropers

*Later, as you become more accomplished in delivering the loop, tie the dummy to a fence to elevate the back legs several inches. Then gradually lower the legs until they're only a half-inch to an inch from the ground.*

learn to throw when the legs are back in a slanted position, instead of up and at the height of the steer's jump. I've never really seen anybody who grew up roping those dummies who had great timing.

When it comes to being really good at heeling, timing is the most important thing. A lot of people can develop the mechanical skills, but developing the timing aspect makes the difference.

I think a dummy should train you; its purpose is to train your delivery. With a sawhorse dummy, you can rope with the legs off the ground or on the ground.

71

It's good to rope the dummy with the legs on the ground at first. Then rope it with the legs off the ground several inches. Later lower the legs until they're a couple of inches off the ground. The better you get, the more you can lower the dummy, until the legs are an inch, then a half-inch off the ground.

If you first start roping with the dummy off the ground, you can get into a bad habit. Kids especially learn to rope and pull the slack at the same time—simply because they can do that when the dummy's legs are off the ground.

This is not good because you want roping the dummy to be a standard procedure. You train yourself to do the mechanical moves so you can be accurate in where you place the bottom of the loop. You gain control and a feel for doing that maneuver. Roping a dummy and pulling the slack up quickly is not a good habit.

Another thing about roping a dummy: At a clinic I can spend 2 or 3 hours working with people and get them to where they can deliver a loop on a dummy. Then they mount a horse and can't do it. So although dummy roping is good on one hand, it's not if you can't transfer the same techniques and use them when mounted.

## Practice Burros

For the last 15 years the best practice for me has been roping a burro. Burros give you an opportunity to make successive runs in a short period of time. If you have a good one and he's trained well, he'll lope just like a steer, and you can train your mechanical skills—your muscle memory. You can throw 30 or 40 loops in an hour and instill that feel and that procedure into your memory.

Most practice burros are just turned loose, and you train them to be tracked like a steer. Actually, to heelers who rope a burro a lot, the burro is the most prized possession on the place. The burro provides the perfect practice. I know several guys who wouldn't take $3,000 for their burros, and they're always looking for another one. If you take care of him, a practice burro will last 10 years or longer.

With a good trained burro, you position yourself behind him to keep him trapped and going to the right. Then, when you do move around behind the burro, your change in position tells him to go left. So it gives you a corner, like a steer who's turning, and he hops like a steer. You time the hop, deliver your loop, pull your slack, and let the burro go.

You don't dally, and you don't hurt him. You just pull up the slack. If you dallied or stretched the rope tight, you'd make the burro not want to work, and he'd be no good to you.

Too, the burros are great for working young horses and good for keeping your horses legged up and in shape. You work at a nice slow lope, time and time again. Cattle costs can be prohibitive, so a lot of people rope cattle only at paid practice sessions. But a burro is easy to maintain, and you get a lot of work on your timing.

The sawhorse and a burro keep practice simple. You can get a lot done and progress to a pretty decent stage roping with only those two elements.

## Focus and Concentration

Where you look when you're heeling is important. People have direct eyesight and peripheral vision. You can put your concentration on either one.

In heeling, the key is where your concentration lies in relation to those two things about your vision. That's really the key. I pinpoint my eyesight on the steer's flank on the right side. A lot of the time, if you're a little too far behind the steer, your horse's neck or head might cover up the middle portion of the steer or his left side. But you can almost always keep your direct eyesight on the steer's right side when you're heeling. So I look with my direct, pinpointed vision at the steer's right flank, just below the hip.

However, my concentration isn't on my pinpointed vision; it's on my peripheral vision, in other words, the whole pic-

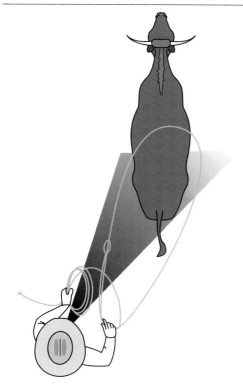

*The key in heeling is where your concentration lies. Although I pinpoint my eyesight on the steer's right flank, my concentration is on my peripheral vision. Then I'm aware of the header, his horse, the head rope, and the steer so that I can read the entire situation.*

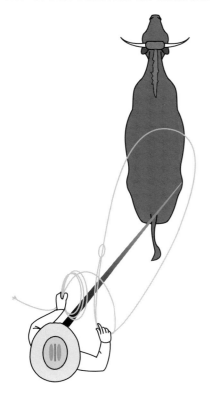

ture. I can look right into your eyes, but my concentration could be focused on everything else around me. That's what I do while roping.

The pinpointed vision keeps my focus localized, but my concentration is on the movement of the steer, plus the header, the head horse, and the head rope. All these things tell me what's going to happen next in the run—before it happens.

You have to read the situation. That tells you when the steer is going to jump, where he's going, where his legs are going to end up. So you have to concentrate on the whole picture versus the direct vision to the hip. But you have to go where that pinpoint vision is taking you, in order to take advantage of any situation.

Novice ropers need to train themselves to keep their eyes on the right flank of the dummy or the steer. But they also need to learn to concentrate more on the steer's back, the legs, the ground surface, etc.

## Setting the Trap

At first when you're roping the dummy, start with the back feet on the ground and learn to throw a trap. If you can throw a good trap and learn the timing for that, you can be a good heeler. Later you can learn to make the transition to other angles of entry.

In the trap, the bottom of the rope lies right in front of the hind legs; it's a straight line across. As the steer moves forward into the top of the loop, the bottom of the loop passes under his legs. At the end of the delivery, the steer is in the loop.

73

*A sequence of three.*

*1/ Before learning to deliver a loop from other angles, first learn to set a trap with the dummy's legs on the ground. After swinging and feeding your loop, bring your hand down to begin the delivery.*

Having the dummy's feet on the ground forces you to look at where your loop hits. When you can lay a pretty consistent loop across and in front of the feet, and you have enough tip-through, which means the rope is proportioned right, then it's time to elevate the dummy's feet off the ground.

By tip-through I mean the amount of loop going across the hind legs and through to the far side; it should be big enough to take in the steer's left leg. You want the loop proportioned evenly on both sides of the hind legs. The more you can lay your trap so the legs are in the middle of it, the more consistently you catch.

*2/ As you continue the delivery, think about directing the tip of your loop toward the open space between the legs. If you can learn the correct angle of entry to throw a good trap, you can become a good heeler.*

*3/ Pause a moment after your delivery and study where the loop landed. In a trap, the bottom of the rope should make a straight line, right across and in front of the hind legs. During an actual run, the steer will continue to move forward into the loop, and the bottom of the loop will go under his feet.*

74

# Reading the Loop

You also should train yourself to hesitate or pause at the end of your delivery, after placing your loop. Then take the time to study or "read" your loop and learn what the position of the loop can tell you. Doing that will help you learn how to throw a trap, or any loop.

So pause after you deliver your loop, to see where it lands. Don't pull the slack. Roping the dummy with the legs on the ground will take care of that because you don't have any feet in the loop. You deliver the loop and analyze it while you're standing there.

When you learn to read how the loop is lying, it all comes back to angles. How the loop lies is the last angle you put on the rope—whether your hand was like this or like that, which way your hand turned, which way the rope came in, what direction it was going. Reading how the loop lies will tell on you—if you learn what to look for.

If you have more loop on the right side of the hind legs, for example, you are either losing power on the delivery or you're hitting the ground too early with the bottom of your loop. The power isn't moving consistently enough or far enough in the follow-through in the delivery of your loop. The momentum of the swing doesn't carry the loop far enough to the left, or the loop just hits the ground, which stops it too quickly.

On the other hand, if you have more tip-through on the left side of the steer's legs, you're using too much power in your delivery on the basic trap.

Try to place the loop so the steer's hind legs are in the center of it. This also holds true if you're roping at a 90-degree angle from the right or scooping up the legs from behind.

# Raising the Legs

Now you can get even closer to simulating what you do with a moving steer when his hind legs are off the ground. After you learn to lay a trap, pick up the dummy's legs, about 3 inches at first. You can experiment with the different types of delivery, but what you're trying to do is to pass the bottom of the rope underneath both legs cleanly without interfering with them. You want the bottom of the loop to end up behind the legs at the end of the delivery.

*A sequence of three.*
*1/  When you read this loop, you can see too much tip-through to the left. This tells you there was too much power in the delivery or the bottom of the loop wasn't set down early enough in the delivery.*

*2/  This loop tells you that there wasn't enough power or follow-through in the delivery, or the bottom was set down too early.*

*3/  An ideal loop is proportioned evenly on both sides of the hind legs. The more consistently your trap is made this way, the more consistently you'll catch.*

*A sequence of three.*

*1/ When the dummy's legs are elevated, your practice more closely simulates what you will do when roping a moving steer. Begin by using an angle of entry and rotation of the loop similar to those used for setting the trap. However, the bottom of the loop now will go underneath the feet, so you'll have to become more precise in your delivery.*

*2/ Although you're no longer setting a trap, you still concentrate on the open target area between the legs and direct the tip of the loop there.*

3/ *The bottom of your rope should pass underneath both hind legs, as it would if a steer were hopping across the arena. Just as you did when all four sawhorse legs were on the ground, pause a moment and read your loop. If the loop is offset, your delivery is off.*

When the dummy's legs are off the ground, the bottom of the rope should come behind both legs and the rope should be evenly proportioned.

If the loop is offset, your delivery is off; the direction or angle you're using to bring in the loop isn't correct. The bottom of the loop ought to come under and come under clean, even though your angle can make the rope drift so it's offset around the legs.

Elevating the dummy legs makes you more accurate. Now you're not just setting the rope down in the delivery. Instead, your rope is moving, going totally under the steer's legs in the delivery. You must learn to make the transition from setting the trap to making the bottom of the loop go under the legs. This type of practice gives you more ability to control the bottom piece of your rope.

After elevating the dummy, practice delivering your loop from all positions—from the back and to the side. Again, pause after each delivery and read your loop. It will tell you what's happening.

# Angle of Delivery

With the heel loop, a lot of different techniques work. But one thing that's common, no matter how you do it, is this: You have to accurately place the bottom of the loop on a pinpointed spot, and you have to be accurate with it at the right time.

Heeling is mostly timing and accuracy. You time the steer's movement; when his back legs are elevated off the ground, the bottom of the loop has to hit or swing through that pinpointed position, based on the angle you're roping from.

You have all the points of entry in delivering the heel loop and—this is hard—the swing, as you rotate it in a 360, has to be turned to change the angle of the loop. You set the loop on a different axis or angle as your hand rotates. The loop is rolling the

*A sequence of four.*

1/ When the point of entry for a heel loop changes and comes more from the side, for example, the loop's plane of rotation must change too.

2/ In this case, because the angle of delivery is different, the bottom of the loop will pass more from one side, underneath the legs, and to the other.

3/ As the loop passes underneath the legs, the tip first comes more directly across because of the angle of delivery, rather than traveling through and toward the front or the back of the dummy.

4/ When the angle of delivery changes, not only is the swing different, but also the heeler's follow-through with his right hand, which also comes across from right to left.

whole time. When it gets to the point of impact, or delivery, the top and bottom of the loop have to be at a correct angle.

It all has to do with angles—how the heel loop comes into position. The point of entry for the heel loop can come from different areas around the perimeter of the right side of the steer. You have 180 degrees of area, from the steer's front all the way around to the back end. The loop can come in on a diagonal from behind the steer, from a 90-degree angle at the side, or from all the way up toward the front.

You can bring your swing in a number of different ways, but whichever way you bring in the loop, the bottom of the loop is what catches the steer's legs.

When you come from the side of the steer or from the back, at the time of impact—when the loop hits—you have to make the bottom of it pass underneath the steer's feet and across. Then when the rope reaches the other side of the feet, the feet are in the loop, in the middle of the steer's jump.

Or if you throw a trap-style loop, you lay the bottom of the loop down on the ground in front of the legs. Now the steer, in the transition of making his jump, jumps into the loop. As he moves forward, he moves into it. You're coming in at a more forward angle when you set a trap.

The more the delivery of the loop comes from the back, the more it changes the loop, and the more the bottom of the loop starts rolling under. This is more like scooping up the steer's legs in mid-air. You're trying to do something different with the rope now, but the angle of your entry still dictates the angle of the loop.

Think of an airplane landing. It should hit on the back wheels first. It's the same with a heel loop. You want to hit on the bottom. If you bring it in and let the tip hit, the loop nose-dives and crumples to the ground. At a certain point, you have to change the angle so the bottom of the loop hits the right spot and allows the top or tip of the rope to continue and follow through.

Heeling cattle is the manipulation of this angle of the loop, which is dictated by the angle of entry—where you're bringing the loop in from. Most people have to learn that, but they get really good at it; they learn to feel it. That's what I do—I feel the loop into position.

For example, you're against a fence and can't deliver without the loop hitting the fence. Then you use more of an angle in delivering the loop and make it come from the back and under.

With a steer who's trotting or shuffling, you have to lay the loop out in front because he has a leg on the ground at all times, like a dragger. You can't slide the bottom of the loop under his legs; you can't go from the side or back because you can't physically get the loop to go under both feet at the same time. So you come more from the front portion of that 180 degrees, as your point of entry, and lay the bottom of the loop out in front of his hind legs.

When I deliver a loop, I probably stay generally from 90 degrees up toward the front. I'm not much on coming under the steer's hind feet from behind, but sometimes I have to go under if I have lost position. The steer might get out too far ahead, or the horse might have shut me off. Something has happened, and now I have to change the angle of delivery just to get the loop to the feet.

I change the angle because I have to shoot the rope out farther and get it more level. It's like shooting a gun; when you aim at a target, the farther away it is, the more you raise the barrel of the gun. Changing the angle of my heel loop is the same thing. The farther away the steer gets, the more I have to raise the tip of my loop. That puts me at a different angle on the release because the tip of the loop is now up. Otherwise, I would already be starting down with the tip, and the steer would be beyond that range of delivery now.

Again, this all has to do with angles. Throwing a good heel loop is angles and power as they relate to the mechanics of the swing, the loop, and how the tip of the loop comes down.

A sequence of four.
1/ When scooping up the hind feet, the angle of the swing is altered to fit the different angle of delivery.

2/ The scoop is delivered more from behind the dummy, rather than coming from the side or making a trap in front of the legs.

80

3/ Because of the changed angle of entry, the tip of the loop ends up in a more forward position alongside the dummy.

4/ With its different angle of delivery, the scoop requires a different follow-through. The arm becomes more elevated as it moves from down low on the right up toward the left shoulder.

*A sequence of four.*
*1/ First learn to deliver your loop before you pull the slack. These are two distinct maneuvers.*

*2/ Release only the loop, but maintain your grasp on the slack.*

Put a concept in your mind that pertains to the delivery. What I do is think of the delivery in terms of accuracy, smoothness, touch, feel, consistency. To me, the loop is an art form. The loop must be delivered on touch and on feel with smoothness, softness, and accuracy. If you go about it in that light, you'll get better at your delivery.

When you talk about the delivery in terms of hard, fast, and speedy, then you're taking away from the things that are most important about the delivery—the accuracy, placing the loop smoothly toward the ground, so it doesn't bounce or jump or slide through too much. Smoothness coming out of the swing into the delivery keeps the loop open and in position as it comes down. If you go fast and hard and do things in a reckless style, then

you won't be very consistent in your delivery. It's finesse.

Good speed comes from just being better at the basics. You can be fast, but to be fast and consistent at the same time is totally different. That's speeding up the basics, but keeping things so you can control them with speed. You still throw a nice, smooth, accurate loop, but you can do it a little quicker. It's still the same components; you just speeded up the process and kept it all under control with practice.

## Handling the Slack

Once you learn to deliver the loop, roll your hand and grab the slack. Just lift it. You're just holding the rope on the steer's feet; the steer leaving and your horse stopping pulls the rope tight. Both of those take out slack, but the lift keeps the rope on the steer's feet. Until the slack is out of the rope, keep your hand about shoulder-high. Then you can go to the horn, but you have

*3/ Roll your hand over to change your grip on the slack.*

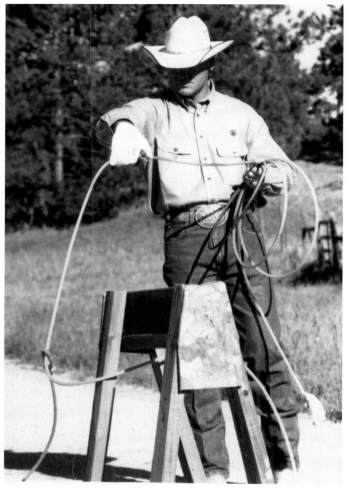

*4/ Lift the slack. The lift will keep the rope on the steer's feet. The steer's forward motion and your horse stopping will pull the rope tight.*

to determine the right time to do that.

The most common problem when people pull the slack: They think they are supposed to pull it up. In order to pull all the way up, as far as your hand can reach overhead, you have to put both hands up. If you don't let go of a coil, this throws your horse off.

So what most people do is pull out a coil, and that's where they get in trouble. Now there's too much rope between their hands, and they go to the horn with way too much slack there. That's not safe.

## Common Problems

The most common problem I see when people rope a dummy: They just kill time

and don't really work toward anything. They're throwing loops, but aren't really focused and thinking about what they're doing or trying to achieve. They don't really analyze what it takes to get better at roping. "How can I change this or that so the loop ends up the way I want it?"

Another common problem I see applies to headers who switch to heeling. They get too much roll in their swing. They may be trying to make the loop figure-eight and come back over the steer's back, as headers do.

The bottom of your loop is what you are concerned with in heeling. If it rolls away and up every swing—away from the feet—then it's hard on the last swing to get the bottom of the loop down and stabilized. The bottom of the loop in the heel swing must be—should be—a straight piece of rope controlled and felt all the way through the rotation.

It has to be accurate. I can't wave it and roll it too much because I will lose control, and obviously I won't have control of it the last swing. Headers typically have a swing where they really roll it because they have been throwing at the horns.

If you're not focused on trying to perform a particular function or maneuver, I think that too often you can create bad muscle memory—bad habits. The right kind of practice does you good. If you play around, you don't practice certain things that you know you should to get the job done right.

So practice with a goal in mind; practice the right things. When you heel the dummy, set a standard for how you want your loop to be. Then try to see how many times you can perform that in a row. Build the perfect shot—10 in a row or 5 in a row. Challenge yourself.

All this leads up to competition. You're actually practicing on your focus and concentration, building your confidence and the mental aspect of roping. If you're focused and know you can control your rope to throw a good loop 10 times out of 10, then you have enough confidence to say, "I can make 5 practice runs in a row on my horse and do the same thing." You build on that, and you have the confidence to move to competition. "Well, if I can do that on the ground and in the practice pen, then I can do that in this competitive situation." They're all building blocks.

People ask how I deal with the mental aspect of roping competition. Mental preparation and physical preparation all go hand-in-hand, from the very start, up until you go for the money. You have to know what you can do, and what you must do to get the job done. Then you have to focus your attention on those things, and keep them in your mind. That's what it takes to compete.

# Dummy Roping From Horseback

I can rope a dummy on the ground and get a feel for my swing and my loop, work on some things, and have a good time doing it. I can also transfer those skills when I'm mounted. But a large percentage of the ropers can't do that at first. Those who can are usually the ropers with natural ability, who have learned a feel for their loop. They can rope and easily throw the same loop from a horse.

But most of the guys who learn heeling at an older age can't—right off the bat—transfer their roping from the ground to the horse. That's where a lot of frustration comes in. They come home from work and spend 2 or 3 hours roping the dummy and get good at it, and they gain a lot of confidence. Then they get on a horse Saturday afternoon at a jackpot or practice session, and they can't throw the loop right.

My suggestion is that they sit on a horse and rope the dummy—deliver the loop, pause, and make adjustments the same as they did from the ground. The angle from the horse is different. The steer's feet stay in the same position, and the ground is still down there, but you have raised yourself 4, 5, or 6 feet in the air. It's totally different.

Set things up where you can practice roping the dummy from an elevated position. It could be from your horse, or you might build a barrel or some device where you put yourself at basically the same height.

The neck of the horse is another element that can cause problems. Now you have to

*No matter if you're practicing on a dummy or roping a steer, think about the open space underneath the body and about the tip of your loop coming over the back.*

swing the loop over his head. And your delivery, where the loop goes, is now basically under his chin and neck. So you're also going to work around that obstacle.

When you're practicing horseback at the dummy, focus on the steer's right hip. The horse's neckline now is an obstacle to you. The neck needs to be lying along the steer's left side, so you can look down and have a window, right down the horse's neckline, to the top of the steer's back and hips.

When you're horseback and roping the dummy, also think about the steer's feet and the open space underneath the steer. The loop has to travel through that open space; you can't hit the front legs or the hind legs because that will restrict the loop. The circumference of your swing comes over the open area.

The edge of your loop comes across the middle of steer's back and shouldn't go in front of the steer's withers or behind his hip. So the distance between you and your dummy, or steer, should be measured by where the tip of your loop is. If you have a 25-foot loop, of course you have to be farther back from the dummy.

A top roper can compensate if the loop is off because he really knows right where the tip of the rope is. If he is a little out of position, he compensates by drawing the hand back or reaching more forward with the arm. He knows what that distance is.

But a beginner wants to hit that area between the steer's front and back legs and swing the tip of the loop over it. That keeps him from having to make adjustments. When he swings the rope over the top of the back and delivers it, it goes right under the belly, where he wants it to go. So he should position his horse in relation to the dummy according to that, and then offset him to the left.

What's the best position? Be where you can barely see the left leg, but still see both legs clearly. The left hind foot of the steer will be just inside the neckline of your horse, or directly in front of the outside of the point of his shoulder.

So set those types of things up, where your simulation in practice is really close to actually heeling a steer. Then you're more capable of transferring your ground work to your horse.

# JAKE ON HEAD HORSES

LOOKING BACK to when I didn't know any better, when I won, I thought it was mostly me. Now, the older I get, the more I see how those great horses make great ropers. A good horse makes roping so much easier. When I have a lesser type of horse, my consistency and confidence go way down.

So the next step for an aspiring team roper is getting a heading horse. Where do you buy one? I hate to see a guy who wants to learn to rope but doesn't get any help or instructions about buying a horse. The

horse traders just drool over a new roper who doesn't know anything about a horse.

When he does look for a horse, he usually doesn't take his time. It's like buying a car; he's compulsive and he wants to get started. So he ends up getting a bad horse. No one wants to lose money, and you hate to have your hard-earned money ripped off, so you make the best of a bad situation and tough it out. That's just pride. You are better off taking a loss and getting a new horse.

Take your time and make sure the horse is the right kind of horse to fit you. Get

*The older I get, the more I see how great horses make great ropers.*

with somebody you trust, who knows something about the business and is not going to rip you off, to find a nice horse. Roping is fun. If you can find a good horse who is fun, then roping is a great sport. But if you have a dink horse, one who is hard to ride, it takes all the fun out of roping.

# The Novice Roper's Horse

Most people learning to rope say, "I'm going to buy a young horse so we can learn together." That's setting yourself back 2 or 3 years. And those people often end up getting hurt. The horse doesn't know anything about roping, and the person doesn't know anything about training a rope horse. It's a wreck from start to finish.

Get a horse who absolutely won't get you into a wreck. He's not too slow, but he's not too fast either. He's one who can basically get into position and keep a guy out of a wreck. That's the most important thing. That good horse is the most important tool you can have, just for the fact that he won't be as likely to get you hurt. Most guys don't buy the right type horse and then end up spending a lot more time in the hospital—instead of spending the time to find the right horse to start with.

What I usually suggest for a beginner is an older horse—a baby-sitter, so to speak. Once in a while you can find a younger horse who can do the same job, but younger horses seem to have more problems because they aren't as seasoned. An older horse, though, has been through all the wrecks. He knows exactly how to keep himself out of a wreck and how to conserve his energy. And he has a lot of rate. That's not to say you couldn't have that with a 7- or 8-year-old horse. But a seasoned, mature horse with a good, even disposition is the perfect horse for our perfect new roper.

# Size, Conformation, and Bloodlines

I'm pretty tall—6 foot, 3 inches—so I like a head horse from 15 hands to 15.1, who weighs anywhere from 1,200 to 1,300 pounds. He's small enough to be athletic enough to do the job, and still large enough to handle the steer. He has the

*A good head horse is the most important tool a roper can have. The better the horse is to ride, the more you can enjoy the sport.*

durability to withstand the jerks.

A shorter, more compact horse has a shorter stride. A finer-boned, smaller horse without quite enough weight to handle the steer has a tendency to anticipate the turn to try and protect himself. If a little horse who's kind of dainty gets a couple of hard jerks the wrong way, then he has a tendency to try anything to avoid that jerk.

But I think a lot of it is the size of the horse's heart. A little horse who has a big heart—and doesn't know that he's little—can do the job that a big horse can. But roping is more demanding on the little horse physically, so he may have a tendency to take shortcuts, to try to save his body.

Something really important to me is having a horse with a short neck. Then you have a clear shot at your target, and the horse's head isn't up in your face. That changes the angle of your swing when you have a horse with a long neck or high head, especially for someone who is shorter. You can get out over the front of a short-necked horse a lot easier.

I have an advantage because I have long

*Although he doesn't have to be huge, a good head horse must be stout enough and tough enough to handle a steer.*

I've also seen horses with perfect pedigrees and conformation who can't do anything.

I think a lot of people get carried away with breeding and such, as far as pedigree and conformation are concerned. I'm sure it helps with certain traits. But then you'll learn about a great horse whose breeding you never heard of; it just happens. When a college starts recruiting for a team, they don't look at the athlete's family; they look at the job he's doing on the court or field. So I don't look for anything specific in a rope horse, just performance and his willingness to help us win.

I like a horse who can run and is big-boned and tough. And I'm sure there probably are certain bloodlines that are better, but I don't think our (team roping) industry is big enough yet to concentrate on certain bloodlines—maybe someday. If rope horse futurities get started, then we'll get into bloodlines. That will really help, but we haven't crossed that bridge yet, even though we're getting closer.

## Disposition and Performance

I like a horse who is obviously gentle, but I will put up with a lot from a horse if he is a winner. I also prefer a horse with a low-key disposition. However, a head horse usually has a tendency to be hyper, more like a race-horse with the speed, the big motor. He must have a lot of run and power.

I don't like a horse who is broncy, or one I am afraid is going to buck me off. I will respect a horse who has some spunk and a little sass to him if I can get him ridden down. But I don't like a horse who is going to buck me off and hurt me if I don't ride him enough. He isn't worth 10 cents to me. If there's a chance he could hurt me, I don't want him. I can't afford to be laid up.

A little fresh on a horse is all right. I can saddle one and leave him saddled awhile and then lope him. And as long as I am hauling him, I can keep the edge knocked off. But one of those horses who's just laying to hurt me or kick me is not worth it.

A horse must be able to score good and

arms and I am taller. So I can get a loop out and over the top of my horse's head a lot easier. If his head is farther out, it makes it harder to swing your rope, and you have to adjust your swing. Just think of how easy it would be if you were roping off a horse who didn't have a neck at all.

From a selling standpoint, the nicer-looking a horse, the easier he is to sell, but roping is all performance to me. It is not a judged event, so I would ride a plug with no tail if he could do the job. Of course, I would love to ride a great-looking show-type horse—who has all the skills—but you don't see that very often. A head horse is more a work-type horse; his job is pretty physically demanding.

When you talk about pedigree, breeding, or speed indexes, those things don't concern me that much. I look just at a horse's arena performance. I have seen some horses with the worst conformation in the world who are great roping horses.

have an extreme amount of speed. And once he gets to the steer, he will rate on his own. Those two things a head horse must have.

You can find a horse who has a lot of run, but that doesn't do any good if he won't rate on his own. If the steer slows down and the horse wants to run by, then you are defeating the purpose. He must have some natural rate.

Also, when you rope the steer, the horse needs to plant his hindquarters somewhat, to set and turn. It's important, too, that a horse use his hind end. He should have a natural stop, with no bounce. I like a horse who's had some calves roped on him. When you rope and dally, he really drives his back legs underneath him and stays balanced to slow the steer—not to a complete stop, but a gradual set. Then you have control of the steer, and as the horse slows, he begins to make the lateral move to the left.

The horse used for rodeo roping and the one used for an eight- or ten-head average roping are a little different. At an average roping, I want a horse to use his hind end a bit more, to set and take hold, more like a calf roping-type horse.

At a rodeo, I'm trying to make a fast run. I don't want a horse to set a whole lot there. He might also drop his left shoulder a little more because I'm trying to be quick. I get the dally as I'm leaving the hole to make the turn; that's where a roper starts eliminating the fundamentals. So although the rodeo horse takes shortcuts, I'm going strictly for speed. This type horse is a little more gritty and thrives on being almost a little too strong and doesn't have as much finesse.

When I try out a horse, I want him to travel really smooth and level on the ground. I can lope a horse around and tell, pretty much, if I am going to like him or not. If he's kind of flighty in the front end, with his front feet coming way off the ground when he lopes, that tells me he's going to climb with his front end when he runs to a steer. I don't like that. I want a horse who travels level and smooth.

*The nicer-looking a horse, the better, but roping is all performance to me. I'm not too concerned with pedigrees and speed indexes as long as the horse can do the job.*

## Level of Training

The more I get into horsemanship, the more I like a broke horse, so the more I work to keep a good handle on the horse.

There are certain things I think a horse must be able to do. He has to be broke enough that you can move him with your legs, side-pass one way or the other. That helps you to maneuver him in the box, and you can also use the cues he's learned when you face. That's pretty basic stuff—teaching a horse to go away from leg pressure and to give to the bit.

Also, teaching a horse to give well to the bit is important. In the roping box, we tend to pull on those horses too much, trying to position and hold them in the box. The more you pull, the more the horse pulls against you. Then the horse

*A good head horse must have enough strength and power in the hindquarters to run fast to a steer, set him, and make the turn, then tow the steer so the heeler can take his throw.*

learns how to brace against the bit, and it becomes a tug of war. The horse is much stronger, so you end up having to get a bigger bit or start jerking his mouth more to get the horse to respond.

I have learned, more and more, to be a little softer with my hands. I want a horse to be soft in the bridle and give to me. Then I don't have to put as much pressure on him in the box.

I don't claim to be any kind of horse trainer at all, and my schedule is pretty demanding. I can straighten out my own rope horses or fine-tune them, but it takes more than just roping. We could all use more horsemanship skills. There are

horse trainers who train horses for a living. I rope for a living. I think it takes a certain breed of person to be a trainer.

## Head Horses, Past and Present

Looking back, both Clay and I had great horses at the time we were winning so much. I had an unbelievable rodeo horse—Bullwinkle. I don't know what his breeding was, but he got the job done. He had a lot of talent, but a mind of his own. He was at his best at the rodeos. However, he wasn't a great horse at an average roping. He was a hot-tempered horse who couldn't take a lot of runs in a row, but he was one of the best when it came to roping a steer fast.

If I could get out of the box without breaking the barrier, we had a chance to win. He was big and strong, and he faced extremely well. One of his weaknesses: He was very temperamental.

Although he was a great horse, I hated to practice on him. He was one of those who did his job. I have to admit that I was as hard-headed as he was. If he hadn't been so tough and bull-headed, though, he probably wouldn't have lasted long at all.

When you saddled him, you could tell that he was in a certain mood. Sometimes I could tell, when I warmed him up, if he was going to give me trouble in the box that night.

He scored terribly, as if he was claustrophobic in the box. I kept changing things up, trying to relax him in the box. I was always trying to find new little gimmicks and things to occupy his mind. Somehow or another, I did whatever I had to do to get him to score.

I would always think, "What's going to happen this time?" It was like that every run. Yet every time, we would win, win, win.

I always heard that you're lucky if you have one good horse, a good woman, and one good dog—and I have been real lucky. Since that horse, I have looked for 10 years for another one like him. Although I've had a lot of good horses over the years, I am really happy with Mr. Freeze, the horse I have now.

I feel that he is simply a great all-around

horse; I also feel that I'm really competitive at the average ropings on him. He really uses his hind end, scores good, has a lot of run, and faces great. When I rope, I have plenty of confidence that he's going to do his job, and I can concentrate on mine. I don't like to rodeo at a one-header on this horse, though, because I don't want him to learn to drop his shoulder and take shortcuts.

I have another horse, Rooster, to make my rodeo runs on. His attitude: "You let me do my job, you do yours, and we'll get along." He's more of a business partner. I don't mind asking him to do the dirty work. He gets in the trenches, and he'll do it.

For example, if it was really muddy, I probably wouldn't ride Mr. Freeze, my best horse; my second horse, Rooster, would get the call. He's a bigger-boned, more rugged horse and reminds me of the old foundation work horse. Day in, day out, I would rather have this horse under me just because I know he won't go lame. He's going to hold up. Soundness is important.

## A Perspective

With my horses, it is strictly performance. I don't fall in love with a horse. That's just the nature of the business I'm in. Sure, I would love to get attached to a great horse. But I've found out that whenever you have those good horses, you tend to baby them too much. You feed them too good; then they start trying to mess you around when you start trying to save them. It seems as if the horses you don't really care about are the ones who work so well.

That was the way that my old horse was. I wasn't afraid to go for first place on him—no matter what the conditions were. He wasn't very good at the big average-type ropings; that wasn't his strong suit. I wish horses came in an all-in-one package—for rodeo, average ropings, and practice, then you'd have it all. Keep dreaming. Very seldom do you see that.

Rodeo roping has a tendency to ruin those really good horses; you start short-cutting the fundamentals for speed. It's more a roper's ability then, and that's when you have to sacrifice your horse. A really good horse stands out like a sore thumb.

I usually try to keep an average horse, a

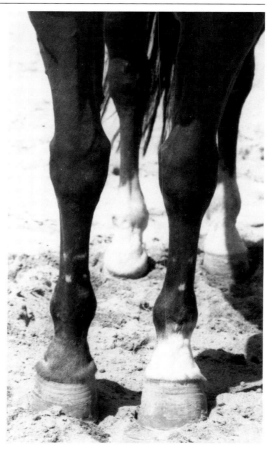

*Although this horse isn't standing on completely level ground, you can tell the legs are straight and durable enough to hold up to the work.*

rodeo horse, and a practice horse. Obviously, when you haul a lot, you like to haul just one horse, but that's hard to do. Usually a horse is either one way or the other. Ideally, I would like to have a couple of each type, so I could rotate them, and they would last so much longer.

I have had a lot of horses come in and out at my place, mostly just to have something to practice on. And I might improve one and then sell him. But you can't ever stop looking for a better horse, and you never know where he's going to come from. That's why I go through so many horses. I am always trying to find a better one.

# 8

# CLAY ON HEEL HORSES

FOR WHAT I DO, I can't have a green horse. I must have a horse who knows his job, who's reliable, tough, strong, and able to withstand mentally what I do on him. The horses I've won the majority of my money on, the ones I've gotten along with best, have been over the age of 10. I've had several heel horses that I liked really well. The last few years I've kept just one or two horses for rodeoing, and I have two I'm hauling right now. But it seems like each of the horses I've hauled had similar characteristics, or qualities, that I liked.

## Novice Roper's Horse

Many novice heelers make the mistake of learning to rope and trying to train a horse at the same time. There's the perception that they will learn together. That can't happen; probably the horse just isn't going to make it. And your arrival as a roper will be way farther down the road than you could have made it with a trained horse.

*This is Ike. Of all the really great heel horses I've ridden, he's one of my favorites.*

92

*My heel horse must be reliable and able to handle the stress of competitive roping.*

If a green roper starts with a green horse, it usually doesn't pan out too good and isn't going to be easy. Roping won't be as enjoyable as it will if you find an older, patterned horse who knows his job. A horse will learn a pattern. If you climb on that horse and just leave him alone, point him in the right direction, and cue him right, then you can have fun.

Mostly, the good horses for learning to rope on are the ones people think are getting a little bit too old, anywhere from 15 to 20. The roper might feel the horse is losing a little bit of his get-up-and-go or his ability to perform at the top level, so he sells that horse to somebody who's learning.

Those horses are hard to find. That's probably the horse most in demand—a good, solid horse anywhere from 15 to 18 years old. But he has lots of good runs left if you take care of him. Maybe they won't go at top speed or be really fast and athletic. But that's not what a guy who's learning needs. He needs a solid, patterned horse who knows what he's doing.

For the average horseman who's just beginning to rope, I recommend something gentle and broke pretty good. The novice roper needs a solid horse that a 10-year-old kid could rope on. Actually, that's what I would rather rope on. There's no

junk about a horse like that, nothing you have to put up with. You can go saddle and warm him up, back him in the box, run 10 steers in a row, and you don't have any problems—no flare-ups, no not wanting to do the job.

That's the ideal situation with the type of horse I enjoy riding. With that kind of horse, you can enjoy the roping and work on correcting the things you need to and not worry about the horse. That horse knows how to cow, how to pattern, and goes where he's supposed to go, but if you want to maneuver him, he'll also respond to that.

*Ike is not only well-balanced in his conformation, he's also rugged and sturdy. That's why he's lasted as long as he has in the competitive arena.*

## Size, Conformation, and Bloodlines

As for size and conformation, I like a horse right at 15 hands, not much taller and not a whole lot shorter. I like a horse who is a little bit higher at the withers than he is in the hip, and I want him built with a hind end that he can move and slide up under himself well.

I like a horse who's not too wide in the front end, so that he has a good smooth stride. A horse who is built too wide and who is too heavily muscled will be too rough. But I do like a good-sized heart girth. And I like a horse with a thin throat-latch and a short neck, not real short and not long-necked either.

One of my heel horses now is maybe a little bit thick in the throatlatch, but he is big and strong in the right places. He's correct through his shoulders and up through the withers and heart. Then he tapers off behind and has that smooth stopping ability. So he's rugged up front and smooth behind.

He's got a great stride so he can line up with a steer. The length of a heel horse's stride is important. You don't want it too short because that's rough and choppy. Too long, and the horse is a little too late in stopping. Gathering him up in the corner and getting the timing and stride right in the turn is hard. That's why I prefer a middle-of-the-road-type horse. He fits the stride and timing of most steers.

I'm really picky about the way one looks, the way he is built. I want him balanced in his structure. I can show you better than I can describe it. But I can pretty much look at a horse and tell you

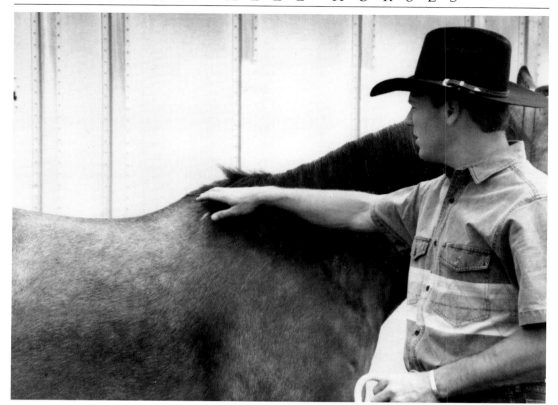

what he will feel like to ride.

One of the really good horses I rode for several years was a Red Man horse. But, since I'm from Arizona and have friends who breed and raise Driftwood horses, that's what I'm more familiar with. My wife's using two of them for barrel racing, and we can rope on both of them. They are half-sisters to my Driftwood heel horse.

Ike, my heel horse now, shows some of the Driftwood characteristics. He toes out some behind, but he's a really big slider. He can really drop his butt to stop. He has good high withers, higher than the hips. I like the way his neckline comes out basically straight; it doesn't rise too much. That gives him the ability to make a sharp corner and bring his front end around

good. This horse can use his front end and his back end both.

I tend to lean more toward the older foundation horses. I like their size and their bone. They have sturdiness, a ruggedness or toughness. There's a little bit more depth to them as far as staying power.

Some of the people interested in breeding and raising horses are going back to that foundation breeding for rope horses. The reining and cutting horse people have had their bloodlines going for a long time, refining them. And I've ridden some Doc

*I really like a horse with a quiet disposition, who also can be all business when the time comes.*

Bar horses. In fact, I've had several in the past few years, and I've seen some decent roping horses with those bloodlines.

## Disposition and Performance

The first thing the horses I really like have in common is a pretty calm, laid-back disposition. I like that, but at the same time, when you back them into the box, they are all business and ready to go. They put forth a lot of effort in the run.

Another thing important to my style and my roping is a horse able to work off his hind end and slide as I'm delivering my loop. When that's done, his rear end is down, and we're anchored. So when the load comes and I dally, the horse can take the hit really good.

Even though he has the ability to drop down in the hind end, he can still keep the front end up and keep moving through the corner. He has to make a transformation in the turn. You're going straight down the arena, then turning and going across, and the horse has to stay balanced.

I like a horse with a smooth stride, a collected way of going. But he has to know your timing and have good timing himself when you throw. He has to go into the stop and know how to read things—when you throw the loop, or when you're going to cue him. Then he also must go into the stop without jarring or throwing you forward. That timing just comes with hours in the practice pen.

I prefer geldings, but I just bought a mare and really like her. Which one, a mare or gelding, I work in the arena makes absolutely no difference to me. But with a gelding, I can pretty much tie him anywhere and leave him anywhere; I don't worry about him. With a mare, you worry about where you tie her, or who's riding

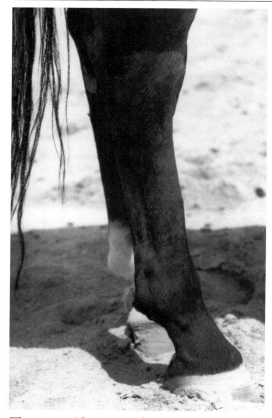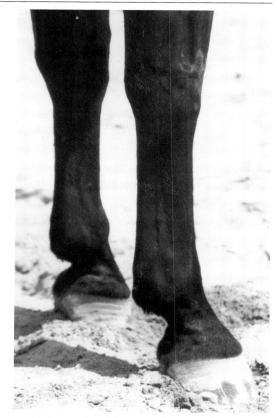

*These are side views of Ike's front and back legs, which are durable enough to withstand the stress of roping.*

up behind you. A mare will back her ears and get kicked or kick somebody else.

A good heel horse needs a lot of cow in him. That's where your rate, the ability to back off and to anticipate, comes from. You don't have to maneuver for those because the horse is doing those things on his own. When he gets to the steer, the horse backs off. Then he rates at a certain position, or he stays to a certain side—wherever you train him to be. That cow sense enters in because that's an anticipated move on the horse's part, and nothing that the roper has to do physically.

If you don't have that, you have a horse who can only perform maneuvers. And he responds only to you moving him. He has to be broke and handle well so that when you move him, his head doesn't come up and he doesn't get out of position anywhere in his body.

Roping is tough on a horse because a lot of the maneuvering is at full speed. A calf roping horse, for instance, runs hard and stops hard, and then you're off of him. Then he backs up and holds the rope. The reining horse's work is done on commands, but it's not all at full speed, so to speak. Those horses are trained so there is very little movement of the reins or the rider's feet. The horse is cued to make the maneuvers and knows you are cueing him, but the person watching doesn't really see what's taking place.

In roping, the horse is running, and you have to move him and control him at a dead run. He has to stand in the box and score, then run hard and maneuver to position—left, right, straight, whatever. Then the header ropes, and his horse has to take weight, transfer that weight and keep going at a run, then swap ends, and face.

The heel horse must score good, run hard out of the box, and rate, or let you rate him to stay in position until the header ropes. Then the heel horse has to turn, come up to the steer, be honest enough to give you a good shot, and then take a big hit from the steer you've roped.

If the steer was perfect every time, you could pretty much turn your heel horse loose; he'd learn the pattern and you could get by with very little maneuvering. But arenas have so many different sizes and shapes, and the cattle range from fresh to roped-out. They run all over the arena, so you have to maneuver and change your horse's direction—pull him off, slow him up, turn him—all that while going fast. It takes a special kind of horse

to take all that maneuvering around and then have the load hit him.

## Level of Training

None of my top horses were trained by a cutter or reiner; they were pretty much just broke outside, then arena-broke. They were all ranch-ridden and worked cattle. But they were broke horses to start with.

The best ones I've had, I didn't really train. I would say I put the finishing touches on them as far as adapting them to my style of roping. But they were already well-rooted in a pattern—the way they left the box, cowing to the steer, in the stop, and in being strong on the end of the rope. There were certain little things I did to my heel horses in given situations—where I altered the horse a little bit to fit my particular style.

I do like a well-mannered horse. You can walk into the pen and catch him without having to chase or corner him and hem him up. He stands and lets you halter or bridle him without hitting you in the head with his head. A well-mannered horse stays away a respectful distance, but he isn't afraid of you. You can lift a hand without him flying back.

You can lead a well-mannered horse; he doesn't try to lead you. You can tie him, and he stands there. You can brush him, clean out his feet, do whatever. When you saddle him, he's not squirmy or cinchy. You can move him with your hand or with a cluck, step him over or step him back. You can maneuver him safely, and wherever you put him, he stands and stays.

That's the most desirable horse for me to be around. A well-mannered horse has no extracurricular activity, and doesn't move around, looking for something to distract his attention. That just gets in your way. I try to keep my horses on an even keel, right where I want them. They feel good and they are ready to perform, but they are not so high that they are uncontrollable or cause problems.

# Heel Horses, Past and Present

The first horse I ever roped on was Baldy, a big, bald-faced sorrel who belonged to my stepdad, Gene O'Brien. The horses I learned to rope on were Sleepy and Suds, two palominos.

I consider four heel horses among the best I've ridden in my career.

Blue, a blue roan, was an awesome horse who scored perfectly and had plenty of speed. He had a smooth stride, a great stop, and was super strong. I won the '85, '86, and '87 championships on him. He was by a horse called Dallas Allen and out of a Red Man mare. Blue was raised and trained by Doy Reidhead in northern Arizona.

A light sorrel horse, Elvis was just about the perfect heel horse for me and my style. I bought him from Wayne Baize in El Paso, Tex., and rode Elvis when I won the '89 championship.

I bought Ricky, a dark sorrel, blaze-faced horse from Lee Woodbury. Ricky was a good rodeo horse and could really run and make a smooth corner. Although he was a little bouncy in his stop, I won a pile on him, including the '88 championship and the Bob Feist Invitational that year. I sold Ricky to Allen Bach, who then won the '91 championship on him.

I'm riding Ike now, a buckskin I bought from Ozzie Gillum in Oakdale, California. Ike scores good, loves to run, and has an awesome stop. Because he's tough and rugged, he's made a great rodeo horse and outlasted them all. Ike has a great personality, is very well-mannered, and is one of my favorites. He's by Mr Bar Truckle and out of a Driftwood Ike mare.

# A Perspective

A certain caliber of roper, the one who ropes to make money and make a living, puts added pressure on a horse that a lot of other people don't. That roper asks more of the horse, and the horse must be able to perform. That pressure would bother a young horse, who isn't mature to a certain degree. Ultimately, he would look for a way out, away from the pressure, versus staying hooked, staying solid in his work.

There also is a certain amount of maintenance that goes along with keeping a good, mature horse working. You have to be careful of the amount of runs you put on him, and what kind of runs you make in the practice pen. To me, the more runs you make on a horse, the more runs you take out of him. Most of my good horses require very little practice; it's mostly keeping them in shape, keeping them feeling right in the bridle.

I usually buy my heel horses. It's hard for me to take the time to really train one. I can take a young horse from not knowing anything and get him to the point he pretty much knows what's going on in a roping pen, and I can take him to the jackpots. But I can't take that type of horse and go to the rodeos because I make my living rodeoing. I have to ride the horse who's not going to make a mistake.

I can't take a green horse to the next level because I don't have the time, and I don't go to enough little ropings to put that kind of seasoning on a green horse. If I go to a good roping, I'm going to ride my good horse. If I go to a rodeo, I'm riding my good horse. I'm not going to ride a green horse. So I can only take a green horse to a certain point, and it's enjoyable for me to do that. But to take that horse and sacrifice what I can win for what he's going to learn—I can't do that. One of these days, when I quit traveling hard, I look forward to training and seasoning my young horses for my kids and others to use.

# 9 GEAR AND EQUIPMENT

Having a good selection of gear and equipment is important to team ropers, or any competitor.

## Jake: Saddles

REGARDLESS OF the type saddle, the most important thing is that it fits the horse and doesn't hurt his back. I'm the same way about my saddles and bridles as I am about my horses: Whatever fits and works the best is what I am going to use. The saddle might be an off-brand, but as long as it fits the horse well, it's okay.

I think most of the stress and the strain comes on the head horse's withers, on the right side, right above his shoulder. A rodeo head horse takes a lot of hard jerks, which is why he will begin to drop his shoulder—to get away from that jerk. With a rope wrapped around the saddle horn, when a horse takes that jerk, I think the bar of the saddle really mashes right into his shoulder blade. So, the horse tries to drop his left shoulder to take the pressure off the right shoulder.

But as a header, you have the opportunity to make a horse work right. If he does, then there is less of a stress factor. You can rope, go to the horn, and let the horse get his hindquarters well underneath him, and take the jerks straightaway, rather than off to the side.

A lot about the saddle fit depends on the horse's withers. Some horses are round-backed, and I don't care for that. When a horse doesn't have any withers at all, your saddle is always rolling. Those horses are hardest to fit. After you make a run, you always have to pull your saddle back up and into position.

*My wide roping stirrups are set short enough that I have a slight bend in my knee. If you're unsure about your stirrup length, there's an old rule of thumb that the bottom of the tread should hit around your ankle bone. Start there, and then raise or lower your stirrup until you find what's comfortable for you.*

*The swell of my saddle should be large enough that I can brace my thigh against it.*

Most dally horns are 3 to 3½ inches tall. I don't particularly care for a really tall horn, but I don't really like the little snub horn either. I can get by with a smaller-type horn when I am hurrying and can rope going nice and easy. But if you are roping and hurrying at a rodeo, and your horse ducks, then your hand often will go right over the smaller horn; it's just harder to find.

But for rodeo roping, a really tall horn sticks up so high that when I rope and have to hurry back to the horn, often I hit my hand. That breaks my motion.

I don't like really big swells on a saddle, up so far that, if I get thrown off balance, I hit them. But I do want the swells big enough that I can get my thighs up against them and brace during my run.

I use the big roping stirrups. I set my stirrups at a medium length. I don't want them too long; then I am sitting on my rear. But I

don't want them so short that I get jacked out of the saddle. I set my stirrups just short enough that my knees are bent slightly.

After you have ridden a saddle any period of time, the saddle seems to get slick, seat and all—even a tooled saddle. I don't like a seat that has any type of varnish or a seat that is slick. I like a rough-out saddle.

That's what I'm riding now, and after it has been ridden a while, I'll use a rasp on

*Check your latigo and the hobble strap between your cinches often and replace them when worn. Keep the back cinch snug on your head horse; it will help distribute the pressure more evenly across his back when he takes a jerk from a steer.*

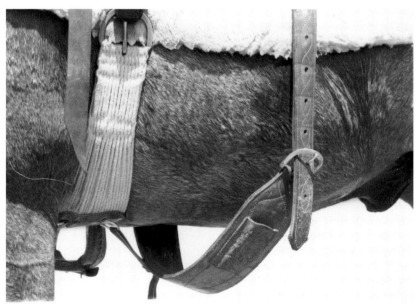

*When a back cinch is too loose and a steer hits the end of the rope, it's more likely to pinpoint the pressure on the horse's withers.*

the fenders, to rough them back up. I began to do that a year or two ago with a new horse who broke out of the box really hard. With a slick saddle, I was all over that horse. The rough-out gives me a little more bind. It's like a saddle bronc rider using chaps and rosin on his saddle so he can get a better hold.

As far as cinching a horse, obviously the front one keeps the saddle in place. So I use a nylon latigo there because you don't have problems with those very often. But it's a good idea to check it regularly. If it has some wear, a latigo isn't very expensive to replace.

I am a firm believer in making sure the back cinch is tight. That's a must for a roper. When a horse takes a jerk, if the back cinch isn't tight, it increases the chance for the front of the saddle to go down and into the horse's withers. That pinpoints the pressure. The back cinch holds the saddle down and distributes the pressure more evenly to keep everything from rocking onto the horse's withers.

One thing that I am also real cautious about is the hobble strap between my front and back cinches. That strap breaking is a common problem, especially at ropings. I don't care how gentle the horse is, if the back cinch slides to his flank area, he's going to buck.

A leather hobble strap will rot from sweat. To avoid the problem, I braid poly hay twine into a pretty wide strap, a three- or four-plait. It might look a little funny, but it won't rot and will never break.

I would hate to be in a position where I was about to win the Bob Feist Invitational or a world title and have that leather hobble strap break. If could be a costly mistake, and it is preventable. That hobble-strap problem is one of the little things you can control and avoid.

## Saddle Pads

In the past I have used a regular Navajo pad. Now I use a Navajo type with a closed-cell foam pad. The bottom layer is a synthetic wool that doesn't absorb moisture. It's basically like a Navajo. But most real Navajos absorb moisture, and they get sweaty and crusty and hard. With the one I use, the moisture runs out of the blanket when my horse sweats.

The majority of us try to adjust the saddle fit with the saddle pads. With a horse who is round-backed, you use less padding. If you have a horse with higher withers, put more pads on to protect his withers.

## Bridles, Bits, and Reins

When it comes to bits, I think that bit selection is like fitting a saddle—you have to listen to your horse. I have a barn full of different bridles, and there isn't one in particular that I use most of the time. However, I do like to use a chain bit. The mouthpiece consists of small chain. The shanks are medium length and have some play. It's a relatively mild bit that works more on the corners of the mouth than the bars, more like a snaffle.

I look at a bit differently than most. I don't know much about bits, so I try to relate to a horse and how it would feel if someone stuck a bit with a port on the bars of my mouth. To me, it seems like a bit can hurt a horse's mouth more than was ever intended with its use. That's why a horse gaps his mouth—because it hurts.

When I rope, I do hold a horse steady in the box. I want to hold him snug. So I feel I need a jointed mouthpiece or something that isn't going to hurt a horse's bars if he pulls against my hand. That's basically for scoring. The only place where you might need more control with a bit like that is when you set the steer or stop. That's what I like about the chain bit. I can make it as light as I want or as severe as I want.

However, I change bits all the time on my horses. I try to let my horse tell me what works for him. He might score better with a certain bit, but he might work better out in the arena with a different one. If it's not enough bit, I try a different one. I need less bit in the box and more bit out in the arena, so I'm constantly working to get that combination and have the control I need.

As for the shanks, again, the horse is basically going to tell me what works after I lope him around and stop him or make a

*This chain bit is one I often use.*

practice run. If he slings his head and gaps his mouth, that's too much bit for him. I switch bits. One might be loose-shanked; one might be solid-shanked. It all depends on the horse.

I don't believe in punishing a horse with a bit, but we all have done it. We take hold of a horse too much, and that's hard on the horse. Can you imagine having someone jerk on your head and your mouth like that?

That's one reason I am not real crazy about mechanical hackamores. A mechanical hackamore always puts too much pressure on a horse, and in the box you are putting pressure on his head all the time. I will say a hackamore is decent out in the

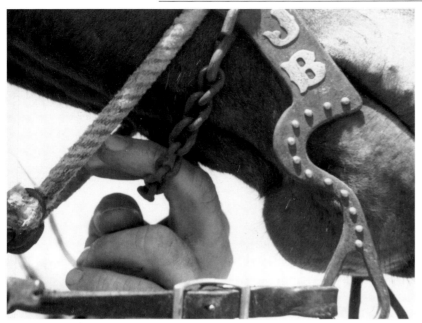

*Don't set your curb chain too tight. The old rule of thumb: You should be able to put two fingers under it.*

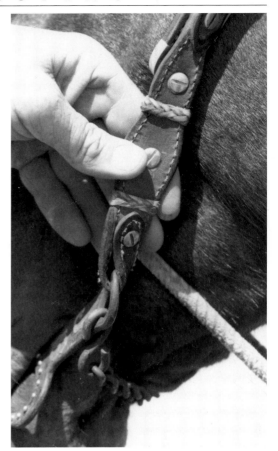

*I check the Chicago screws on my headstall regularly and sometimes glue them.*

field because you need more stop there, but I have always thought hackamore bits are just too severe.

However, some horses do work better in hackamores; some work better in jointed mouthpieces. Another might work better in a Rutledge roper-type bit with a flat mouthpiece, and some horses work better in a chain bit. Usually I have mature horses coming into my barn, and I have to deal with the mouth and the handle they come with. So I can't be set one way or another about headgear. I have to listen to the horse and see what he likes the best.

Regardless of the bridle or bit, the first things that I always check, and quite often, on my headstall are the Chicago screws. I have been really fortunate to never have a problem with one coming loose, but I have seen it happen. At the National Finals one year, Charmayne James lost the Chicago screws in her bridle. That's one out of a million times

that it could happen. Her horse Scamper finished the run, and Charmayne wasn't hurt. But with the majority of horses, you will get in a wreck and get hurt.

You can avoid that problem. On my bridles, I glue the Chicago screws, and I also have taken them completely out and put rivets in their place.

And I regularly check my curb strap. I don't like using leather curb straps either. I use nylon to avoid the chance of something breaking.

But I don't like nylon reins because, when they get wet from sweat or rain and then dry, they become stiff and really hard. I don't like that feel; I want something soft and easy to manage.

I prefer leather reins, just smooth leather without the plait. I like a smaller type of rein so there is less bulk in my hand. With

*A flat leather noseband for a tie-down is mild and often works well for a horse who has lots of rate.*

*Because it has more bite, a rope noseband usually works better on a chargey horse who's on the muscle.*

the coils in my hand, wide reins make it harder to handle everything. Of course, leather reins can get wet and then get hard and stiff, but you can oil them.

## Tie-Downs

It is an absolute must, I think, to use a tie-down in roping events. In the competitive arena, I don't care how broke the horse, you will get in a position where you take hold of his head too much. And the first reaction of any horse—no matter how broke—when he's jerked wrong or off-balance, is to throw his head straight in the air. When his head goes into the air, you are out of control.

The tie-down should be for balance. In the arena, if you jerk a horse the wrong way and the tie-down is snug, he at least can't get his head past center, so to speak. He can only go so far and the rest of his body must respond to bring things back into balance. But if a horse gets his nose up in the air, then it takes you forever to recover.

Which tie-down noseband to use— how wide or narrow—depends on the horse. If I have an older horse with a lot

of rate, I put a soft tie-down on him, usually just barely snug. I might even give him an extra notch. The tie-down is a balancing factor, but a horse with a lot of rate usually won't get himself out of balance.

If I am riding a chargey horse who has too much run, then I might put a rope tie-down on him. It has a little more bite to it than a leather noseband. I don't believe in messing up a horse's nose or cutting it, but I do believe in putting something there that he can feel and respect. Then he is basically punishing himself when his head gets out of position.

When I adjust my tie-down strap, I set it snug. Then, when I take hold of a horse, his nose won't tip up and get on the hori-

*A tie-down can help a horse make a quick recovery if he's pulled off-balance when you're roping. This tie-down is set so my horse can't get his nose up and on the horizontal. When that happens, the tie-down is too loose, and the roper begins to lose control of his horse.*

zontal. I don't want his nose going up at all because when it goes up, you lose all your control.

Here's something else important. I see guys run the tie-down through the breast collar and then down to the cinch. I don't do that. I want a direct pull from the ring in the tie-down noseband straight to the cinch and my saddle. When the tie-down strap goes through the breast collar, you aren't getting its full effect.

When I warm up a horse and lope him around, he tells me how I need to set the tie-down. If he wants to be a little chargey and I have to hold him, then my tie-down is too loose, and I might have a hard time controlling him.

So I shorten his tie-down strap.

A lot of times, when a horse is fresh, he naturally is going to be on the muscle and wanting to go. So I might tighten his tie-down and lope him around for a while. But when I feel him relax, start dropping his head, and act more normal, I might let the tie-down back out. Then I rope a practice steer. If the horse doesn't feel like he is running hard enough, I might give him a little more slack in the tie-down strap and see if that doesn't allow for more run.

Or I may have the adjustment too tight for a horse who wants to lope around nice and easy. If he is not wanting to run at all or isn't really moving out freely, then I let my tie-down out. Your tie-down really controls your run. It creates a balance point with the horse's head, and it affects the length of his stride.

## Breast Collar

I believe a breast collar just keeps your saddle from scooting back, but it won't

106

eliminate the problem of a saddle rolling on a mutton-withered horse. I do think your saddle needs to be adjusted and reset as you rope, no matter what type horse you ride. When you're pulling a steer, the saddle is naturally going to work back somewhat. I won't reset my gear after every steer, but I should pay attention to my gear, especially if I latch onto a heavy steer.

The breast collar needs to be set up and over the point of a horse's shoulders. The main thing: Be sure that it doesn't get pulled up to the base of the neck tight enough to cut off the horse's wind.

## Protective Leg Gear

I am very protective of my horse's legs. That is just like having an insurance policy. At one point or another, a rope horse is going to get himself in a bind—he is going to cross-fire, take a wrong step, or get a wrong jerk, and then he bumps himself.

So I use bell boots and splint boots on my horses. They're leather with neoprene lining. The thing I like best about them is that they're light and easy to put on—just three straps. Some of those leg wraps like they use on racehorses can be pretty time-consuming.

Leg gear is another place where technology has really changed things in the last few years. I have used the neoprene and synthetic foam-type boots, and I think having that suspensory support is a great idea. But I also think that there is too much bulk and a lot of restriction there for a running horse. It seems to me that it would be harder for a horse to turn and move with them. But that is just my personal opinion.

What I'm looking for is protection from a blow, to keep a horse from whacking himself, and to keep him from pulling a tendon. I have been real lucky, I haven't had very many horses hurt.

Another thing: When I'm at a roping, I don't believe in leaving splint boots on a horse all the time. I think that creates too much heat on his legs. So whenever I rope

*Every time you saddle up to ride, check your gear and equipment closely. Worn equipment can prove costly in the competitive arena.*

a steer, I usually pull off my splint boots between my runs.

I think that maintaining a rope horse is just common sense. A lot of horses get hurt because they become fatigued; they've roped too many in a row. But the odd thing can always happen. Use your head, watch what you're doing, and keep your horse in good condition.

I guess, too, the older you get the smarter you get. I was always the one who roped way too many cattle in a row on my

*The more rubber you have wrapped on your horn, the better your rope binds on it. However, if you pull the wraps too tight on the horn, the rubber will get a hard feel to it, and your rope won't bind as well.*

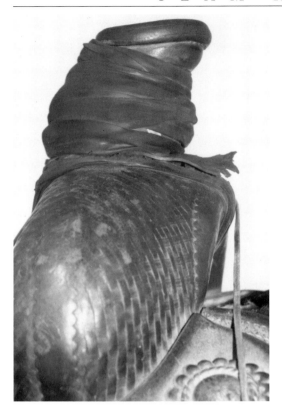

horse. I thought you could rope on a horse all day long. Now I try to let my horse tell me when he's had enough. If I make five or six runs on a horse, and he works good, I'll quit him for the day.

I also do a lot more scoring than I did before. I see now that not taking the time to score cattle in the practice pen will cost me in competition. It's all in how you go about it.

## Rubber Strips

Most ropers don't use enough rubber on their saddle horn.

Most of us, and I include myself, don't ever have enough rubber. Rubber is the cheapest equipment or tool you can have in roping. You can go to the tire shop, and they will almost pay you to haul it off. But go to a roping, and everyone is always asking if you have any rubber.

I use about a 1½-inch-wide strip of rubber, and plenty of it on my saddle horn. At some point, if I don't have

enough rubber on the saddle horn and a steer wants to drag, it just naturally makes my rope run. The more rubber you have, the better the bite and the bind you get with the rope.

I don't think you should put the wraps on your horn too tight. If you do, it makes the rubber too hard, and you don't get as much bite or bind.

I do like to wrap the rubber smoothly around the horn. Some ropers are very particular about putting on a smooth wrap, and others just start wrapping and twist it any way. I like my wraps smooth, but that's hard to do.

## Common Problems

When people come to our clinics, we always look over the horses and gear. The most common problem I see is that the tie-downs are not even close to being adjusted right. The horses are not real balanced, and the horse's head is right in the roper's face when he's trying to rope.

Another common problem is that people don't choke up short enough on the reins when they back into the box to rope. You can't control your horse if your reins are too long. As your horse gathers up and runs, his head comes back toward you, and then your hand comes back to your chest because your reins are out long.

Another common problem concerns the padding. So many people don't have enough pads on their horses; the saddle is sitting right on top of the horse's withers. Other people overpad to the point that the saddle will roll.

Something else really common is a loose back cinch. You can see daylight between the horse's belly and the cinch.

Too, participants sit around at roping clinics for hours. Instead of getting off their horses and uncinching them between runs, they leave them cinched up and keep sitting on him.

The lack of leg protection is another problem I see. You make a horse last as long as possible. He's just like a car. If you don't take care of it, then pretty soon it starts breaking down. When you have a new car that you like, you polish it up and take care of it. It's like that with your horse. If you take good care of him, he is going to respond better than a horse you don't take care of.

# Clay: Saddles

I like a saddle that's comfortable and gives me balance the way I want. I want to sit a horse with my upper body pretty much straight up and down. I don't do a lot of leaning out, or forward or back, but am fairly stationary when I heel a steer. I don't stand up out of the saddle, so I don't get my balance from my lower leg; I grip with my thighs around the horse.

I do get a lot of my balance from my thighs and my contact in the seat of the saddle. And where I get my balance, especially when turning during a run, is from my left thigh bracing against the swell of the saddle. This allows me to push up with my upper body and keep it up to compensate for the turn. So I like a saddle with a good front end on it or good swells.

I have a variety of saddles that I use. Every one of them is different. I have handmade saddles and production-line saddles. It all just depends on how a saddle is made and how it fits each horse. The important thing is the fit. I use the saddle that is proportioned right in relation to how a horse's back is made.

I think there are a lot of good saddle-makers who make attractive and well-built saddles. The main thing with your saddle is that it fits your horse right and doesn't cause soreness. Looking at the top 20 ropers and analyzing their gear and saddles, you'll have a pretty good range of styles in seat, swell, cantle, horn, everything.

I like a good-sized horn on my saddle for heeling. I don't like the smaller horns coming out today. I like a good cap and lip around the top of my horn, and a 3- to 3 1/2-inch-high horn, for a dally horn.

I also like a good-sized swell on the front of the saddle so I can brace against it with my thigh. As for the ground-seat, I prefer a saddle that feels narrower and doesn't spread you out when you sit in it.

A saddle must be made of good leather and have good cinches, especially a good thick flank cinch. That's important because my saddles do take a lot of torque and pull when I rope.

When I cinch up for roping, my front cinch is tight, almost as tight as I can get it. On a scale from one to ten, with ten being just as tight as you can possibly get a cinch, I probably use about eight. That

*By bracing my left thigh against the swell of the saddle, I can better balance my upper body to compensate for the turn when I'm roping.*

means my saddle is right to the point where it has little to no movement. However, when I cinch up a horse snug, I can still move the saddle slightly. Obviously I could go even tighter, but that would just cut the horse in two.

I set my flank cinch tight, too. That helps keep the pressure spread out, rather

*No matter what type saddle and padding you use, the important thing is that your saddle and pad fit your horse's back well and don't cause any soreness.*

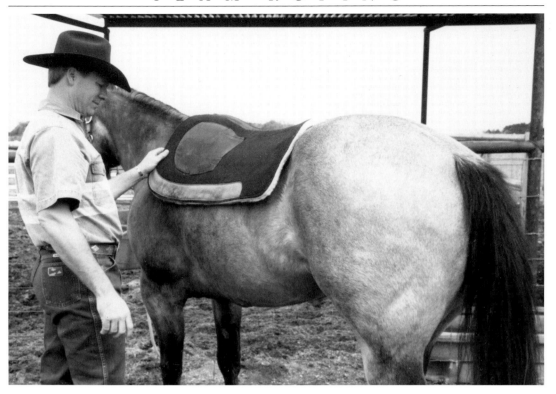

than pinpointing it on my horse's withers when I heel a steer.

## Saddle Pads

When I use a regular saddle, I use a Navajo blanket with a felt pad on top. But with the flex-panel system that some of my saddles have, I can use less padding.

## Bridles, Bits, and Reins

I have probably 40 bits, and I will use all of them occasionally, but I tend to use maybe 3 or 4 the most. The right bit, to me, is just what feels good when I ride, and what I like when I ride a particular horse.

I think everybody has a certain style of riding or a feel for a horse's mouth; the way each person uses pressure on the bit is different, and every horseman is differ-

ent in the type bit he likes to use. Some like a loose-shanked bit, and some like a chain bit; others like high-ports, low-ports, or big bars. I think bit selection is just what you feel comfortable with and what fits your style of riding.

I don't know a lot of technical stuff about bits or about how they work or what they're supposed to do exactly. But I do know my feel for things and what I like or don't like—as far as how a horse responds to a bit—and that's all based on how I use my hands.

I often use a medium-shanked bit, probably 5 or 6 inches long, and usually put 1 to 2 inches of play (slack) in the curb chain. I can rotate that bit back to me and then have it connect pretty solidly. I usually leave that much play in the curb as a warning to the horse. With a lot of people, there is no leeway in their curb chains at all. And there are some people who can pull the shanks straight back, and the message still doesn't get to the horse because the curb's too loose. The 2 inches of play seems to work for me without creating a tug of war between my

The bits I use most often, such as this one, are loose-sided with the shanks curved back and have a port made from big stock. When the bit mouthpiece is made from smaller, thinner stock, it can be too hard on the bars in the horse's mouth.

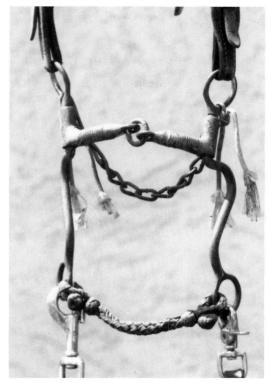

This loose-shanked bit has a jointed mouthpiece. I often use a smaller curb chain with this type bit.

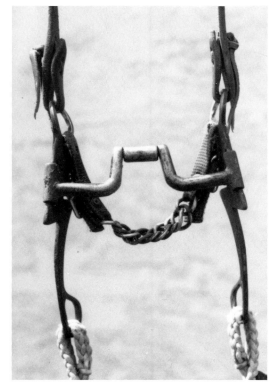

Here's another bit I like that also has loose, swept-back shanks. The broken mouthpiece has a port.

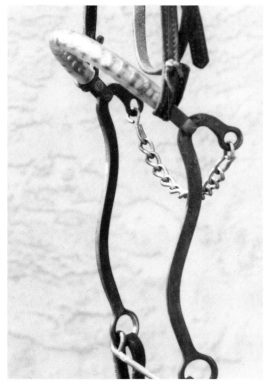

Mechanical hackamores are often used on rope horses.

*Adjusting your equipment properly is important every time you ride. You can be a more effective rider, and it's less likely that you'll gall or sore your heel horse.*

hand and my horse's mouth.

My heel horse, Ike, needs a pretty good bit, yet even it's not severe. I do like using a broken mouthpiece on really light-mouthed horses. And although it's broken in the middle, the two pieces are bent and shaped in a U, so the bit doesn't have that scissor effect found in some snaffles with the straighter pieces joining in the center.

I generally ride bits with a broken mouthpiece with a smaller curb chain. With some bridles, I use a woven curb chain, which lays flat and doesn't bite into a horse much.

The three or four bits I use most are loose-sided, and the shanks are curved back. I've gone toward a ported bit with a pretty wide gap in the port, which gives a lot of tongue relief. I also like bigger bars on my bits. I don't like the 3/8-inch or smaller bars. They're a little too thin and, therefore, too hard on the bars of the horse's mouth to suit me.

With the larger bar on the bit, a rope horse can get hold of it, and he's not scared of it. He can even run against it to a certain degree; that's easy because of the big bar. I want my horses to take hold of the bit and run against it a little, but I still want to have control. However, every now and then I have to back a horse off the bit, or he'll start to run through it. To do that, I run the horse up into the bit, then take hold of him with it and show him that I'm still there.

But because my horses are not over-bridled, they do seem to move freer, and I can still regulate their speed. I usually find a bit that works and then mainly stay with it—whatever works on that particular horse.

I used to switch bits all the time. But I think you can rate yourself as a horseman when you put a bit on a horse and find it works. If you can maintain that same rig on that same horse, and that horse keeps working the same, that says something about your ability as a horseman.

## Tie-Downs

The tie-down I use pretty much depends on the horse. I try to get away with a leather noseband if I can. That has less bite to it than a rope noseband. With one of my horses a leather tie-down isn't enough; he's just too strong

*I adjust the tie-down strap snug when the horse is standing in a relaxed position. After warming up the horse and loping him some, I readjust the strap if I think it's necessary.*

through the neck. He has a big head on him, and he's just tough-mouthed and strong. So I have to stabilize him and take a little of his leverage away by keeping a rope tie-down on him and cinching it down pretty tight.

With my other horse, I can ride a fairly loose tie-down with a leather noseband because she has so much rate. She never goes beyond what I want when she's working. With the gelding, I always have to be sure that he's under control; he goes all-out.

How tight or loose I set the tie-down strap usually depends on how the horse is made, how he travels, how he gets into the ground, and how he turns. It also depends on how a horse is balanced.

When I first get on the stronger horse and have the tie-down set pretty short on him, it feels like he has his head right between his legs. But as I ride him and warm him up, his head comes up and into better position. That's where he's

balanced, and he works good there. With the mare, she feels better with the tie-down set looser and her head out, where she can get it up a little and balance with it.

I look at a horse and usually adjust and fasten the tie-down strap when the horse is standing in a relaxed, comfortable position. I make the tie-down snug, and then I go lope the horse to see how he feels with that adjustment. Some horses, just from the way they are built or the way they react, can get their heads up and back to you—even with the head tied way down. It depends on the horse.

113

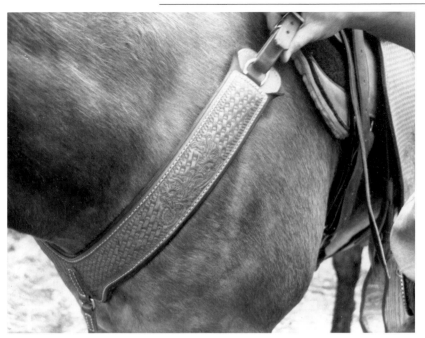

*The breast collar should fit above the point of the horse's shoulder and rest comfortably at the base of his throat—without choking him or restricting him in any way.*

*I use splint and bell boots to protect my horse from the bumps and bruises that can occur when we're hurrying to complete a run.*

## Breast Collar

It would be hard to rope without a breast collar, although whether you need one depends so much on how your horse is built. For heeling, I want to have a breast collar on all the time—not a big bulky one, but something that will keep the saddle from sliding back.

The two good horses I'm riding right now are higher in the withers than in the hip. They each have pretty good, high withers and without a breast collar, the saddle would just keep working backwards. When he's heading, Jake needs a

breast collar because of the dragging and the pull on the horn. In heeling, the pull is the other way, so the breast collar works more to keep a saddle positioned where I want it on my horse's back.

When you set the breast collar, it needs to be up and over the point of the horse's shoulder. I want the breast collar tight, not hanging down. I adjust it so that it's comfortable in the V at the base of the horse's neck.

## Protective Leg Gear

What I've used the most for years are leather splint boots with three little straps, and the red slip-on bell boots. That's pretty much all I've used for the last 10 or 15 years.

I've never really had a horse get crippled in any of the areas that have been covered by what I've put on him for protection the past 15 years. And the gear is all easy for me to use. But it's more for protection from a slam-bang-type injury, when a horse bruises the coronary band or bumps it, rather than for

*I use quite a bit of rubber to wrap my horn—enough that I have about an inch thickness around it from top to bottom.*

*Dallying eventually chews up the rubber wrapped around your saddle horn.*

suspensory problems. I try to pick pretty straight and sound horses, and I've never had many lameness problems.

## Rubber Strips

I use quite a bit of rubber on the saddle horn, probably about 1-inch thick from top to bottom. Depending on where you dally on the horn, the rope will chew up or burn off a portion of your rubber from one run to the next. Then the rubber has to be replaced with another ring or rewrapped to even out the surface.

## Common Problems

When people come to roping clinics, we see a lot of problems with ill-fitting equipment. Usually the saddles don't fit, or the horse isn't padded right.

More than anything, most horses are either way underbridled or way over-bridled. Sometimes the horse is so over-bridled that he is apprehensive and will hardly go forward because he is so scared of his rider and the bit.

Some people don't have any clue; they just hang any bridle on a horse, and then they don't know why he isn't stopping or working right. Or they don't have the curb strap tight enough to touch the horse; it doesn't even come close. Or the tie-down is so loose that the horse's head is straight up in the air.

People overlook the obvious. And many people don't think about the gear and equipment at first. They start thinking something is wrong with the horse. A lot of the time, if they will look over their equipment, they can help correct the problem.

# 10 JAKE ON HORSEMANSHIP

IT'S BEEN SAID that Clay and I are some of the best ropers in the world. We have taken it to another level. We have accomplished more team roping to this point than anyone else. We are always striving to get better.

As far as the roping goes, I think we have mastered that, but as far as horsemanship goes, that's another story. I feel Clay is much farther along in his horsemanship than I am, but we can always become better horsemen.

As for the fundamentals of roping, I honestly feel there is not a lot I can change in the mechanics of that; as for the horsemanship, the fascination is really coming now. To me it all revolves around the horse. We get so much credit for the ability we have as ropers, but the horsemanship in team roping is the weakest area of the event.

Here's something I suggest to anybody if they have the time and the patience: Go ride with a good trainer and learn the fundamentals.

I have had some help, but horseman-

*I can always become a better horseman. I believe horsemanship in team roping is the weakest area of the event.*

ship skills are like roping skills: You have to spend many hours developing the skills. In team roping we concentrate more on the roping than we do the horsemanship. I have ruined good horses just because of my lack of knowledge.

More and more I think the roping game is changing a bit. Now everything I do revolves around my horse. The better horse that I have, the better roper I am. I think the better horsemanship comes along with the better horse. And a horse is just like the rider: He can always improve in a certain area. If there is a better technique and a better way to do it, then I am all for it. If you show me a better, easier way of roping, then I'm going to try that too.

Good horsemanship gives you more tools to use in your roping. I know horsemanship is the weakest area in my roping, as it is with the majority of ropers. It's not so much that the fundamentals of roping are that hard, although it is difficult to collect your thoughts when things are going so fast. But if your horse isn't responding, then you have a real problem.

Often a roper has a horse who is automatic, to the point that the roper doesn't have to think about riding. He's going to be a pretty good roper until he loses that good horse. Then when he has to ride and rope at the same time, he's in trouble. A lot more heelers use good horsemanship because it takes more horsemanship on the heeling end. And now you see more headers getting better too. You see ropers flex their horses—for example, for heeling because it's really hard for a heeler when his horse is chargey . . . running into his hand and wanting to run off.

Compare that with a horse who is light in hand when he runs down the arena. Or consider that, because of good horsemanship, a heeler is better able to hold up a horse's shoulder when the steer starts to turn and the heel horse wants to drop in. Heelers are learning those things. Used to be, what the guys did just depended on their roping ability; wherever the steer was, the roper just turned in, stopped, and roped. Now team ropers are really learning to find that sweet spot, to put themselves in a good position for a consistent shot.

# The Complete Roper

A complete roper is one who can ride and maintain his horse's position and still

*The complete roper can competently handle both his horse and his rope at the same time.*

concentrate on what he's trying to do with his rope at the same time. I relate that to a person with two brains.

The one brain doing all the riding is your left hand. The left hand is the most important part of your roping. It maneuvers the horse. It puts the horse in the box, determines how far to score the steer, releases the horse, and then maneuvers the horse into position to make the catch.

You would think that the other brain, which is the right hand that does the roping, would be the most important, but it does the least amount of work. When a roper leaves the box, the right hand goes to work, too, as it swings the rope, catches the steer, and dallies. But that's all that right-hand brain does.

Once a roper gets to the steer, the left hand rates the horse off the steer. Although the right hand ropes and dallies, the left hand sets the horse, slows down the steer, turns the horse, and leads the steer off. And after the heeler ropes, the left hand faces the horse to finish the run.

Around the roping pen, you have probably heard the saying, "You have to have a good left hand." Now you know what that means.

And that holds true whether you are heading, heeling, roping calves, or whatever. Eventually you can do that at a higher level, where you have enough concentration to separate the two hands, and you can comfortably do all these things at one time. Although one hand is just as important as the other in team roping, if you don't have good position with your horse, you won't have a consistent shot at the steer. So the horse's position is determined by the left hand, which sets up everything in the run.

## Dry Work

People don't ride or dry-work their roping horses enough. A lot of horsemanship is done before you ever get to the roping arena.

I side-pass my horses a lot, for example. I also pull a log a lot with my head horses, so they learn to make lateral movements in stride. And I work on stopping, too.

I dry-work a horse on a log to improve his facing. I put a lot of emphasis on a horse facing. At the level where we rope, a lot of times winning or losing is determined by how fast the horse faces. I believe it's best to teach a horse to face on a log first, then transfer that to your run. The horse should pivot on his front end and swing his hind end around when facing the steer. I don't want him to plant his hind end and swing the front around because, when he comes around then, he usually comes forward, which puts slack in the rope.

To loosen up my horses, I flex them a lot using a snaffle bit and a pair of split reins. That helps keep them flexing to the right or the left, suppling them so they aren't so stiff. I do that when I feel a horse is getting a little strong in my hand. Also, when I'm just riding around, I always make my horse flex one way or the other—even when I'm sitting on him in the box.

When you start flexing a horse, asking him to give his head, you can't recognize it very easily when he responds. I am getting better and better about recognizing when a horse gives his head to me. It's pretty neat once you understand how it feels when you and the horse get on the same wave length. You're able to tell when he starts to give, and you give him some slack. Pretty soon, it doesn't take any effort at all. When you ask a horse to give or flex, he does it right away.

A lot of horses are so used to being pulled on that, when you ask them to flex at the poll and give to you, they try to brace against your hand. We see that a lot at clinics where, sometimes, we don't see much horsemanship at all. A lot of guys can't even fathom a horse giving like that, being that responsive. I was the same way until someone else pointed out that you could get a horse to respond to something light.

We pull on horses' heads so much. A horse is so sensitive that he can feel a fly land on his back, yet we put so much pressure on his mouth with the bit and the bridle. A horse is a strong animal, and you're not going to outpull him. But you can teach him to give, and when he does, you give it back. Pretty soon he can recognize a light feel on your bridle rein; then you can just wiggle your bridle rein a little bit and he will drop his head and feel soft in your hand.

Back in the late 1980s, the old horse I was riding had a mind of his own. He was kind of a renegade, and I always had problems with him in the box. He would pull and I would try to pull harder. Sometimes he would rear out of the box with me. After Paul Tierney helped me with the horse, I could get him to relax a lot more. In the box I could get him to drop his head, so he wouldn't be so tense.

It just comes back to the knowledge, or lack of knowledge, that you have and the ability to use it and your skills correctly.

*A sequence of two.*

*1/ I flex my rope horse by asking him to give his head in both directions, to keep him supple and loose. This also helps when a horse is getting a little strong, pulling against my hand.*

*2/ I also ask my horse to respond to leg pressure and move his hindquarters in either direction.*

*A sequence of two.*

*1/ I teach a rope horse to side-pass before I log him so he learns how to make a lateral movement in stride. I ask my horse to move away from the pressure of my right leg and side-pass to the left. Here, he has crossed over with the hind leg.*

*2/ Because I maintain the pressure with my right leg, my horse continues to move laterally and in stride, crossing one foreleg over the other.*

## Side-Pass

I work on side-passing my horses all the time. It's really important to be able to side-pass your horse before you log him, because you are defeating your purpose if he doesn't understand the side-pass. Like everything else, you put the side-pass into your horsemanship program like a piece in a puzzle.

But if you start by stabbing and jabbing, slamming and jamming a horse, he isn't going to understand what you want. So at first I dry-work him slow and easy without a log, and I get him where I can move him off my foot. I teach him at a walk or trot to move away from the leg pressure. Once he understands that, I can gradually start nudging him easy with the spur and moving him a little farther each time. When he understands what a side-pass is and can do it at a walk, I gradually go a little faster, at a trot. Then later I can use a light log and begin pulling it at a walk or a trot.

*Besides being a good conditioning tool, logging can be used to help sharpen a horse's response on facing a steer. Some people circle to the right when pulling a log, which takes the strain off your leg, but I circle to the left because that's the same direction I go when I'm pulling a steer.*

For the side-pass and the facing work, I want to keep the horse moving continually, just like some horses go around a barrel in stride. They keep moving; they don't drop and set the hind end and then turn. After I face a steer, I also want my head horse to keep moving back, to get the rope tight and get as quick a flag as possible. So I dry-work my horse enough that I can move him off my foot to face without him losing his momentum, his speed. The momentum is still there because he's also learned to make that lateral movement in stride.

# Logging

I log my head horses to work them on facing and feel that it's as important as scoring and rating. I use a light log, so the horse doesn't have to strain to pull it. The horse can concentrate on my leg pressure and where he places his feet.

I also side-pass my horse some when I log him, so he learns to handle himself and learns how to place his feet without stepping on himself. But because I use something light to log my horses, I can repeat the maneuvers for 15 or 20 minutes in a row without physically wearing out my horse.

You do need to warm up a horse before you log him. Walk him around a few minutes and then lope him some and get his muscles stretched out. Horses are like people; if you don't spend the time for the proper warm-up, you risk pulling a muscle and maybe laying up your horse for a month.

I don't start many horses on logging. Usually I'm trying to get broke rope horses ready for competition; they already are accustomed to pulling something. They are trained horses to an extent, but they might not face the proper way, for instance. So that would be about all the training that I do—teaching them to face.

Too, logging is a great conditioning tool and a great tool to knock the edge off a fresh horse. When you have a horse with a lot of juice, when he's fresh, just pull that log real slow and take some steam out of him until he lets down.

121

*A sequence of four.*
*1/ This series of photos shows how I use logging to help my horse work better when he faces. First, my horse must be pulling the log forward consistently—before I ask him to face.*

*2/ In the face, I start my horse's front end around to the right by cueing him with the reins and also use my right foot to move his hindquarters to the left.*

3/ I continue moving the horse around to face the log, in effect making a turn on the forehand.

4/ As the horse faces the log, I often let go of the rope so the momentum helps carry his hindquarters around to complete the turn.

When that fresh horse starts trying to respond and trying to get along and do what I ask, I'll give him a chance and go to a lighter log. I give him the benefit of the doubt as much as possible, but I'm not going to give in if he is going to take advantage of me.

I start pulling a log at a slow walk. It's harder for a horse to pull at a walk than at a trot. There is no momentum at a walk. A horse can even lope easier with a log, versus just walking real slow. There's a constant drag at a walk because you are basically pulling dead weight.

I drag a log about the same distance behind me as I pull a steer. I want to give the horse the same feel, when he's pulling a log, that he would have pulling a steer.

I use different weight logs at different times. Usually when I am logging a horse to work on his facing, I use a really light log. I don't try to fatigue the horse. I just let him know something is back there, usually about half of a cross-tie. That is just for my facing drill because I want a lot of repetition then. I usually face the horse between 10 and 20 times. When he starts to get the hang of it, that's when I quit him. Don't overdo this with your horse.

I have also pulled a car tire without a rim. It's small and not very heavy at all. But if I have a horse who wants to be really chargey or too strong, then I go to the heavier log or to a full cross-tie.

I work my horse in a circle to the left when I log him. A lot of people log their horses while circling to the right. That takes all the pull off your leg, and with the log to the inside, it is easier.

But I always log the horse the same direction I go when I'm pulling a steer. That's to the left because I try to simulate the same movements I use during my run. If I'm working to get the fresh off a horse, I move in a really big circle; then I don't have that pull straight back over my hip that comes from making a tight circle. The ideal, if you have enough area, is to make a big circle or go in a straight line. Better yet, go outside the arena. Pulling a log has a tendency to pack your arena and make the ground hard.

Most of the time I try to stay at the upper end of the arena, the same place I would be once I rope a steer. If at times the horse begins to anticipate, wanting to fudge and turn early, I just keep circling him to the left until he relaxes and keeps pulling steady.

The steady pull is what I'm after, and I don't want the horse anticipating at all. I want him responding to my cue. If he wants to do things on his own, I keep going in a circle until he relaxes and gets his mind more on pulling.

## Facing

I won't work on facing with a horse until I have a good consistent pull on the log with him. Then I try to set the horse up, cueing him to tell him that we are going to face now. Usually I'm trotting, but as I get ready to face, I might speed him up a bit into a lope. Just trotting, it's hard for a horse to use his momentum to swing the hind end around. So I cue him for a lope before I face him. But if I feel the horse anticipate the maneuver, I continue loping and bring him around one more time.

If the horse doesn't anticipate anything, I start his head around to the right by neck-reining him on the left side, and I cue him with my right foot or spur while he's still pulling the log. As I continue to bring his front end around with my reins, I continue to use my right foot to move the hind end around. I want him facing in line with the log or steer.

I often let go of my rope as I face, to let the momentum help carry the horse's back end around. He is leaning into that weight as he's pulling so, as he turns to face, he loses his balance somewhat as I undally. So he has to keep shuffling his feet to regain his balance. When done correctly, the momentum of the face propels his back end around his front end, with the motion going away from the steer or log.

And because he is still off-balance as I face, that also gives him the momentum to step backward once he has faced. I always make sure that I take three or four steps back when I let my rope go as I face.

The reason: If a header faces too early or the heeler misses his dally, there is slack in the rope. When that happens, usually the first thing people do is jerk on the horse to make him back up. He doesn't have any idea what's going on, so he comes up in the front end. But if you undally or let the rope slide on the saddle horn and always make your horse take three or four steps back as you face in the dry-work, then he knows what to do when there's slack in the rope. And also, whenever you get in a bind and take hold of the horse, he knows to back up. He becomes like a calf horse who knows that slack in the rope is a no-no.

Actually a great facing horse just naturally learns how to come around on his own. He pulls along, and when he starts to face, he jumps in the air, it seems, with all four feet, like a cat. That doesn't take any time at all and you shave off more tenths. There is no way humanly possible for you to teach a horse to do that. Some just naturally have a knack to do it. If somebody knew how to train a horse to do that, I would send all of my horses to him.

Some people consider it a wrong for a horse not to face off his rear end and set and turn, but that's for horse shows. There, you want the horse to drop his hind end whenever the heeler comes tight, which forces the head horse to spin around.

For speed, you want the horse to pull the steer—almost tracking off on the diagonal. When the heeler ropes, the head horse can still be pulling as he is facing. Then when everything becomes tight, the head horse jumps around and back, which takes slack out of the rope. For that reason, you always want the horse to back up a couple of steps to keep the rope tight.

When I see my heeler rope, I start my horse's head around and cue him with my right foot in his side. That's a cue for him to swing his hind end around and face. He learns to take a shortcut but ends up with the same results and has a quicker time.

You can even face early a lot of times. If a horse really jumps around, a flagger—even though the ropes aren't tight—will go ahead and flag you. You may have shaved off a tenth of a second. And team roping comes down to tenths of a second a lot of the times.

That's where horsemanship comes into play. Having a horse who faces well is just as important to me as having one who scores or pulls good. You must finish the run just like you started it—fast.

# Loping and Leads

My horses always take a left lead no matter what. A team roping horse should be left-leaded and never get into the right lead during the run. The horse I did so well on was a really right-leaded horse, so I had to spend hours and hours teaching him to break in his left lead. I spent lots of time loping in small circles, teaching him to pick up the left lead automatically.

But you are not going to teach a horse to take a left lead when you're running full-blast after a steer. And there's really no way you can control the lead during your run. Once a horse starts out of the box, and you're chasing a steer, you're not going to get him to switch his lead.

The main thing to understand: It is going to be hard for a horse to pull if he is in his right lead. The horse will be weak in the corner, trying to turn off and pull the steer at the same time. Then he has to try to switch from his right to his left lead. And for just an instant, he'll bog down in the corner and not be able to pull. That's really hard for a horse, especially since the weight of the steer hits him at the same time. That's when you get injuries to your horse's legs. Also, I've seen horses fall trying to switch leads in the corner.

A head horse must take a left lead. However long it takes for you to teach him to stay in that left lead, do it.

## Stopping and Rate

I do a lot of stopping with my head horses. I lope them down the arena and try to teach them to stop on their hind ends. That fits right in with what I need them to do when I set a steer. If a horse doesn't have a natural smoothness in his stop and starts bouncing, I lose control and also break the rhythm of my run. I am not going to get a very good handle on the steer for my heeler. That's why you usually can take a good calf roping horse and convert him to a head horse; he has a natural tendency to stop well.

You don't want to build up too much speed with a horse who isn't broke very well when you're working on the stop. If you lope down the arena with a lot of speed and jerk on the horse's head, he throws up his head, which drives his front feet in the ground and hollows out his back. He's going to feel like a jack-hammer.

I suggest instead that you lope your horse around slowly and tell him whoa. Then take hold of him gradually and set him up for the stop. Don't get in too much of a hurry; let him figure out what you want. Then he won't be so resistant and stiff in his spine.

If a horse is really chargey, I lope him first in little tight circles before I work on his stop. I get him to the point where he does a little hobby-horse slow lope and relaxes and drops his head. This means he'll flex at the poll and give to me instead of pulling against me when I work on his rate and stop.

Something else I do with a horse who is a little green, or one who wants to be a little chargey, is work him on a lead steer or a donkey in the arena. I track the steer or donkey and lope the horse behind until he rates off the steer.

That's the way a lot of guys learn to heel. To pick up the timing, they get a slow

126

*At home I sometimes rope the heels to help my head horse improve his rate.*

steer and lope behind him, just following him around. When the steer slows down a little, the roper can get his horse close enough to rope the steer's back feet, and then he can teach the horse to stop when he throws his loop.

Even though I'm trying to get a head horse to rate when I do this at home, I rope the heels. It's basically the same position. Otherwise, if I head, I have to take the rope off the steer's horns. This way, I still can follow the steer, rope, dally, and make the horse stop and back. And the horse also learns how to take that jerk when the steer reaches the end of the rope.

Too, I try to simulate that same type of stop without the steer and work on stopping alone. When I stop a horse, I want him to stick his back end underneath him. I want to teach him to use that natural stop, not a bounce. This kind of dry work sharpens a horse on both his stopping and his rate.

It's so important when a horse has that natural rate; he can collect and balance himself. But if he has too much run and

gets too close to the steer, you have to put more pressure on him to rate him back. Then when you turn the horse's head loose, he's out of balance. That's why, with a head horse, it's so seldom that you find one who has both a lot of run and natural rate. That's a combination you don't see very often.

Usually a horse has a lot of run, but doesn't have a lot of rate. Or if he has a lot of rate, he usually doesn't run very fast; you're always having to push him. So when you find that combination in a horse—a lot of run and a lot of rate—he is usually a really good horse.

*Risk is involved whenever you rope or ride, but you can help avoid a wreck by using good horsemanship and common sense.*

# Seasoning and Practice

If I have a young horse who's a little green, I might need to rope on him every day to bring him along and season him. But I don't want to fatigue him. A maximum of 10 steers is a lot for a horse at any one time. Whenever you get beyond that point, you are doing him more harm than good.

Give the horse a recess. A young horse has a tendency to get mad sometimes when he's worked steady; his adrenaline gets going, or maybe he's a hot-blooded horse. A lot of guys believe in working a horse through that, but not very many young horses give up when they get hot, and then

it's just a big fight. You are better off tying up the horse for a little while or even waiting until the next day to go back to work.

I've done it too—tried to ride a horse through a mad spell. But I feel I've become a better horseman now. I can recognize when a horse has had enough. I'm like everybody else—I start roping, it's fun, and I don't want to quit.

If I don't have enough horses to do that, I keep roping on the same horse—knowing that I am messing up. I've never been on drugs, but roping, it seems, is almost like an addiction. When you get started, it's hard to stop. Usually your horse is the one who pays the price.

You can rope four or five steers in a row on a horse and then tie him up, let him catch his wind, and in 30 minutes, rope another four or five. You can do this and rope on him all day long, and you won't hurt him. That's how you can get in a lot of practice and not ruin your competition horse.

Whenever I'm practicing for my rodeo runs, I use my practice horse. He's a work horse and that is his job—to rope a lot of steers in a row. He is a sacrifice to relieve my good horses, so I have them tuned, fit, and ready for the money runs.

Of course, that all depends on the good horse. Maybe one needs a lot of roping to keep the edge off and to keep him working good. But a good horse with a good mind might not take a lot of work; he just needs riding. With a really good horse who has a good temperament and who doesn't get too high, I may rope only two or three steers on him once a week. So about all I do with him is exercise him and keep him in shape and score lots of steers on him.

## Taking Risks

When you rope and have good instruction, you are upping the odds that you are going to have a successful day. But I don't care what level horseman you are, there are extreme risks whenever you deal with animals. So there are certain precautions you take and wisdom that you must use when you ride a horse. You use a lot of common sense to avoid as many wrecks as possible.

As far as getting my hand caught in a dally—I can live without a finger or thumb. But the thing that scares me the most is falling and slamming my head into the ground, or having a horse roll over my head. I don't want that to ever happen.

That type accident often is caused when the head horse gets too close to a steer. The steer then tries to cut in front of the roper to get away. If you are riding a green horse or a horse a bit out of control, that steer is going to trip you up. The horse's front feet will hit the steer's hind feet; the steer gets turned sideways in front of the horse. This, in turn, drives the horse's front end straight down; then you are at the mercy of the Lord.

Roping can be extremely dangerous. If you don't take precautions, you could get in a wreck. Many people don't think about that. They worry so much about their roping that they quit riding their horses. They concentrate too much on roping and not enough on riding safely.

# 11 CLAY ON HORSEMANSHIP

*Your horsemanship helps determine how consistent your performance will be as a team roper.*

ON ANY GIVEN run, your horsemanship might not make any difference at all. But when you're talking about the ability to make run after run and perform consistently as well, then horsemanship enters into your roping. Horsemanship also determines whether you ruin your rope horse and have to buy another one, or if you can ride the same horse for 10 years.

Certain things in horsemanship, and not only in the arena, affect the longevity of your horse—what you can get out of him and what you can do on him. Your horsemanship plays a part in how you maintain your horse and whether you add to his ability. A lot of horsemanship is not teaching the horse what to do so much as just showing him what you want. Then once the horse does that maneuver, you have to know how to maintain him so that he'll do that same thing every time.

Most of the great horses—and those with the ability to work at the level where I can make a living—are not trained per se. Eighty percent of it is all natural—the horse's athletic ability, disposition, conformation, and cow sense. All that wrapped together makes the great horse.

Yes, you can ruin a horse like that, but if he's in the right hands and he's the right type, he will make a good rope horse. His rider shows the horse the right things, then leaves him alone and doesn't crucify him or mess him up when the horse doesn't understand what the rider wants.

Those good horses are born, not just made. And I've heard reiners and cutters talk the same way: The great ones are born.

A sequence of two.

1/ I try to maintain the performance level of my heel horse by paying attention to the little things when I do dry work. During my warm-up, for example, I'll ask my horse to give his head to either direction. I can check his response and be sure he'll be as responsive as I'd like before I get to the roping pen.

2/ In the same way, I also check to see if my horse responds well when I ask him to move his hindquarters away from the pressure of my leg.

# Horses and Horsemen

First, let me put the kind of horse I'm riding in context for the reader. At my level of competition, the horses I buy are really good natural athletes and also trained ones. They know their leads, are responsive to whoa, can back fluidly, have a turnaround or at least some lateral control, and are responsive to a neck rein. I do the finish work on my horses, the little things that make them better suit me and my style of riding and roping.

As far as I'm concerned, I think there are horse trainers and horsemen. A trainer is somebody who is always training on a horse. He's always trying a different bridle on the horse, or poking and prodding and trying to teach a horse something.

A horseman, to me, can take the horse, use him, and maintain the horse at a performance level so you can continue to compete on him. That horse will keep working at that level, without ever decreasing his level of performance and without the rider having to prod him all the time to do his job, or having to keep him from finding a way to avoid the job.

There's a fine line there. You do have to correct a horse, but there are ways to do it that don't tear down his confidence or break the rider's communication with him. Sometimes a horse trainer can break down all communication with the horse because the trainer's approach is either "my way or no way." The horse must do the maneuver because the trainer's going to make him do it, one way or the other.

I think there's another aspect in horsemanship: A good horseman communicates to the horse what he wants, but lets the horse figure things out, rather than making him do things. This horseman also has a calm manner; he might correct his horse, but you never really see him doing it. His approach instills confidence in a horse instead of tearing it down.

To me, a horse's total mental realm is either one of confidence or the lack of it, and he is either comfortable or uncomfortable in his work. It's one or the other. When you put a horse in an uncomfortable situation where there is no confidence on his part, he will search until he finds a comfortable place, and then he'll relax. That's what a horseman accomplishes.

That's the rewarding thing for me about horsemanship. I love working with my horses, being around them, doing maneuvers with them, trying to learn more about how to communicate with them with my riding techniques.

# Dry Work

Basically, between rodeos I just keep my good horses fit. I trot and lope circles on good ground. I stop and maneuver a horse around some, maybe roll him back. I fool around with that kind of thing, and I enjoy doing it.

For one of my horses in particular, that type work is really good for him because he tends to get on the muscle; he can get a little strong in the roping pen and then isn't as responsive as I'd like him to be. It's good for him to stop, or for me to flex him and do rollbacks to help keep him responsive to my feet and hands. And I might do

a little bit of two-tracking. But the type of dry work I do all depends on the horse. Some horses need more of that type work; some don't need it much at all.

If, for example, a horse is getting stiff in one area of his body or sluggish in performing a maneuver, he needs to be a little more flexible and free-moving. So I break that stiffness loose in whatever manner I determine might be the best. Whether it's rolling back on the fence or just stopping the horse . . . whatever the maneuver . . . I work to flex and loosen him up. I want him to give more response in that area, no matter if he's responding to the bridle, my feet, or any other cues.

The mare I've been riding recently rates well and is cowy, but I really don't know her yet. So far, I've just kept her in shape. She doesn't need a lot of runs, but she does need to be in shape, and she needs some loping to make sure she's not high. A lot of mares, it seems, have a tendency to be a little high-strung. So I want to ride her enough that she's in really good shape and to be sure she has the edge knocked off; then she is really ready to work. But I won't practice roping a lot on her unless it's under the right conditions.

I have a little ritual I do with my horses; it's like a tune-up or a systems check. I usually walk a horse a good way, just easing him around at first. Then I pick up with my inside rein and use my inside foot, and let him take a step over—still walking—to the outside. I just block the horse on one side until he responds and steps over to the other side. I'll work him like that in either direction at both a walk and a trot.

Then I may ask him to lope and do the same thing in small circles at a slow lope. I may again ask a horse to go off-track and step to the outside of the circle, while using my inside rein and foot to cue him. Or I might ask the horse to go to the inside of the circle, stepping across the circle. Then I pick up the other rein and use the other leg and ask him to step across again, to the opposite direction.

A sequence of two.

1/ As part of my systems check, I use my inside rein and foot to cue my horse, asking him to step over, to the out-side, and maintain his stride. I do this first at a walk and then at a trot.

2/ Then I might ask my horse to perform the same maneuver at a lope, again using my inside rein and foot to move him off-track, to the outside.

When I'm heeling, sometimes I need a horse to move out as he turns, but at other times I need him to cross over inside the corner with the steer. Sometimes it's a sharp corner; sometimes it's a rounded one. So I like to build that kind of quick response into my horses, where they pay attention to my cues so they can handle the corner, whatever it is. I do that kind of dry work all the time with my heel horses.

Usually a lot of my dry work goes, ulti-mately, to the left. Every now and again I might lope a horse in a couple of circles to the right, or do a maneuver to the right. However, I'm usually going straight, or maybe even angling to the right—with every intention of crossing the horse over in some way and going to the left. In a maneu-ver like two-tracking, or a side-pass, I work my heel horses and bring them across and over to the left to work on the way I need them to make a corner on a steer.

*A sequence of two.*
*1/ Side-passing a horse helps him learn how to handle himself so he can make a corner on a steer. Although I'm working to the right in the photo, I'll change direction and also work to the left.*

*2/ My leg cues block the horse's motion in one direction and direct him to move in the other or add impulsion to a maneuver. My hands on the reins also help direct him and either block or release his forward motion.*

## Taking Control

I'm looking for a good response from a horse without an over-reaction from him. I like to have control, but I don't like a horse to be overbridled. In fact, I probably underbridle a horse more than I over-bridle one.

When I'm competing, I'm riding the horse with my hand all the time, usually working somewhat against his mouth. So I have a certain amount of pressure most of the time on the bit. A rope horse must get used to that. For me, he has to be bridled so he can rest against my hand, but be comfortable. Yet when I pick up on the rein, I can still get some response.

And if I really pick up, I can bring things to a stop. Sometimes that's hard to do with different horses. They all have different levels of tolerance, and it depends on the individual horse's mouth.

## Leg Cues

When I use my feet and legs to cue a horse, I'm asking the horse to go some-where. If I block his motion with a left rein and use my left foot on his side, then I am asking him to go to the right. It might be on a diagonal or straight across. That depends on how much I block his forward motion with my rein hand.

My feet ask the horse for impulsion—to go forward or go faster. But my feet can also work as a block. If a horse is moving to the left, then I can use my left foot as a block in that direction. Or, for example, for a pivot on the hind end, usually my feet are asking a horse to step away from the block. When I block his motion to the right side with my right foot, for example, he can still move, but it's to the left.

I use my feet also for stopping, to gain more slide. While I lift or elevate a horse's front end with my hands, I use my feet and legs to drive his rear end up under him in the stop. This helps him learn to walk in front and slide with the hind end.

## Rate and Stop

To help improve a horse's rate, put him behind a slow steer at home, or use a practice burro. Then turn the horse's head loose, so to speak, and see what he needs to get him tracking and rating well. Then you set the horse's head and handle him so he learns to position himself where he should be and rate himself behind the steer. But you have to know what you're looking for and how to help the horse.

A lot of people try to put rate on a horse by pulling on him. But that can teach him to run against your hand too much by bracing against it. You don't ever see a reiner or a cutter, for example, pull on the horse a lot, because then the horse learns to push hard against the rider's hand.

But roping is a little different because another element enters into the equation. To be a top roper, you have to be able to maneuver the horse at a run, so he does rest against your hand, somewhat like a race horse does. But there's a fine line between feeling one resting his mouth against the bit and your hand and pushing too much against the bit.

At the same time, a roper must be able to take hold of a hard-running horse's head and maneuver him—without the horse over-reacting or running off, running through the bit or the rider's hand, as it's sometimes called. When that happens, the roper either is holding the horse's head too much or maybe isn't using enough pressure on the bridle rein. Either way, the horse is really pushing against the bit and the rider's hand, rather than resting against them.

As for rate, I think you get a lot more rate when you put the horse in a situation

*A sequence of two.*
*1/ Another way to check a horse's responsiveness is to stop him . . .*

*2/ . . . and immediately roll him back in the other direction.*

135

*A sequence of two.*
*One of the best ways to help a horse learn to rate is by tracking a slow steer, which can also help relax an experienced rope horse. Either way, ride quietly toward the steer until the horse is where you want him in relation to the steer.*

*Keep positioning the horse until he learns that where you want him to be is the most comfortable place.*

where he is trapped, so to speak, and has to figure out things on his own. That works best when there's nothing but the horse, the fence, and the cow. You back the horse off the cow and get the horse positioned where you want him in relation to the cow, and hooked on the cow. Then you're pretty much able to turn the horse

loose. You just cruise him around behind the steer, or even your burro, until the horse finds out that when he cows and rates, everything is comfortable.

"Cow" in a heel horse is a factor. That's where his rate, the ability to back off the steer and anticipate the steer, comes in. You don't have to physically maneuver your horse because he's doing it on his own. The cow sense gives him that. That's good. If you don't have that kind of horse, you have a horse who only takes orders. His response is to you moving him. He's got to be broke and handle well enough so when you move him, his head doesn't come up or his body doesn't get out of position.

As for positioning the horse behind the steer, if he's really green, like a colt, I position him dead behind the steer, especially when a colt might have a tendency to crowd the back of the steer a little bit, maybe even click his feet against the steer's hind feet. The horse will start watching, especially after he's stumbled a couple of times.

Or if you use a pretty tall steer to track, a green horse isn't as likely to run up too close and bump his head against a tall steer. So that also teaches a horse to stay back. If you can position the horse dead behind the steer and hold the horse there, he will learn to stay back far enough to keep his head in good position, so he can watch and keep himself from stumbling because he's too close. Then he'll learn to track a steer, rate behind him, and develop that cow instinct.

You handle things a little differently, for example, with the 12- or 15-year-old solid rope horse who's carrying a novice roper, but not rating really well. That charginess comes from the horse's speed; he's anticipating things and getting in too big a hurry because he knows what's coming. So you back off and quit running so hard on cattle. Use a slow steer and just fool around with him, taking things easy to relax the horse. You track the steer and rate the horse, but there's not a lot of pressure on the horse.

Sometimes you might have to actually stop the old horse in a certain spot during a practice run to get his mind off charging up too close on a steer. You can teach a horse to back off that way, too, but then you're also teaching him more to respond off your hand, not to really rate behind a steer.

There are two ways horses stop. A horse stops on his hind end or on his front end. At impact, with the rope on the steer, the horse should be at a dead stop either way.

I like my horses to stop gathered up and on the back end. The reason: That type stop doesn't bounce my delivery when I throw my loop; the bottom of my rope doesn't bounce on the ground.

Right at the moment of impact is when the horse comes to a complete stop. If he stops hard on his front end, that jars me just as I am trying to set a loop down nice and smooth. All of a sudden—bam. That's going to bounce my rope on the ground, or make it increase in speed all of a sudden. So my rope will hit and bounce or not hit the mark at all. Plus that kind of stop throws me forward.

When a horse slides with his hind end tucked under, it's like a shock absorber. He takes all the shock out of the stop, so it keeps my delivery smoother through impact.

How well a horse stops depends a lot on his conformation. Either he is built to stop well with his hind end up under him, or he's not. If a horse doesn't stop all that well, you can try to lift his front end by elevating his shoulders and keeping them up when doing your dry work. Then, perhaps, the horse will learn to drop the hind end first when he stops.

But you have to be careful when you start dry-working a horse on stops. You have to know your timing and what to do in that situation. Otherwise, if you are too severe on his mouth when you ask him to stop, you just make the horse apprehensive. Then he's thinking about protecting his mouth. So he'll stiffen his spine and brace against the bit and stop on the front end.

At clinics, I can tell ropers what I think might help to improve a horse's stop. But in stopping you must know what you are doing to really get good results. That maneuver can be so individualized. It depends so much on the horse, how he's made, how his mouth is, how the horse has been handled, how his pattern for stopping has been set, and how he was trained to stop. Some horses are built so they can't physically stop well. But many stopping problems are related to how the horse was broke.

Sometimes if you can see that a horse might stop a little better if you did this or tried that, then try it. Maybe you can alter your headgear—let out the tie-down, or take off the tie-down altogether, change the bridle, adjust the curb strap, for example. You can try anything you think might help. Or maybe this particular horse is really green right now, or maybe he isn't saddled right. When your saddle hurts a horse's back, that can cause him to not stop right. Those are all the things you have to evaluate.

# Practice Burros

I dry-work my heel horses a lot with my practice burro. I do this type heeling work in a slow lope.

The best part: I can rope the burro on my good horse, the gelding, who sometimes gets too keyed up with roping practice in the arena. Roping a burro isn't like a real practice run, yet it is in some ways. I get my practice, and Ike gets his exercise, but roping the burro doesn't get him all keyed up like it does when he's leaving the box and really running a steer. There's none of that. He just stays laid-back mentally and lopes into position.

Roping the burro does two things: It gives me practice and gives my horse exercise. Those two things go hand in hand. Roping out of the box a lot does give me practice, but isn't always good for the horse.

While roping a burro can be really relaxing to some horses, such as Ike, others get keyed up when worked on the burro. Anything similar to going toward a steer can get some horses chargey. It's trial and error. Each horse is a completely different individual. You just have to read the signs and see what you have with each horse. He'll tell you. (For more about practice burros, see the chapter on roping the heel dummy.)

# Seasoning and Practice

When a horse gets too hot mentally, he's much too strong on the bridle, for example, or prances, or simply works the bit, pops his head, that kind of thing. Knowing when to quit when working a horse is probably the most important part of horsemanship. You have to recognize when the horse has had enough, about all he can take, and give him a break mentally. There's the fatigue factor, too, when you can feel a horse physically struggling; that means it's also time to quit work.

Most horses learn to protect themselves when they're overworked by somehow expressing their stress or fatigue. A horse may come out of the box and run through the bridle, or he might start chewing on the bit. Or maybe he just gets mad and shows it in some way. In the box, for instance, he won't stand or won't give you an opportunity to start him off right or set him up right. During the run he might feel like he's running off or running too hard. Once a horse reaches that point, when he's too hot mentally, he will do something wrong.

Too, once a horse reaches that point, most people think the horse is working bad. So that person's next move is to correct the horse. The rider puts the horse in the box and jerks him around or spurs or whips him. The rider thinks he's going to fix that problem.

Understand, now, the horse got to that mentally hot point because he'd already had too much work. Right now, he's already had more than his brain can understand or handle. He's uncomfortable and doesn't understand what you're doing. All he knows is that you're going to back him into the box and run again and again. Now that he's shown you how uncomfortable he is, you keep backing him into the box and correct him or whip him on top of it. He doesn't understand what that's all about: "You're whipping me because I'm tired and confused."

So now the horse is also trying to figure a way to get away from the spurring or whatever. First, he was just trying to figure how to get away from all the runs; now he's going to figure a way to get away from you abusing him. And you've just escalated the process—getting him hotter mentally.

A lot of times it's best to uncinch the horse, go tie him up, and let him sit for 30 minutes. You go shoot the bull with the other ropers, or get on your other horse. Let the first horse cool out mentally and physically before you come back and make another run or two on him.

If later he goes right back to work and makes a good run, you know you quit at the right time. The horse still has good runs left in him, but his attention span and his brain can handle only so many successive runs. Maybe his limit is only seven runs instead of the ten runs you wanted.

That's usually true on pretty good, mature rope horses. They have a tolerance span for seven or eight runs and up. Some of the good rope horses may not be the greatest in physical ability or how they work, but will let you run 50 steers in a row. Those horses will back in the box the same way every time and run steers again and again; their tolerance level extends that high.

The next horse may go only to 10 head, and with another horse, the number may be 13, and another may handle only 8. Some horses have only a two-run tolerance. You have to be smart enough to know and learn what your horse can handle.

You can increase the number of runs your horse can handle—if you don't punish him when he's past his limit. If you stop roping at that point on a regular basis for the next few days, maybe 2 weeks down the road you might get a couple of more runs out of the horse. You can keep progressing with a horse to increase the number of runs he can make.

Sooner or later, you're going to hit that spot where the horse does something to tell you that last run was enough. What you do from that point on is important. How you handle things then determines whether you make any progress beyond that point with your horse, or if you are starting to ruin the horse.

But you can rope on a horse all day long if you run four or five head, uncinch, and slow down for 10 or 15 minutes. Let the horse catch his air and forget about the arena and roping. Let him look over the fence and at the grass and trees. Then come back and cinch him up a little later. You might be able to do that all day long and never hurt him a bit.

But if that horse has a tolerance span for 10 runs, and you try to make 11 or 12 runs on him that day and freak him out, you have taken away from the horse. You haven't maintained the horse's level of performance or built on anything with that horse.

Nowadays, if I go try a horse, I'll rope until I hit a spot where, physically, I know that's enough. He's sweating, he's panting, and he needs a breather. But most of the time a horse reaches that used-up stage mentally before he reaches the physical stage.

When I go try a horse, I might try to run 10 steers in a row, but very seldom will I run 10 head on my good horses, or even a practice horse. Maybe seven or eight is about it. But I will try a horse on up to about 10 head sometimes, just to see where he is mentally, how much he can handle. I try his engine out, see what I

*Knowing when to quit—no matter if you're doing dry work or roping in the arena—is the most important part of horsemanship. How you handle things when your horse is exhausted mentally or physically helps determine how willing and relaxed a partner you have the next time you rope.*

have, and see what he can take. And that tells me a lot about a horse.

If you back in the box after four or five runs and the horse won't look at the steer, or he's leaning the wrong way, or doing anything that says, 'I don't want to,' you know that's all a horse has—a four- or five-run limit. You might progress through that and beyond four or five runs with that horse. The problem: You really don't know what was going on before you got him—what his training process was, what kind of abuse he might have experienced, whether the horse is just green, or if that's really all he can handle.

So accept what a horse gives you. Asking for too much is the most common mistake I see ropers make and what ruins more horses than anything.

# 12 ROPING CATTLE

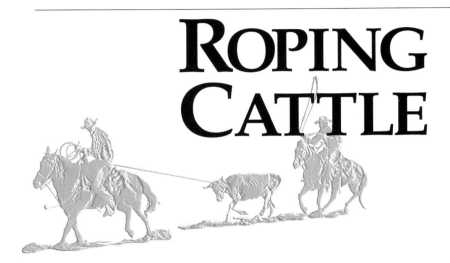

## Jake: Practice Cattle

MOST PEOPLE don't want a lot of cattle around because of the expense of feeding them. Yet, I rope every single day, and if I don't have a lot of cattle, they burn out quickly.

The practice cattle I try to get, and that seem to last the best, are bigger steers that weigh anywhere from 450 to 550 pounds, 600 maximum. Usually a smaller steer won't last near as long as a bigger steer.

Often I take a loss on cattle. If I buy fresh steers, they will last only a couple of months. For example, if I have 15 head that last 3 months before they are completely worn out, I'll lose a couple of hundred dollars a head plus my feed.

But a lot of hobby ropers buy their cattle really small, and they might rope only two times a week. Their cattle will last them a season. Mine won't.

So I try to shop around for bigger cattle. Most ropers think that when cattle get to 450 or 500 pounds, they are too big. I might buy a set of 25 used steers. Then I go through that set and sort off about 10, mostly the black ones and maybe some brindles—the saltier cattle that never got roped down.

They make great practice cattle. They are big and strong by then, and I can rope them for 2 or 3 months. They might even gain a little weight. When I'm through with them, I can ship them and keep my money together.

I very seldom buy fresh steers for practice. The loss on them is too much because I rope them up so quickly, and their feed bill is too expensive. The bigger cattle stay good for practice for a longer period.

I like black cattle, not Angus, but Corriente cattle and also the brindle-type. I want black cattle because they stay good for practice a lot longer than most, and they are harder-running cattle.

But at rodeos I prefer to stay away from black cattle because they usually are more aggressive and harder-running. I want to draw some other type. It's really important, too, at rodeos that you can read a steer by his type. You can often determine, just by the look of him in the pen, if he's really wild or not.

*Black, Corriente-type cattle are great for practice because they last longer than other kinds of cattle. However, Corriente steers can also be more aggressive and harder-running than most.*

*First turn a fresh steer out of the chute and haze him to the catch pen several times so he learns where to go when he leaves the chute.*

Longhorns, for example, aren't quite as gritty as black Corrientes. I like them best, the ones that look like fighting bulls, for practice. But I try to stay away from the paint-colored, Holstein-type cattle with dairy blood in them. Those cattle usually don't last long.

The type cattle I want to draw when I'm competing are those that don't run very hard and who seem to want to play the game. I don't, for instance, want to draw Brahma cattle because they have a tendency to run. I don't want steers that try to outrun you or duck and dodge—the more broncy cattle. They have their own game plan—figuring out how to get away from you.

# Clay: Practice Cattle

For practice cattle, I would say 400 pounds up to 500 is the ideal range. I like Corrientes the best. Probably Longhorns would be next-best, but they are pretty wild, run harder, and are a little smarter. Corrientes or Longhorns are what most people rope.

The Longhorns are smarter than some cattle, so they figure ways out of things. Longhorns either start setting up and stopping, or they outrun you. They learn to cut to the left, or they drag. They rebel. They are smarter than Mexican steers.

The best kind of steers to practice on are those that can learn how to lead and to follow the head horse. There are some things you can do with your practice steers—the way that you break them in and train them—that will impact how long they last.

For example, you need to show your practice cattle the back end of the arena really good before you start roping them. Run them through the chute four, five, or six times so they really know where they are going. When you turn one out, make sure you haze him and put him where you want him to run all the time. Don't let the steers turn back. Fresh cattle can turn back on the fences, and that generally messes up one for practice.

Next, put a head rope on a steer in the chute and let him come out. Then you might bring him to a slow stop, really easy. If he fights the rope, try to encourage the steer to turn and head to the left and jump across the arena. When he gets through doing that, you can undally your rope and let it go. You teach the steer how to make the turn and jump out of there. The steers that learn to hang back on the end of the rope will learn to drag, and their heads will get sore because they are resisting.

I have even heard about people tying a heavy cotton rope, large in diameter, around a steer's horns and then tying the steer to a fence. This breaks him to lead. Then, when he gets roped around the horns, he leads well.

141

*With fresh practice cattle, put a head rope on the steer in the chute. Then handle the steer easy and teach him how to make the turn.*

In a pen of 10 steers, there will always be 2 or 3 that learn to lead, and 2 or 3 that will learn to drag. You'll have one or two that learn how to get away on the left fence, and one or two learn how to get away on the right fence. So you get to practice on everything.

The steers will learn ways to get away from you, to keep from being caught. But with practice cattle, you don't want to hurt them. If you do know the steers are wild and pretty juicy, then you might dally them on both ends, too, and stretch them, just to kind of temper them down a little bit.

Once a steer gets a good pattern for practice, though, if the heeler dallies him, the header should undally. If the header doesn't undally a steer, then the heeler should not dally. To keep practice cattle

fresher longer, don't stretch them every trip unless you have an overabundance of steers and are rich enough to afford it.

How long a steer lasts for practice depends on several things. You can rope steers that have a good pattern even if they weigh 650 pounds because that kind of steer won't hit or pull on your horse so hard, especially on the heading end.

The header has to rope and turn the steer. If the cattle are big, 600 to 650 pounds, and the steer hits the end of the rope every time, or if he drags, then you are hurting the horse. And you might be putting yourself in a bad position. If something goes wrong with your dally, for example, it's going to be bad news.

Instead of the heeler letting his horse take that hit, the roper can heel a steer and let his rope come off the saddle horn. And he still gets good practice that way.

But if you have cattle that are trained well, that follow and lead good, then you don't have to deal with the steer's weight on the end of the rope. Once he's roped, that kind of steer will follow and lead as the header takes off.

Many guys get rid of the steers that are soured for practice or are too heavy and big. But these same ropers will keep the bigger steers that have a good pattern when they leave the chute. They always come out clean and run a good pattern down the arena, and then follow the header.

A roper can keep that kind of steer for 2 or 3 years because he has such a good pattern. If you take care of your steers and practice wisely, you won't burn them out, and they will last longer.

# Jake: Knowing Your Cattle

The steer usually dictates your run. The better your cattle are, the better you can perform. Good cattle do make roping a little easier, but we don't always rope in ideal situations.

When I'm at a roping, I try to study every steer, but there is no way to remember every steer. So I try to remember the hard runners and the slower steers and if they have any tricks or are hard to catch. If I don't remember them, they are probably right down the middle, the average in the herd. Knowing my cattle allows me an advantage. Some ropers sit in the stands until it's their turn to rope, but I'm going to take advantage of every situation.

If I know what my draw is, it's not so much of a guessing game. I study the cattle to find out if one has a sore horn, a sore ear, or ducks his head. If he does, I will try to rope that kind of steer around the neck. Whatever his pattern, I'll try to react so that my heeler and I don't have a handicap.

At ropings I study the cattle as they go through one at a time, but when there are a couple hundred head, it's a lot harder. I pay attention, though, because I never know when I might draw one of those steers. At a five-steer average roping, for instance, I know I'm going to have five steers in that pen. I don't know which ones, so I study all of them.

But that's an advantage for me. In team roping nowadays, if you want to dominate, you must have an edge in every area. There are a lot of great ropers now, but only a fine line separates the guys who are great from the ones who are really good.

# Jake: Slow Cattle

As for slow cattle—I love them. I can be faster on slow cattle because they're easier to catch. To me, team roping is a race, and the slower the steers, the quicker I can catch them and the faster my times will be. The faster a steer runs, the farther down the arena I have to go, and the longer my time will be.

Although I like slower cattle, I don't want a steer that just walks out of the chute and wants to stop; that's too slow. When a steer doesn't run very hard, I can rope and turn him off pretty well. That steer basically gives me a good handle because he's not going a hundred miles an hour.

The easier cattle to handle are those who don't run as hard and who are a little timid. But because you can rope them easily, I think some people get into a poor habit of roping and turning off too quickly. A roper can ride up on slower cattle, rope, turn off, and dally—all at the same time.

Usually this type steer has already learned to lead. When you rope him, he starts turning on his own. So your horse never really uses his hind end to take hold of the steer, and everything seems to move along on its own. But if you rope like that all the time and then get into fresh cattle that run hard, you're in trouble.

*On a trotter, the header needs to speed up so the steer begins to hop, which makes it easier for the heeler to catch the hind feet.*

*I like slow cattle because they're easier to catch and usually give a good handle. But a header can develop poor habits roping such cattle because he can rope, turn off, and dally almost simultaneously.*

Another consideration with a steer who doesn't run hard: If you run up, rope, dally, and set him, you are wasting time. By the time you start the steer's head around, your horse has set. So that steer stalls on the corner, and then you have to jerk him out of the hole.

With a slow steer, rope him, get to your horn, and keep moving. Then you can use the steer's momentum to keep him hopping through the corner. But you won't have to pull him very fast or hard; he's basically going to handle himself, and your heeler can get a quick shot.

## Jake: Steers That Set Up

Experience plays into your heading when you have a steer that sets up leaving the chute. However, the only time a steer ever sets up is when the header and heeler crowd him too much. So you have to stay far enough back and rope from far enough back that the steer doesn't want to set up. Hold your horse back and rope the steer out in front of your horse. Even if the steer checks off a little bit, trying to set, you can still catch him, and you can still turn him. You still have something you can work with.

When a steer sets up, your odds for a good run are cut down, and those steers sense when something starts getting too close. If your horse is a little chargey, he ends up too close to the steer, or the heeler could ride up too close. Whenever that happens, the steer will set up. You have to really concentrate on your horse so he doesn't over-run the steer. You also have to get your rope up quicker and be ready to rope before you get to the steer. Then you know you have enough distance to rope him without the risk of him running behind you.

## Jake: Fresh Cattle

A fresh steer naturally handles faster and wilder than an older steer, so with fresher cattle you build more speed. If you've been roping slow, easy cattle that handle themselves well, your horse may already be in the habit of moving left as you throw. Even though he can still handle the slower cattle this way, that won't work with fresh cattle.

As a rule of thumb, the faster a steer runs, the farther down the arena I go and the more I need a horse who really wants to set and use his hind end. Then I can slow down the steer and break his momentum before I make him come across in the turn and bring him out of the corner nice and easy.

Another possible problem with a hard-running steer: By the time I get to the back end of the arena and rope, the horse will be ducking off. Then I have to get a fast dally. But there is so much speed and momentum built up with the hard-running steer. It's hard to slow down everything before you leave the hole and make the corner. Then the steer's hind end pops around and swings out—and he takes off running again. So that, too, is sometimes a problem with fresh cattle.

You need lots of experience in roping fresher cattle. Sometimes when a fresh steer hasn't been roped very much, you also should take time to make sure he gets his balance before you turn him off. Otherwise he generally runs so hard that when you rope him, his momentum turns him sideways. Because he doesn't have any

*A fresh, hard-running steer usually handles faster and wilder, but I can use my horse to set the steer and break his momentum before I come across in the turn.*

balance or idea about what's happening, he usually falls over; he doesn't know how to maintain his balance at this point.

This is where it's really important for the header to set his horse and bring the steer's head around and control him. You'll be a hair slower, but you'll give your heeler a better handle.

Sometimes with fast cattle, you're forced into doing things differently than you would like. Say you're at a rodeo with fresh cattle, and someone drew a steer that didn't run very hard. When the guy ropes him, the steer just rolls around there, and the heeler ropes him right on the corner.

There are enough good team ropers today that whoever draws that steer will take advantage of it. For instance, it might take a 5-second run to win that rodeo, and my steer might run really hard. I won't have an opportunity to rope and handle him like I want and make sure I give my heeler a good handle. If I do, our time will be too long.

So I have to take a chance. I have to reach way out there and rope the steer, and I have to move out quicker than I want. Now I'm just hoping that— maybe—the steer will maintain his bal-

145

ance. But a lot of times I will jerk him down—just because I am forced into a game of all or nothing.

That's why I prefer average ropings instead of roping one head, where a lot is simply the luck of the draw. Too, anybody can luck out sometimes—reaching out, roping one, turning him off, and having a heeler catch two feet. Those guys are hard to beat. Sometimes we all can do the same thing, but it's just luck.

So I like average ropings. Then the better you rope, the better the horse you have, and the more knowledge you have about handling a steer, the more it puts the odds in your favor.

## Clay: Fresh Cattle

Fresh cattle make ropings easy, probably because they are harder to catch. That's where the header comes more into play—his ability to handle and control his horse and the steer. After the header ropes, he tries to steady the steer and not let him jump away from the heeler. After a header makes a turn, squares up, and gets in position, then the fresh steer is likely to jump out and away. He wants to run on his own, as compared to just following the header.

The heeler has to be ready to rope. When you come around and into position, when the fresh steer is trying to leave, you either have to catch him right then or follow him across the arena until he's controlled again.

It takes more ability to control your horse and hit the right spot at the right time off the corner when you throw. But that's going to be your best shot. Obviously when you are running faster down the arena on fresh cattle, you also have to hit your positioning at the right time. This all gets back to horsemanship—where the

ropers are running wide open and the horses must respond quickly.

## Jake: Broncy Cattle

Broncy steers are hard to rope; they're wild and crazy and hard to handle. A steer like that obviously will give some resistance.

He might, for instance, throw his head up and give you a slow corner because he is already starting to set back on the rope. And because he is starting to put pressure on his head, he naturally starts leaning back against the rope more. So he pulls against you more, and you have to drag him.

You can take the broncy steer's head away from him, so to speak, but sometimes when you do, he might want to come up the rope. He's going to handle a lot faster and be more aggressive, and that kind of steer will also come out of the corner on his own. What happens all depends on the steer. Some steers might get their heads down and run up the rope, and others might resist and just not want to be led.

When broncy cattle want to run up the rope, just try to stay out in front of them. The rope doesn't even have to be tight. When a steer runs, his feet are basically together; it's the heeler's job to cowboy up there and make sure he gets the heels caught.

Don't ever turn in a circle when a steer runs up the rope. Think of a guy driving a ski boat and what happens to a skier behind the boat when the driver turns hard to the left. It naturally swings the skier out wide to the right.

What you do—no matter where you go in the arena—is take that steer in as straight a line as possible. The more you turn, the more it swings the steer away from the heeler and makes it harder for him.

The worst thing I could do as a header is stand still or have a steer on a loose rope because then the steer gets around me. And when the heeler moves up there, he's going to hit me in the back of the head with his rope.

So when a steer comes up the rope, I just try to stay out in front of him as much as possible. I don't even care if the rope is so loose it's hanging down on the ground, as long as I'm in front.

*Some broncy steers really resist being led. If I know a steer has a problem with a horn or a sore ear, I'll rope him around the neck.*

## Jake: Used-Up Cattle

I don't like to practice on worn-out, used-up cattle that duck their heads or drag. True, it's good to be able to rope and catch those problem cattle. But if all your practice cattle are bad to rope, then you always second-guess yourself and what you are trying to do. Your roping becomes a guessing game because you're always trying to outsmart and outguess the steer.

Another consideration: If I was going to a big competition and had been practicing on problem cattle and not catching them very well, I wouldn't have a lot of confidence when I went to that big roping.

## Jake: Draggers

When you're heading, how well you handle the steer that drags goes right back to your being able to think. You must be able to react to every situation.

Think about what causes a steer to drag. When you roped him, you might have pinched his ear between the rope and a horn. Or when you rope a steer around the neck, he might hang back on the end of the rope; then he begins to choke and will start dragging.

Usually the steer drags because of a sore horn, a pinched ear, or the loop is around both eyes. When you turn him, you put pressure on his head by setting your horse. At that point, you can tell how the steer will react or handle. If you see the steer slow down when the head rope goes on, that's a signal that he's going to stop or get heavy on the corner or possibly even drag.

On the other end, the heeler sees the same thing you do. He knows the steer is about to get heavy, so the heeler's reaction is to hold up his horse and try to get a quick shot.

However, if a heeler cuts in too soon, it can also make a steer drag. Then the steer sets back and hangs back until the header pulls him beyond the heeler or until the steer jumps past the heeler.

Think about it. The heeler reads the same thing the header does: The steer is getting heavy. That heeler's got to try his shot pretty quick. On a dragging steer, two or three jumps is all the heeler gets out of

147

*Usually a steer resists or drags because he has a sore horn or a pinched ear.*

him; then he's almost impossible to heel. There is no way humanly possible to catch the steer's feet when they are dragging on the ground. The only way to catch is when the feet clear the ground. Sometimes his feet might clear by only inches.

When a steer starts to get heavy, you could slide him some rope, then jerk him out of the ground. But that usually screws up your heeler so badly that it's almost impossible for him to catch.

When the steer drags, the heeler's reaction is to pull off and try to set up to throw. He wants a fast throw because each jump gets worse with the steer dragging more. There's progressively less jump and more drag, and usually by the third jump, a steer is dragging so badly there's no way to catch him.

So the header slides the steer some rope before he jerks him out of the ground. But when he does, the heeler's momentum carries him right on top of the steer because the steer isn't moving forward at a steady pace. Now you have a steer dragging, and you also have a

heeler right on top of him. Because you have given the steer slack, the heeler now has over-ridden him and lapped up on the steer, almost side by side.

The heeler's reaction: "Man, I'm too close." The steer really starts to drag now, so the heeler sits back on his horse, and he looks down, underneath—where he's been riding up so close on the steer. All of a sudden, the header tightens his dally, and the steer jerks away from the heeler.

The heeler already was off-balance with his horse checking back, and then everything goes away from him. All of a sudden, he has to catch up, but there's no way to make it work. It's just lucky if the heeler happens to reach out there and catch in that situation. So it's not good to slide a steer rope when he starts to drag.

Here's how to handle that situation best, when the header sees the steer getting heavy. First, the header has to speed up somewhat, to give the head horse some momentum, because now he's pulling dead weight. Then the header wants to try to maintain a consistent pull throughout, to create a rhythm or hop for the heeler. Even though the steer is getting heavy or dragging, he still will come up eventually.

The heeler's reaction is to try and stay back and be ready. Then when the steer's feet do come up and off the ground, the heeler can try to rope him. The header's job is to try to keep the dragger moving, without giving him that really hard jerk, which makes the dragger resist even more. He can resist a little bit, but if you and the horse keep him moving, he will hop a time or two. It's the heeler's job to recognize that and hurry to get his shot, so the situation doesn't get worse.

If I'm at a roping and know a steer is a dragger, I also have to communicate with my partner. I tell him that when I rope the steer, instead of moving out fast, I will try to bring his head around and let him float down the arena, not putting much pressure on his head.

A dragger has already learned this pattern and that he can make the heeler miss by dragging. The steer has resisted—not once, but two or three times before—and it worked. So he knows he can drag. The more pressure I put on his head, the more he will resist and try to drag. Instead, I try to bend his head around, changing his direction as he goes toward the catch pen. I change his direction so it won't be a crossfire, and I have the steer in forward tow. But there's not a lot of pressure on his head. Then the heeler can come into position and rope him by two feet.

Another thing I will try is to rope the steer around the neck, eliminating any pressure on the sore horn or pinched ear that can cause a steer to drag. Then most of the time he just hops off and lets you lead him as if nothing is wrong. In all these situations, knowing what to do falls into the category of knowing your cattle.

# Clay: Draggers

With a less-than-perfect steer, what's going to catch the steer is your precision and ability to get the loop in position. With a dragger, whether you try to set a trap for him or not depends on the steer. A steer can be heavy and dragging and still have a rhythm to his motion and have both feet together when they come up and off the ground. As long as you can slide the bottom of your rope into place, that type steer is just as easy as any.

But you must have good position with your horse; that's really critical. You only

have a short time to get the loop into place. The timing of your throw has to be right on, and you have to be in the right position with your horse to get the loop there at that precise time. You have to be really deliberate, and you have to deliver a good loop.

# Jake: Head-Duckers

For me, the hardest steer to rope is one that tilts his right horn down. You can't get the bottom of your rope placed where you need to. You're over on the left side of the steer, and it's hard to get close enough to rope up underneath the right horn.

What you want to do, and this is the only time you would ever want to do this, is position your horse over close to the steer's left side, so you are up against him. Then try to swing your loop parallel to the steer's horns. If the steer has his right horn tilted down and the left horn up, you swing your loop on the same plane as the horns. The horns dictate the plane of your loop.

What if the right horn is up, and the left horn down? Pull your position out farther to the left of the steer. Now swing your loop at that plane, the same plane as the horns are tilted. The plane of your rope must match the angle of the horns.

Now and then you get a steer who just runs with his head low, ducking his head. He doesn't tilt, but runs with his head down so far that you can't even see the horns. He hides his head.

Now it's really important that you ride for position—up close—and swing with the tip down. You must swing with a lot of pitch to your loop when a steer's head is down. But you have to make sure that you're positioned close enough to him. If you are too far back and throw, you'll throw the loop over the top of his horns.

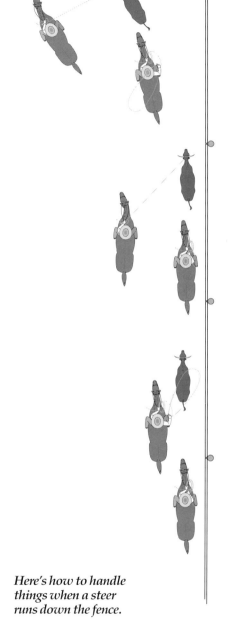

## Jake: Steers Close to the Fence

When the steer comes out and the heeler misses the haze, the steer will travel away from the header, to the right. Often those steers will get up against the fence. I've even seen steers drag their horn on the fence. It is pretty obvious when that happens that you're not going to catch him.

But usually the steer leaves about a foot between him and the fence. When a header keeps his position close to the steer and throws, his loop will hit the fence. The closer the header, the closer the loop is to the fence. What you should do is pull your position out a little farther, so your loop doesn't hit the fence. You try to stick the loop between the fence and the steer's right horn, but most guys keep their position in too tight, and the rope hits the fence.

## Jake: Bad Cattle

Everyone needs to learn how to rope bad cattle. When you have a set of cattle, say 20 head of steers, you end up with half of them being problem cattle anyway. There will be one of every kind in there. A couple will be really slow, a couple will duck their heads real bad, some are going to drag, and a couple run up the rope. So you have a combination of all problems

*Here's how to handle things when a steer runs down the fence.*

*Study the cattle. Team roping is so competitive today that you need to take every advantage you can.*

unless the cattle are really fresh and haven't been roped very much. Even then it doesn't take very long, if you rope them every day, for the steers to start figuring out tricks.

In many beginners' practice pens, the cattle get bad because they don't get caught enough. They get smart and figure out how to get away. They learn how to duck and dive and outmaneuver the beginning roper who has trouble getting into position. Consequently, the roper ends up taking a bad shot and will miss. These steers will learn these patterns early because they very seldom get caught.

# Clay: Bad Cattle

It is better and safer for the novice to rope good steers and avoid bad cattle.

However, it could benefit a novice to practice some runs on a few bad steers, just so he knows that it's not really a trick to rope those cattle, but good basic proce-

dures. It's still maneuvering your horse to the right spot at the right time, although the steer is being more difficult.

On the other hand, if you try to rope a bad steer, and just throw fast and out of position—doing things that are contrary to building good habits—then the steer hurts your roping. You can't make very many runs on a steer like that because it is really hard on the head horse to pull and drag the steer, and it's hard on the steer.

I would rather rope 10 perfect steers because then I am simulating my practice on good conditions, building in the right muscle response I want. So it's all right for a new roper to expose himself to bad cattle a time or two, just to find out, "Yes, I can deal with a bad steer," and think and ride himself through it. But he will gain more by keeping the better steers around.

# 13

# JAKE ON HEADING PRACTICE

THE WHOLE KEY in heading practice is discipline. Discipline yourself to ride for good position and to take a good consistent shot. With lots of preparation in the practice pen, you can have a clear shot with your rope, and it will be easy for you.

I want the odds in my favor every time. If it takes a 4-second run to win the go-rounds at the NFR, and I can't make that type run in my practice pen, there's a good chance that I'm not going to make it at the Finals. Perfect practice puts the odds in my favor.

I think a novice roper should approach the practice pen with some intent to get to a higher level—not just to rope. I believe you can enjoy roping as a stress release, which a lot of people do, but you can also rope to reach a higher level of skill.

Even I sometimes get frustrated with my roping, and when I am, it's not fun. Roping is a great sport and great fun when you catch and win, but nothing is worse than not being able to catch—and you can't figure out what's going on. When you start missing a lot, you're a magnet; you attract "coffee-shop" theories from everybody. Every theory is a little differ-

*The practice pen is where you develop the good habits to become a consistent roper.*

ent, so you try everything, but you don't really know what to do.

Instead, when you have problems with your roping, go to one man who is knowledgeable about roping and say, "Could you help me pinpoint exactly what I'm doing wrong?" But don't start taking advice from every Tom, Dick, and Harry, trying this and that. If someone wants to give you advice, sure, it's all right to listen. But make sure he explains things at a level where you can understand his advice and it makes sense to you. And if it makes sense to you, you might try it.

Although I've been successful with my roping, if somebody else comes along with a better theory, I'll sure say, "Maybe I ought to try that. It looks like it might make my roping a little better or easier. This might fit my program."

I'm not saying my way to head a steer is the right way or the wrong way; I've tried to create the roping style that is easiest for me. This book holds the fundamentals and the mechanics of what works for me. My way might not work for everybody else, but it's my theory that works from everything I've seen and learned about roping.

And those things don't come from Jake Barnes alone. Throughout the years I've taken bits and pieces from different ropers—a little horsemanship from this man, a little knowledge about a rope from another. I gathered the information, but the style is how I use that information.

# From the Dummy to the Arena

Somehow a person gets into roping; maybe he has a friend who ropes. So the new roper buys himself a horse—usually the wrong kind of horse. The guy has roped the dummy a little, but that's boring, and it's hard. Who wants to go do that for 2 or 3 hours every day to really learn?

But he has a horse now, and he wants to rope in the arena. He doesn't know what to do once he catches a steer, how to pull the steer off, how to handle the steer, or what the steer's going to do. He's setting himself up for a lot of heartache—if he doesn't lose a finger or get a rope under his horse's tail and get bucked off. How many head is he going to catch anyway?

His next step totally amazes me: He enters a jackpot. He doesn't have the slightest idea about what he's doing, but he wants to compete and puts up his hard-earned money. Never, ever have I gone to a roping where they paid me when I didn't catch.

If you can't catch four in the practice pen, how in the world can you do that in an average roping? Are you going to survive on luck? I'm not. Luck will starve you to death. But that's the way most people learn to rope.

Most people don't know when to move from roping the heading dummy to practicing on a horse in the arena. Usually they make the change way too early. Then the novice roper chases no telling how many steers until finally he catches one. The first thought when he catches: "Now I gotta dally!" The first thing he does is look down at the saddle horn and turn off his horse with the left hand.

The horse is going one way, the steer's going the other, and the new roper doesn't have any idea about those things because he's looking down and trying to get a dally. He gets his hand in the rope and cuts off some fingers. It's amazing that there aren't more wrecks and accidents in roping.

Some day you will catch a steer, but do you know what to do with him when you do?

# The Ideal Novice Roper

In my clinics, I try to take things one step farther. I want to teach a novice roper how to go that step beyond catching the steer to knowing what to do with him after he does catch. I'll describe the ideal novice roper here and how I would build the perfect roper.

Before a novice switches from roping the dummy to being horseback in the arena with live cattle, the first thing required is horsemanship. He must be able to ride and maneuver a horse. That includes having some understanding about the horse, how he thinks and how to handle him. This is really important.

153

*A sequence of three.*
*1/ Before he actually ropes a steer, a novice header should put a rope on a slow steer in the chute, then turn him out. This allows the roper to learn to handle both his horse and the steer—at the same time.*

But the whole key to roping is learning how to handle cattle in every situation—how to deal with slow cattle, what to do with cattle that simply run or those that run up the rope, and how to deal with draggers.

To start a real beginning roper horseback on cattle, I want really slow cattle that trot out of the chute. Fast cattle make everything happen so quickly that the steer is gone before you realize what's happened. Use slow steers to get started.

After my ideal novice roper backs into the box and positions himself correctly, the first thing I have him do—without a rope—is track a steer in position. I turn out a steer, and the roper gets into position and follows him to the far end of the arena. The novice learns how to move into position with his horse and how to maintain that position everywhere the steer goes. When the steer slows, the roper slows; when the steer trots, the roper trots. It might take 15 or 20 runs until a novice is comfortable with that, but that's how he can learn to stay with the steer and concentrate on keeping the horse in good position.

Now you put a rope on the steer's horns in the chute—the same slow steer—and give the tail of the rope to the beginner in the box. Open the chute gate, and as the steer comes out, the roper comes out with the steer and gets into position. But he now practices coiling up the rope as they go toward the catch pen, changing his horse's position as necessary. He has to coil the rope quickly enough so that the horse and steer don't step over the rope. He learns to maneuver his rope and his horse so that he won't get in a wreck. He stays right with the steer and learns how to handle both, and he does that until he's really comfortable doing it.

A little later, the novice roper can use the same slow steer and learn to cross his hands over the horn, when he starts to dally, and to stop his horse and the steer. It's really important that he learns—step by step. He picks up with the left hand to keep the horse from turning off and moves his right hand to the left, coming underneath the left hand. His hands cross over; then he begins his dally, and stops the horse. He doesn't even need to turn the steer off right now.

2/ *As he tracks the slow steer, the new roper learns to pace his horse to match the steer and becomes comfortable with having a steer on the end of his rope.*

3/ *Gradually, the new roper can draw closer to the steer and begin to coil his rope. Because the steer is a slow one, the novice has time to think about positioning his horse and handling the steer.*

Most people perceive that when you rope and dally, you turn off at the same time. But when you turn off too quickly, the horse's left shoulder drops. Your horse isn't balanced as well now, so he gets a harder jerk when the steer hits the end of the rope. Turning off too soon will build in problems down the road.

First, you want the rope to be tight on the saddle horn—before you turn off. As you start to pick up on the horse to slow him down, the steer's head begins to come around. When that happens, then you make your lateral move to the left, to make the corner smooth as you turn off the steer. The horse doesn't take near as hard a jerk if you make the horse set the steer first, before you turn.

You do these things over and over, step by step, to develop muscle memory. When you practice something with enough repetition, it becomes second nature to you. You don't have to think about it. But if you move your hand over, look down at the horn, and dally enough times, you're memorizing a problem.

*A sequence of two.*
*1/ Again using a slow steer at first, the ideal roper takes the next step. He tracks the steer...*

It's just as easy to memorize the right fundamentals as it is the wrong ones. This goes right back to discipline. If a novice roper learns the right fundamentals to start with, he is less likely to get himself into a bad storm or to create bad habits.

By now we have our ideal roper to a point where he can come out of the chute, get into position, coil up the rope, pull his slack, dally, and stop with the steer just trotting along. With practice, our roper can do all these things right away—second nature. He's ready to move on.

So we advance to a little faster cattle, and everything speeds up a little more. Doing everything with speed is a little harder, but how much harder depends somewhat on the person's natural ability. Anyone with more experience in any aspect—horsemanship, cattle, or rope-handling—might pick up on the procedure a little quicker.

When our novice header is really comfortable doing these drills, we can put a heeler on the other side. But now we drop back to the same slow steer with the rope on his horns because we're adding another element—the heeler. The novice now learns to turn off with a steer in tow. What our roper tends to do, now that the heeler is in the picture, is turn off quicker—before he ever sets his horse. Everybody has a tendency to do that at first, and it gives the heeler a bad handle.

But at this point I don't really worry about the shot the heeler gets; I'm trying to train my guy to head. When he has the procedure down pat for handling a steer, step by step, we advance again to a little faster cattle. Another new element: Now the header starts riding with speed. Before, he didn't really have to ride actively because the steer was slow, and the roper could be just a passenger on his horse. Now he has to think more about riding.

When the novice masters all the steps, with the rope on the steer in the chute, the fun starts. He gets to try to rope the steer's horns. But we've added another element, so we take away the heeler for a while. Now our ideal roper concentrates on get-

*2/ . . . and learns to take a dally. He practices crossing his hands correctly and builds good habits.*

ting his horse into position, swinging the rope, and throwing it. Then he reaches the point where he can catch the steer.

Once he catches the steer, the header goes right back to his fundamental drills—right back to where he was when we first put the rope on the slow steer in the chute. That's where that type work fits into the program; we're combining the drills like a puzzle.

After our ideal roper practices enough, he can catch every one of the slow steers, cross his hands over, dally, and stop correctly and safely. Then we advance him to the faster cattle. Each step in the training process takes less time as the novice gains more experience and confidence. And even with the next step—the faster cattle—he ropes, dallies, and stops. It's right back to the fundamentals, the drills. All the steps fit together, and the roper never gets in too big a hurry or into a panic situation.

So we can add the heeler back into the picture again. By this point, though, we can probably eliminate the really slow cattle and use the medium-range cattle because, when our ideal header ropes now, all the fundamentals fall into place. And our ideal roper has never started bad

*Whenever the ideal roper adds a new element—the heeler, for example— to his drill, it's better to practice with slower cattle at first.*

habits that might take years to overcome. He's off on the right track.

You must be fundamentally sound in your roping technique before you ever work on speed. We teach that in our schools, and seldom do our clinic students try to rope fast; they work on fundamentals. Our ideal roper, by working on the basics, ought to be able to start catching consistently on average cattle with medium-size horns, who make average runs without ducking and diving.

However, when most people start adding speed to their runs, they start eliminating fundamentals and take shortcuts. They don't get the rope tight on the steer's horns, for example, or they begin to allow the horse to duck off or don't ride to position before taking their shot. That's when the roper's consistency falls off.

We might watch a rodeo performance and see, maybe, two or three fast runs out of twelve. That's because 10 of those ropers are using too much speed, trying to eliminate steps. If I make that type of run, I will end up ruining my horse because I'm asking him to do too many things too quickly. That's as if I'm trying to rope, turn off, get a dally, get a smooth handle, and give the heeler a good shot all at once.

Then people say, "I have a tape of you at the National Finals." Well, that's the worst setup in the world—a short score, where we try to make a 4-second run. To make that 4-second run, you take all the basics out of roping. You take a lot of chances.

## The Horse in the Box

When I back a horse in the box, I want that horse ready to go and on the muscle somewhat, but I also want him to be relaxed and responsive. I think of a horse in the box

as a rubber band stretched out. I hold him there and determine how far out I want that steer before I release the horse and let him go. While I hold him, even when the gate opens or the heeler takes off, my horse doesn't move. He responds to my hand. Then when I release—whoosh—like that rubber band, my horse leaves the box.

When you ride into the box, get a feel for your horse. Some horses want to turn to the left as they enter the box. When I was growing up, they taught me that you always turn a horse to the cattle, never away from them; that's the Code of the West. But when you ride some horses into the box, they just naturally want to turn the opposite way. I can't see how the turn affects your horse's performance. Some horses go in the box and turn left; some turn right. I can't see making a big fight out of which way my horse turns to set himself in the box.

Your leg cues and horsemanship do become really important in the box, however, when a horse is offset one way or the other or when he tenses and locks up in the box. Use your legs to direct and maneuver him; use that good horsemanship. A horse in the box is so focused and so ready to go because he is in a race; his tension is natural. But if you have a broke, responsive horse, you can adjust his position by using leg pressure.

You see people ride horses forward in the box and then back a few steps, and they do that a couple of times. They're just relaxing their horses. And sometimes it's a "get your mind back on me" kind of a thing. But you also can do it with your feet. By maneuvering the horse around a little bit, you help relax him and take his mind off wanting to go.

You can also do the same thing in the box with your reins—if your horse will flex or break at the poll. When you back in the box, the horse naturally is on the muscle and wants to pull some against your hand. When those gates bang, he really wants to take off. But if you can quiver your rein a little and have him come off the bridle, by breaking at the poll, then he isn't pushing into the bit too much and probably won't take off too soon. This all goes back to the dry work when you quivered your hand and the horse learned to flex at the poll.

A horse scores on different things. The first reaction he has is to noise—the chute banging open. The race is on, so he jumps or wants to take off. The roper either lets the horse go or tries to stop him.

If he lets the horse go, he's liable to break the barrier, so the roper's reaction often is to check the horse. But the rider usually checks too much then, given the situation, which lifts the horse's front feet off the ground. So the roper ends up late out of the box anyway and has a bad start to his run.

When you back in the box, your horse's hind end is in the corner of the box. But most people point the horse's front end toward the chute. I like for a horse to be pointed right at the middle of the box.

At an average roping, for example, where you want to catch a lot of cattle, the ideal positioning, for the pattern you want him to run, begins with the steer going straight. That's the heeler's job, to haze the steer, and he dictates which direction the steer goes. But straight is the ideal direction, which is why I want my horse to come out of the middle of the box.

If you're trying to make a fast rodeo run, for example, the best pattern for the steer to run is slightly to the left. But if you're pointed toward the chute, and the steer runs out and to the left, that puts you directly behind him. You're out of position, and your horse's front feet can also hit the steer's hind feet, which can trip your horse.

Most people say that when they angle a horse's front end over, quartering him to the right, it naturally makes the horse break into his left lead as he leaves the box. That just tells me the roper hasn't spent enough time on horsemanship. Have your horse broke and train him so you can be sure he's in the left lead.

Another reason that some ropers quarter their horses is that the horses don't score cattle well. The horse is too fast out of the box. Because the horse is so quick,

*Using leg cues and good horsemanship is important when positioning your horse in the box.*

the roper doesn't want to break the barrier, so he angles the horse, trying to buy a little time and keep from breaking out. This only means the roper hasn't spent enough time in the practice pen scoring cattle.

True, you can buy a little more time when you turn a horse's front end if he tries to leave the box too quickly. On the other hand, when your horse scores well and you turn him sideways in the box, it takes more time for him to straighten and then go. That's not to your advantage; you're wasting time then.

There's another thing I dislike about quartering a horse in the box. When you nod for the steer, the horse who is quartered will naturally take a step to the left because of his awkward position in the box. As he steps over, his head blocks your view of the steer.

I position a horse straightaway in the box so I can watch the steer on the right side of my horse and at all times. When I leave the box, I always have the steer in sight.

*A sequence of two.*

*1/ Do use a forward body position on your horse in the box and have your reins short enough to maintain control. Use the horn to balance yourself so you don't pull on the reins and the horse's head.*

*2/ Don't make a common mistake and sit up straight on your horse in the box. When he takes off, the momentum will throw you back and out of position. Too, if your reins are out long as your horse gathers himself to run, you'll lack control.*

## The Roper in the Box

When I back into the box, the diameter of my loop depends on the type run that I'm making. At an average roping, for example, I use a medium-size loop to start with. When I'm afoot, a medium-size loop probably comes from the ground up to about my hip, to about my jeans pocket. When I'm on my horse in the box, that puts the bottom of my loop around the tread of my stirrup. Then as I feed out my loop, it goes in size from pocket-high to about my chest height. The exception, for instance, is when I know my cattle have really big horns. I make my loop a little larger to start with.

In the box, a roper has to pay attention to his body posture. A common mistake is to sit straight up, just like the roper's sitting still—which he is. Although he may have hold of the saddle horn, his upper body is still straight up. When the horse takes off, the momentum naturally throws the roper back and out of position.

Instead, your body posture should be somewhat forward. I relate riding and roping to being a jockey. A jockey gets down and forward on top of the horse in the starting gate. When the horse leaves there, it rocks the jockey back somewhat, but he's forward in his position to start with. That helps the horse keep moving. When you make a horse run, it's a lot easier for him when you help him by leaning forward. If you want the horse to stop, sit up straight and put your feet out in front of you and quit riding; the horse will almost stop on his own.

But say, for example, this guy sitting too straight has hold of only the reins, not the saddle horn. When the horse takes off and throws the roper back, he ends up pulling on the rein, pulling on the horse's head for balance. This not only slows the horse, it can literally lift his front end off the ground as he leaves. Either way, he's late out of the box and leaves off-balance.

As you leave the box, pull yourself forward with the saddle horn. Leave there balanced—without having to pull on your rein. Your body posture as you come out is important, just as positioning your horse in the box is.

Sometimes when a roper has problems with his body position in the box, it's because his reins are too long. When the roper falls back, he can't take hold of the horse if necessary. Make sure your reins are short enough. Your strongest pull on the reins is to the belly button, not to your chest.

Too many people hold their reins up too high. When a horse is standing still, his head is lowered and he's relaxed. As he collects himself to go, like a cat getting ready to spring, it creates slack in the rein. But instead of taking up on the rein, the roper moves his hand higher. He has less control with his hand in that position.

Another very common mistake I see, when people back in the box, is a lack of concentration. The heeler has to understand that a header backing into the box should totally be focused on the steer.

Often, however, the header backs in, looks at his heeler, and asks him, "Are you ready?" Then his concentration moves from the heeler to the guy opening the chute, and he makes eye contact with him.

*Here's how I hold my rein and my coils in my left hand.*

Finally, the header nods. That only tells me that the header will be at least halfway to three-quarters of the way down the arena before he ever gets his concentration zoned in on the steer.

We tell our students, "Heeler, get in there and be ready so the header doesn't have to look over and ask if you are ready. If you have a problem over there, speak out."

The header should back in and focus totally on the steer—not the guy on the gate and not his partner. That header must have great concentration. It's so focused that he leaves the box ready to rope—and quickly.

*Scoring cattle is one way to help a horse learn to relax there and that he leaves on your cue, not the rattle of the gate. Position the horse in the box just as you would during a competitive run.*

# Scoring Your Horse

The most common problem in the box is keeping a horse quiet. People just don't spend enough time working with horses in the box. This goes right back to the dry work and the practice pen.

The unruly horse needs more box work, but his rider won't score enough cattle. The box is not a comfortable place for that horse to be; that's why he won't handle quietly there. You have to teach a horse that the box can also be a place to relax—not just a place where a race begins.

Scoring, teaching a horse to stand quietly in the box even when a steer is released from the chute, is how you teach the horse that at the start of this race he must listen to you. During a run, *you* determine how far the steer gets from the chute before you go, so that *you* don't break the barrier.

The head horse's cue comes from you, not the rattle of the gates or the heel horse leaving first. Often a heel horse doesn't have a barrier, or when he does have a barrier, the score is shorter on his side. Usually a head horse hears the gate open, he's ready to take off, and if he sees any movement at all, that's also his first reaction. So there are three cues that it's time to go—the noise, the sight, and the movement—and the head horse is the last one to go. He wants to go; he anticipates it.

When scoring a horse in the practice pen, often a roper won't simulate scoring exactly the same way things happen in competition. He might, for example, back in the box with a really loose rein or score without a heeler on the other side. The horse doesn't gear up to go then; he's not tense.

When I score my head horses, I try to simulate everything just as it is in competition. I get tensed up myself; I move around in the saddle, positioning myself and my horse. When I nod, and the steer leaves the chute, I want my heeler to take off. I want to simulate every one of those cues—the gate banging, the steer taking off, and the heeler leaving.

These head horses are not stupid. If the heeler stays in the box and doesn't move, often the head horse just stands there. He might jump forward a little bit, but most of them are smarter than that. So if the gates haven't rattled and the heeler hasn't taken off, as far as I'm concerned, I haven't scored any cattle.

162

Usually when the gate opens and the heeler takes off, the head horse jumps forward. When your horse does jump, don't persecute him for it and jerk and snatch; it's just his natural reaction. Instead, just bump his mouth a little bit with your rein to stop him. Don't tear off his head. If you do, your horse will get to the point that, when the gate bangs and he does jump forward, he immediately jumps back because he knows you're about to jerk his head.

The whole point in scoring is to make the box more comfortable to the horse. If he jumps, get him stopped, then rub or pet him. Score him until he does relax and handles things exactly the way you want him to.

You might score one steer or two, or it might take ten before you relax a horse. Get him quiet enough that, when the gate opens, he stands there, just like a statue; he doesn't even wiggle a muscle. That's the way you want your head horse to score. Everything takes off, but he's still in your hand, and he can leave the box like a bullet and get a flat start.

Some horses are better at scoring than others. Some seem to have a better concentration, just like people, and naturally work better.

Sometimes a person comes to a clinic with a horse who gets really hot in the box—rearing, lunging, and totally out of hand. What I should tell them: "Get another horse." Some horses probably won't ever score well; they might be too hot-blooded, like some race horses who flip over in the starting gate.

You've probably seen a race horse who scores well. He walks into the starting gate like a little gentleman and stands there. He never wiggles, but when those gates open, he's gone. That's how a head horse should score. Some good horses naturally do it; it seems like it's fun to them. They're the exceptional ones. Others just do it because you make them.

Remember: Some horses just don't make good rope horses, no matter who rides them. There's nothing more miserable in the world than trying to rope and ride a bad horse. Your roping is not enjoyable. On the other hand, the rider himself might be the problem, which goes right back to horsemanship.

## Position on Steer

I feel the highest percentage shot for me in heading is to position myself within a 5- to 8-foot radius of the steer. That's my bread and butter. My horse's shoulder should be just back of the steer's hip and to the left a little bit. I want anywhere from a 2- to 4-foot distance between the steer and my horse. That's my sweet spot.

When you position yourself to track a steer, relax your upper body and lean forward, like a jockey does, to stay over the motion. But don't put weight in one stirrup or the other. If, for example, you do lean to the outside, then an older horse will move away from the pressure of your weight. A green horse probably won't; he'll try to come to you.

If you're behind your horse, when you position yourself and start the swing, your upper body leaning back will pull the tip of the rope up. Then it will take you four or five swings to get the tip back down and get the right pitch on your loop.

The most common out-of-place position on the steer is straight behind him. That gives the steer an opportunity to cut in front of you. You should be to the left of the left hip.

When you are out of position behind the steer, or the steer cuts in front of you, another thing happens. Usually your elbow drops down and you also lean to compensate for the change in position. You can't see the steer well, so naturally you lean over to try to make your catch. But when you lean out, that makes the tip of the loop go up as you swing. You might catch the right horn, but the left horn will be hard to catch—you can't see it. Many times in this situation, you're barely able see the right horn; when you

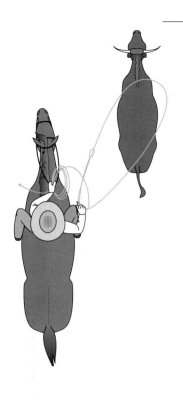

*Do position your horse's shoulder just back and to the left of the steer's hip.*

throw, your rope splits the horns.

When you run up to a steer and your horse starts rating off too soon, it changes the delivery of your loop; it won't quite reach the steer's horns. The same thing happens when a horse charges up too close to the steer—you're going to miss.

But there is a spot where you are going the exact same speed as the steer. Find that spot and learn to stay there. I want to rope as soon as I get to that spot; I don't want to keep swinging and have my horse backing off, and I don't want to try to pull my horse back to keep him from charging the steer.

Usually, as I approach a steer, I take hold of my horse to start rating him down, so I can match the steer's speed. I hold that position as I go into my delivery. But as I throw my loop, I will release the rein some with my left hand.

*Don't follow directly behind the steer.*

*I want from 2 to 4 feet between the steer and my horse.*

## Using the Lead

The lead, the amount of rope between your hands, is just a little more than a coil's length, about 12 to 18 inches. When you start a run, you have about a coil-length plus 6 inches between the loop in your right hand and the coils in your left. But the amount of lead you end up with is determined by your distance from the steer.

When you get too close to a steer, then you feed your hands up next to each other. The closer you feed your hands, the more it restricts your swing. However, when you're closer to the steer, you don't need much lead between your hands because you are so close.

If you are farther back, then your loop must travel farther in distance; you need more extension on your swing. You don't want to feed your hands so close together. Instead, you need more slack between your hands to allow for the longer distance.

But, for example, if you go to a fast steer with your hands close together and are getting outrun, there is no way to make that situation work. The only way you could is by using a reach shot. You have to drop a coil so the loop can travel farther.

That's where the consistency comes in, for example, on my fast rodeo-type runs. I can drop one coil out of my hand and reach and stay pretty consistent in my roping. However, when I drop more than one coil, my percentages drop. It also makes a difference in how I handle and set the steer up for my heeler. The more I reach, the worse the handle I give my heeler, which pulls down his percentages too.

But with a shorter lead and distance from the steer, I'm where I need to be for the best handle. My percentage of catches will be higher, my handles are going to be better, and that increases my heeler's chance for catching the steer.

The most important thing about the amount of slack in your rope: When you go to the horn to dally, don't have extra slack between your hands, or between you and the steer for that matter. For example, when you have a big loop on the steer's

*A sequence of two.*
*1/ Don't drop a coil and try to dally immediately if you're close to the steer. Either pick up the dropped coil or let the excess lead between your hands feed out before you dally.*

*2/ If you don't, you're asking for trouble when you go to the horn to dally.*

165

horns, pull out all the slack before you come to the horn to dally. You can get your hand caught in that slack dangling there. I suggest that you put a coil back in your hand and get the rope tight first. If you go to the horn with a lot of slack, there is a really good chance that you will get your hand wrapped in it.

On the other hand, if you had, for example, dropped a coil to go the distance and make the catch, there shouldn't be a lot of slack. After all, you dropped the coil because the steer is farther out; the distance is greater. So the rope is covering the distance, so to speak.

But you can get into trouble when you're close to a steer and drop an extra coil from your hand because that creates extra slack that isn't needed. That does happen on occasion, when you are close and throw—an extra coil just pulls out of your hand. Unless you are trying to make a rodeo run and really reach out with your loop, you're better off to stick that dropped coil back in your left hand.

This goes right back to the drill when you had the rope on the steer in the chute. When you worked that drill and came out of the box, you gained on the steer in distance, so you actually gained slack in your rope. As you approached the steer, your horse was moving faster than the steer. Obviously, that created extra slack, so you practiced reeling in your rope as you got closer to the steer. Know how to handle that slack. Practice that drill so that you can pick up a coil.

You'll have to pick up a coil in other situations; for example, when you rope a steer, and he slows down. Two things can happen then. You have to dally and turn off and really try to move your horse to take out the slack. And even then, you are giving a bad handle because of the big jerk that comes when the steer reaches the end of the slack. Or when that steer starts to slow down, make sure you can coil that slack back in your hand to get the rope tight and give a smooth handle. You have to learn to read that situation when it happens.

## Taking the Dally

Now that you have caught the steer around the horns, it's time to dally. For most beginners this is a scary situation.

The first thing a beginner does is turn the left hand, which makes the horse go left. So the horse is going one way, and the steer is going the other. Now the beginner looks down at the horn, which he doesn't realize he's doing, and he's out of control. He doesn't have any idea where the steer is or what his horse is doing, which ends up in a terrible handle for the heeler.

This is why it's important to learn to dally first, so you don't pick up bad habits from the start. That's why I like to start a beginner by putting the rope on the steer in the chute, so he can learn how to coil up the rope as he goes to the steer. Once the beginner has the rope gathered and is in position, concentrating on the steer's head, he can cross over with his left hand to help hold up the horse's shoulder.

With my right hand, I like to have my slack just slightly lower than shoulder height, with my arm extended out straight. I don't like to pull my slack down by my hip because then I have to come forward and around my body to get back to the horn, which gives slack back to the steer. With my arm straight and at shoulder height, I can come straight across to the horn without giving any slack to the steer. At this point, the left hand should be roughly about 12 o'clock, and the right hand with the slack at about 4 o'clock.

When you start to dally, the left hand moves to about 2 o'clock. That's because your horse naturally wants to drift away from the steer; he knows he has to turn that steer. You must hold up the horse's left shoulder, so your left hand moves the

*A sequence of four.*
*1/ When you pull your slack, your left hand is at 12 o'clock and your right at about 4.*

*2/ As you start to dally, the left hand moves to about 2 o'clock, to hold up the horse's left shoulder so he stays straight, rather than drifting to the left. Your right hand crosses under the left, and you use your wrist to feel for the horn.*

rein up against the horse's neck, to keep his body position straight as you dally.

Remember: The common problem when people learn to dally is that they look down at the saddle horn. It is a natural reaction. You look down to make sure that you don't get your hand in the dally. That is one of the worst habits you can develop.

First of all, it's like driving a car and trying to pick up something from the floor at the same time. You might run off the road, or veer into traffic and cause a wreck.

The same thing happens when you rope. When you look down at the horn, you don't know what's in front of you—if the steer happens to cut in front of you, it could get ugly. That saddle horn never moves. It's always in the same spot. You don't need to look to know it's there.

You must always keep your eyes fixed

on the steer as you dally. That's why this next drill is so good. You can go at a slow pace and not have a wreck. And even if you do happen to get your hand in the rope, it won't cut off your fingers. This is a good drill to practice even after you've learned to rope pretty good.

Here's the drill. At the end of your run, follow your cattle to the catch pen. Put yourself in the same position you rope from, then pull the slack, dally and undally. Dally and undally. It's good practice.

*3/ Keep your right hand close to the horn as you start your wrap. The left hand is still up, supporting the horse to help keep his shoulder up.*

*4/ As you complete the wrap, continue to feel for the horn with the lower part of your right hand. One dally will hold the steer and also allows you the freedom to slide the rope if anything goes wrong.*

Everybody thinks you should try to dally fast and take big sweeps around the saddle horn. That is not the way you dally—that's the way that you get your hand in the dally or bang your hand on the horn.

Dallying well comes more from feel—doing it as if you were blind. You're looking at the steer anyway, not the horn. When you dally, feel for your saddle horn with the palm of your hand and your wrist. As you dally, continue to feel for the saddle horn and rotate the slack counterclockwise around it to complete the dally.

Taking a big swipe often creates more slack. When you make a big swipe and come around in the dally, that slack can go over your wrist, and your wrist becomes half-hitched to the horn. Then, when the horse drops his shoulder to turn, you are in big trouble. That's why it is so important to hold up the horse's shoulder by keeping your hand up. You have to be thinking—team roping is a thinking game.

So when you dally, keep your eyes on the steer and feel for the horn with the palm of your hand and your wrist. A proper dally is a nice, smooth rotation around the horn—not a panic situation.

My hand is usually more flat with the

*A sequence of two.*
*1/ Do look at the steer when you take your dally, not your horn. Feel for the horn with your hand.*

*2/ Don't look down at the horn when you dally or take a big swipe at the horn.*

palm down as I pull my slack. But when I go to my horn, I then turn my thumb up to dally. I want to be right against the horn when I dally. Remember—not a big swipe.

When I dally, I take just one wrap. A number of things can happen. If the steer happens to fall down and you have two dallies on, you probably can't get them off quick enough. One dally will hold, but still give you the freedom to slide the rope if something goes wrong. Then, if you can get the dally off the saddle horn, you might make a save.

The only time I might take more than one wrap would be if I turned a steer, he sat back and wanted to drag, and my rope started to run—to the point that I couldn't hold the steer with one dally. Then I would try to get another wrap to keep the rope from running.

## Handling the Steer

Handling a steer is an art. Give him to the heeler so that he has an easy shot. If he gets a hard shot, his consistency level goes way down, and his confidence too.

Once you rope the steer, make the horse stay true: Don't let him slow down or speed up, or turn left; you want him to simply stay in position. He paces the steer, going the same speed, and that's only for a jump or so.

Then as I dally, I want my horse to set, and as I set the steer and slow him down, I turn off in a lateral move and start pulling across the arena. I want my horse at a steady pull so the steer isn't changing speed. He's hopping on a nice even keel. Here's where the logging work pays off.

Most guys rope and let a horse turn off too soon. The rider has his mind on the dally and lets the horse go. You can feel that happen sometimes when you're practicing. As you get ready to throw or right as you release, the horse starts to drift. It's almost like driving a car down the road and feeling a tire go flat. When the horse drifts, your handle is going to be too fast, but you are committed to whatever happens and the results.

*Learn to dally safely by having another person hold the loop of your rope while you practice.*

*A sequence of two.*
*1/ Be sure your horse sets the steer first, especially if you're roping fresh, hard-running cattle.*

*2/ Then turn off. Many ropers tend to let their head horses turn off too soon.*

When I feel a horse wanting to drift, I take hold of him and make him go back to the steer and set things up again. Many people don't, and that's also a common problem. Often a header is aggressive in riding to his steer, but when he ropes, he quits riding his horse. When you quit pedaling a bicycle, you start to coast. That also happens to a head horse after you rope and pull your slack; you quit riding and think about dallying, and your horse starts to coast.

In the practice pen, when you rope and feel that horse drifting, keep going. Kick him up to keep him moving and start the dally as you ride.

Mostly, you're working more off the left bridle rein against the horse's neck, holding up the left shoulder. That's why it is so important, when you start to dally, that you cross over with your left hand and

*Try to keep a steady pull on the steer for as smooth a corner as possible, which gives your heeler a good shot.*

bring that rein into position. Even if the horse wants to duck, you can still hold him long enough to get a dally. The rein blocks him.

But when most people start to dally, the left hand goes into left-hand-turn mode, and they turn off at the same time they dally. So the horse actually learns that. It's not so much the horse doing it as it is the rider teaching him to do it.

Some guys get away with it and rope for quite a while like that. But as soon as the horse gets slightly ahead of the rider, the horse's anticipation grows a bit more each trip. Before long, by the time the roper is ready to throw, the horse is already leaving, which leaves the rider strung-out and off-balance.

A roper needs to keep his horse's shoulder up and teach his horse to set and take hold with the hind end, and then make a lateral move out of the hole—not lead with his shoulder.

But when a roper feels his horse drop, his natural reaction is to try to beat the horse to the horn and catch up, so the rider quits holding up the left rein. That enhances the drop of the shoulder even more, and the roper gets a real hard corner and a bad handle.

Don't worry so much about turning off the steer. Worry more about training the horse and teaching him to hold his position until you ask him to change it.

A smooth corner gives a heeler a good handle. When the steer runs down the arena, the heeler gets in time with him. When you start the steer around the corner, you have to hold his head to maintain control. If you can simply slow that steer, but keep everything moving through the corner, the rhythm doesn't change. There will be a time when the heeler can throw on the corner because he and the steer are in perfect time. They are in stride together.

That's harder to do if the head horse drops in the turn too hard and jerks the steer's head. That also makes the steer's back end swing out before he takes a jump forward. The header has broken the steer's rhythm and stride, and the heeler must start his timing again from the corner.

172

To become a really good header, it is so important to know how to handle a steer around the corner and how to slow the action down without breaking the rhythm. Your heeler can become an offensive heeler then. The header can give him a good smooth handle and not jerk the steer away. The heeler can gather his horse, set himself up on the corner, and know he's going to get a quick throw.

But if a header reaches with a lot of slack in his rope or if his horse ducks out, the steer makes a hard corner. Then the heeler has to be in defensive mode to get close to that steer. It's more like damage control.

To control this with my rodeo horse, I spend more time freeing him up in the practice pen than anything. Obviously I'm going for fast times, and my target is a little farther away so I have to reach for the steer. But in the practice pen, instead of getting a dally and maybe letting my horse duck, I'm really conscious of him dropping his shoulder. I hold my left hand up and go another two or three jumps before I handle the steer nice and slow. This is good practice and a horse will respond to that.

In rodeo roping, we all have a tendency to rope fast, try to get a fast dally, and move out fast—to try to speed up the time. You can only rope so many like that on a horse before he starts to anticipate and get quicker and quicker. You end up missing cattle just because your horse moved too quick, or you break stride and don't give the heeler a good shot. But a good header, even when he reaches, will try to maintain his flow around the corner.

Handling cattle well is not just roping, turning off, and the heeler coming in behind you. There's an art to bringing the steer's head around so that he takes nice smooth hops.

Look at the steer's head as he comes around the corner. That's important. I don't watch the heeler; I watch the steer's head. When I start taking the steer's head away from him, the steer gives me a signal. He tells me how fast he's going to

move out of the corner, what he's going to do, and how he's going to handle.

For example, if a steer starts to slow down when the loop goes around his horns, this tells me the steer will be slow on the corner. I can go ahead and push out of the corner a little stronger because he's going to hang back on the end of the rope.

Another steer will basically want to lead. He'll turn and almost move alongside you, almost turning himself. If one does this, I might have to really push out in front of him because he's already starting the turn. Otherwise, he'll begin to circle around me, rather than being in tow.

If you don't have access to a lot of cattle, watch an open roping, not a rodeo. See what the other guys are doing and the way they handle their cattle.

The best way to learn to handle steers is to put your rope on a steer in the chute and turn hundreds of steers for your heeler. This way, you can really concentrate on your horsemanship and your handle.

## Facing

Facing is just as important as scoring or any other fundamental in team roping. You can't teach your horse about facing by just making practice runs.

In the chapter on horsemanship, I discussed how a roper can log his horse to help work him on facing. I very seldom face with my horse in the practice pen, once he's to the point he faces well. When I do face in the practice pen, which is seldom, I make my horse back up a few steps afterward.

After my heeler ropes and dallies in the practice pen, when my horse knows how to face and in the correct way, I undally

*One of the best ways to work your horse on facing is using the log. See the chapter on horsemanship for more information.*

my head rope right away. But if my heeler misses or ropes two feet and doesn't dally and lets his rope slide, I pull the steer a couple of more jumps and then undally.

What I do also depends on the horse. If I feel the horse wanting to anticipate, or if he quits pulling right then, I undally and drive him out pretty hard so he doesn't learn to anticipate facing. Then I circle him back to the left, back toward the chute, before I head toward the catch pen.

I won't let a horse start toward the fence and head right toward the catch pen because he learns to pull off that way, which makes him weak in coming back up the fence to the left. If my steer runs left, and I rope and need my horse to come left, he'll hesitate there, which changes the handle of the steer and breaks the rhythm of the run.

This is something important I've learned. I don't think you are going to teach a horse a lot of the essential things he must do to be a great horse—to score, to run, or to pull. But the one thing you can eventually teach a horse to do and make some improvement on is the face.

A lot of heelers seldom dally in the practice pen, to keep their horses from taking the jerks and to keep from wearing out the practice cattle. So it's hard to work a head horse on facing in the practice pen. That's why I do a lot of dry work with the log; that's where I can teach my horse. I can simulate the pull with the log, circling in the arena where you would be turning a steer, facing the horse on the log, and then backing him.

## Practice and Your Horse

When you rope a steer in a practice pen and feel your horse wants to cheat you, don't continue with the run. This is a perfect opportunity for you to make your horse work correctly. You don't have the luxury or the time when you're competing, but in the practice pen, you are not at

*Sometimes the best practice is when you don't rope at all, but use the opportunity to correct your horse. For example, when a horse is too much on the muscle as he leaves the box, I might not rope at all. Instead, I'll shut him down a few strides out and remind him that he must respond to my direction.*

the horse's mercy. You can correct him. That's what the practice pen is for.

When some people practice-rope, their horses duck off, for instance, and they finish the run just like they would at a roping. They haven't corrected anything. When they go to the next roping, the horses are much more tense and tight; they anticipate that much quicker.

Although I might practice that way for a few runs, before I finish my practice session, I free up my horse, relax him, and go strictly for technique and finesse in handling the horse and the cattle.

Then, when I get to a roping, my horse gives me a little extra; I know he's not going to cheat me. That's the worst feeling in the world—when you're ready to rope, and your horse doesn't run and starts anticipating. You have to try to compensate with your loop.

If you have a seasoned, smart horse working at about 85 percent in the practice pen, he gives about 50 percent in competition. Even though you tune in the practice pen and have him running free, the old veteran might still give you just 50 percent.

It's the opposite, sometimes with a young, green horse. You think you have him ready to go and take him to the rodeo, and he might go the other way. He'll work too freely—take an extra jump forward or be a little late turning off.

With about any horse, if you don't spend time in the practice pen, when you back in the box to compete, he is all muscle. You jiggle your reins, but he doesn't come off the bridle. When you're in the practice pen, don't get in a hurry; make sure your horse gets right in the box. Spend the time and solve the problem.

At home, slow down; take whatever time it takes to do what you're trying to accomplish. If you don't, when you get to a roping, your horse will have a problem there, and you're forced into letting him get away with it. And if you are letting him get away with things in the practice pen, he is definitely going to try the same thing in competition.

# Playing It Safe

As a precaution, be as safe as you can be by practicing correctly. A lot of people just don't think and multiply the chances for losing a thumb or finger for no reason. They get in too big a hurry and don't keep things under control.

When most people get in a tight situation, instead of trying to clear themselves from it, they go ahead and try to finish the run. And they panic even more. That's where they get in trouble.

If you get in trouble—at least get your hand out of there, away from the rope. If you do feel that you have your hand stuck in a dally, or something is not right, the best thing to do is take your horse back toward the steer. Keep things in forward motion.

If you try to finish the run, it makes everything worse. You lose control of your horse, or your horse ducks. And you're still trying to get a dally instead of reacting to make the horse go back to the steer. That's trying to beat the time and beat the horse's move at the same time.

Being safe is where your time in the practice pen pays off. You work slow cattle, and you learn. You learn to handle your cattle, and you learn to handle your rope.

The header has a great responsibility. He has to come out from behind the barrier—not too early or too late. He ropes the steer around the horns, and then has to handle him, slowing him down and making sure his feet are hopping. Then, when the heeler ropes the steer and dallies, the header has to turn and face to stop the clock. He starts the run and finishes the run. There are a lot of fundamentals that must happen during a run. If you want to be a successful roper, you must master each one of them.

# Making Your Heeler's Practice Better

As a header, try your best every run to give your heeler the best handle you possibly can under the circumstances. A good heeler always looks for a good shot—and as quickly as possible—to throw his loop, and he's aware that a bad handle can occur. How good a run is made, to a certain extent, is within a header's control. But when things don't go as planned, sometimes the heeler must really ride defensively—for damage control.

Over time, a heeler can gain more confidence in his header. The better the header handles the cattle, the more offensively the heeler can rope without simply reacting to problems created by a bad handle. The more careless or reckless the header, the worse the handle, which puts the heeler in a more defensive mode; he must try to salvage a run that isn't going well.

Practice runs tell a heeler what kind of handle to expect from his header. Given a bad handle, the heeler, instead of taking an easy throw for a fast time, must think more about what the steer might do. But that's also a part of being a header—being able to read each steer and respond to what he does, so you can set things up for the heeler.

My objective as a header is to be a quarterback. My first job is to put a rope on the steer's horns and put the team in a potentially winning situation. My second job is to handle the steer the best way I possibly can without losing that winning situation.

No matter how good or bad the handle, I think a good heeler also must be aggressive enough and have roped enough cattle to read and react to any situation. That's why Clay and I have been so good roping together. Even when I gave Clay a bad handle, he was cowboy enough and had enough "charge" to him that he could still make a great shot. On the other hand, because of his experience, when I gave him a great handle, he really capitalized on it, and a winning time was that much easier. That's what separates the good heelers from the great heelers: No matter the handle or what a steer does, a great heeler will somehow catch him. Even if he doesn't get a good handle, he never has any excuses; he always feels he should have made the catch.

As a member of a team, a header must understand that consecutively bad handles, time after time after time, cause his heeler to rope late or miss altogether. When that happens, you must do something about it in the practice pen, where a good team works to make every run a potentially winning one.

A good roper should be like Michael Jordan, capable of making a slam-dunk, a free throw, and a 3-point shot. He also must be able to play defense. I don't want to be a one-dimensional roper who does well only in certain situations. I want to be a great header no matter what type of run needs to be made.

You want the same thing in a good heeler too. If the team has plenty of time, he won't take a bad throw and risk missing. But if your team needs to make a 4-second run, a good heeler won't track the steer so long you'll stop the clock at 5 seconds. He takes his shot. It might be a hard shot and he might even miss it. But at least you and your partner have put yourselves in a position to win.

When I go to the practice pen, it's strictly business. Some ropers go there to socialize, and that's fine too. But I am intense; I'm in the battle to become better in my roping. My competitive juices flow even in the practice pen. That's another reason we have been a successful team; Clay is as intense about practice as I am.

Early on, when Clay and I practiced roping together so much, we seldom said a word to each other for 2 or 3 hours at a time. We each did our thing, and when I rode out of the arena, Clay always said, "Thanks." That was it. We focused on our roping. Even now, as far as team roping goes, we both are still on the same page and can be because of our time in the practice pen.

*A sequence of six.*

1/  Both header and heeler position themselves
in the box. The steer's head should be straight
in the chute before the header nods for the release.

2/  After the steer leaves the chute, the heeler
moves into position to haze the steer, and the
header begins to move toward the steer's left hip.

3/  When the header is in position, his horse rates
the steer until the header throws his loop. The
heeler continues to haze the steer until the header
makes the catch.

*1*

*2*

*3*

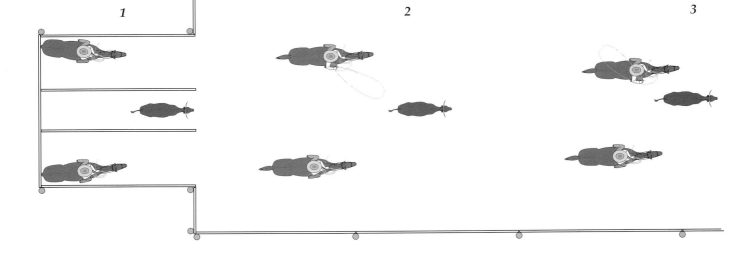

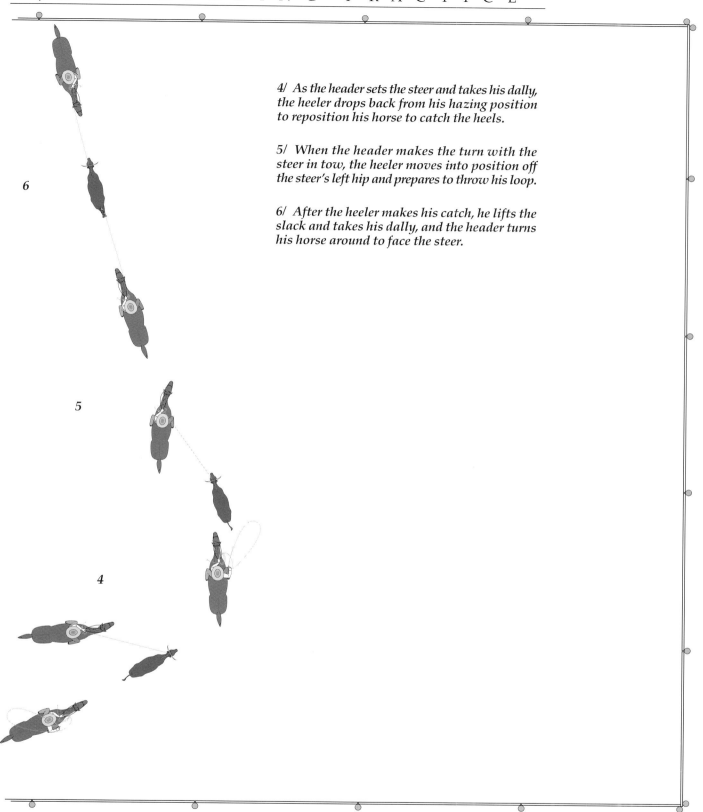

4/ As the header sets the steer and takes his dally, the heeler drops back from his hazing position to reposition his horse to catch the heels.

5/ When the header makes the turn with the steer in tow, the heeler moves into position off the steer's left hip and prepares to throw his loop.

6/ After the heeler makes his catch, he lifts the slack and takes his dally, and the header turns his horse around to face the steer.

# 14 CLAY ON HEELING PRACTICE

WHEN A NOVICE roper can heel the dummy well, it's time to practice horseback in the arena. At this point, the roper understands the heeler's correct position in relation to the dummy and knows how to control his loop. He can come in from a 90-degree angle and send his loop where he wants it, or from behind and scoop up the hind feet. Or he can trap the steer's feet from the front angle. He also knows how to handle his slack. Now he can combine all the steps he's practiced at the dummy and progress to roping a steer from horseback.

## Rein-Hand Position

At first, it's awkward for some people to handle the bridle rein, the coils, and the loop. Here's how I do it.

I hold my reins so I can adjust them while running down the arena. I wrap my left hand in a fist around my roping rein, with the loop coming from the bottom, up through the top of my hand. Then I hook my little finger through the rein. My roping rein is set pretty long so I have quite a bit of excess rein that flips over the top of my hand.

*When he gets horseback in the practice pen, a roper combines all he's learned about positioning himself in relation to a roping dummy, handling a rope, and riding a horse .*

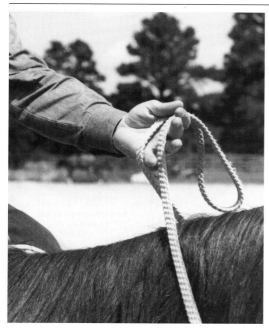

*I hook my little finger through my roping rein. Because my rein is set long, more excess than usual flips over the top of my hand.*

*Here's how I hold both my rein and my coils in my left hand.*

If I need to make adjustments as my horse runs down the pen, I pull the excess rein with my right hand, sliding it through my left, to shorten the rein to get closer contact with my horse's mouth. I also can adjust either the left or right side of my roping rein. Because of the extra length, if my horse stumbles or something goes wrong, I can let the excess slide through my hand. The rein won't come completely out of my hand because I have my little finger hooked through it.

Compare this with having your entire hand wrapped around only the roping rein. I don't like that because you have to set the length of your rein ahead of time, so you can't really adjust it as you need to during a run. With the shorter rein, if the horse stumbles or takes his head away from you, he can pull the rein out of your hand. At the least, he pulls your hand down as his head drops, putting you out of position to rope.

On the average, my rein is set far longer than most ropers set theirs. I have a good 6 inches to a foot of length coming over the top of my hand. That's a lot of excess, but it works for me.

When I'm just riding around, I ride with a fairly long, loose rein. When I stop, I also can put the rein over the horn, and it won't restrict my horse or pull him back. He can stand in a relaxed position, and if he shakes his head, the rein won't flip over his head or fall down where he can step in it.

## In the Box

I know how I like my horse to sit in the box, but each horse has a little different pattern to the way he wants to stand there. His pattern is based on what he's been allowed to do or has been taught to do in the box.

I like a horse who's no-nonsense; he does what you tell him. You ride him in the box, turn around, back into the corner, and position him where you want him. Then he stands quietly on ready, with you holding him, until he breaks with the steer.

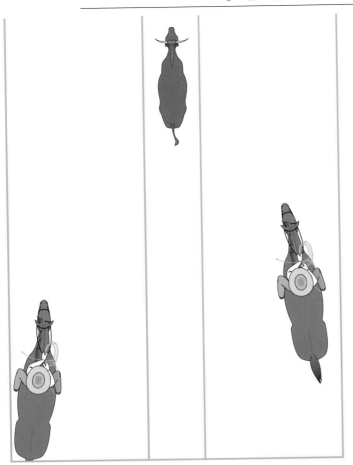

*Here's how I like to position my heel horse in a long box.*

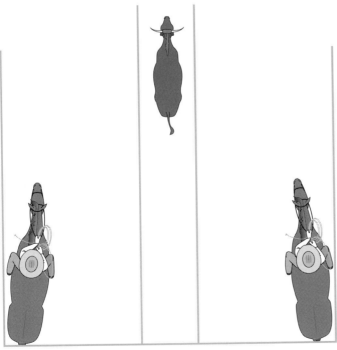

*When the box is short, I usually position my horse in the far right corner.*

A horse should stand square on all four feet and be balanced in the box, not leaning one way or the other. Although I usually like a horse to tilt his head to the inside a little, toward the steer, I like his body to be straight. Then he can break straight out of the box. Another thing: Anytime I pick up on the rein for any reason, I want my horse to respond—in the box or outside.

Depending on the length of the box, I position myself so that when the steer comes out of the chute, he can see me immediately. The way I present myself to him has an impact. My position causes the steer to travel in the pattern I want. Straight is good in this case, and just a little off-center is good also, but I don't want a steer coming over to the right as he runs down the pen.

If the box is short, I usually position my horse back in the far right corner. If it's a long box, I move myself up a little closer toward the open end.

Although I do like a horse to stand straight and square in the box, I'll let him tip his head to the inside. Sometimes, allowing him to do that seems to help trap his back end somewhat against the side of the box. This means his body is straighter, and he stands more the way I want.

A rope horse is sometimes apprehensive and always ready to go in the box. Many times, if you hold his head totally straight, his hip tips to the left, out of alignment, because he's so ready to go; it's difficult to hold his body straight. However, if you cock the horse's head a little to the left, it helps align his body against the right fence so he stands with a straighter body position, which means he's also more square on all four feet.

Many people seem to think that a horse in the box should have each foot in place, standing like a statue and in the ideal position to leave the box. Usually that type of person rides into the box to set his horse and prods, pulls, and positions the horse constantly; he never lets up.

Once the horse is in position, the roper immediately asks for the steer, and the horse has to perform. Most riders also make too many runs before giving a horse a break. After three or four runs, the horse figures out that when he finds the perfect position, he immediately has to perform again.

*Make the box a comfortable place for your horse to be. Let him stand there for a moment and relax.*

So, why would he want to be in that position? The horse has never found one comfortable spot the entire time since he's been there.

There must, of course, be some type of communication or signal between horse and rider that it's time to go. However, when a horse backs up and stands in that ideal spot in the box, it should be a comfortable thing for him to do. That spot should be a comfort zone for the horse.

But 90 percent of the ropers, without ever realizing it, teach their horses something else altogether: That it's the performance spot. All the horse knows is that when he's there, things get fast and furious. He has found no reason to want to be there, and the rider has continued to prod, poke, and maneuver him the whole time.

Watch horses in the box. Some do everything possible to avoid being set in that position. They might even hit the spot for a split-second, but they keep moving and go through it; they don't want to stay there. That's because after all the maneuvering, when the roper finally positions the horse, he immediately nods for the steer. The next time the roper tries to position the horse, the horse thinks, "No way. I'm not going there."

*Set a pattern when you ride in the box so your horse knows what to expect. The pattern also tells him when it's time to get down to business and focus on his work.*

183

Some horses can tolerate more of that kind of handling than others. Some can stand there and make run after run after run, but most horses can't.

You must signal or communicate in some way to set a pattern so that when you ride your horse into the box, he relaxes there. He must hit the good spot, but also learn that he's not going anywhere for the moment, so he can relax. Only later is there another signal that tells him, "It's time to go somewhere and do something."

Too, when you position a horse in the ideal spot, don't leave the box every time. Pet him, rub or reward him, and let him stand there and enjoy the moment.

When you make a run, before you ask for the steer, take a step up or in some way move your horse out of that relaxed mental setting before you prepare him to break from the box. Pick up a little of the bridle just before you nod or as your healer nods.

The next time you back your horse in the box, he probably won't be as afraid or apprehensive about being there. "Oh, yeah," he thinks, "this was a good spot last time. I didn't have to leave just as soon as I got here, give all I had, get spurred and jerked, handle the steer, and do it all over again and again."

When I have a problem in the box, what I do depends on the horse and the situation. I might just work with a horse in the box, or I might try scoring some cattle.

When a horse does something in the box that he doesn't normally do, there's a reason for it. You've roped too many steers, maybe, or the horse is hurting in some way. Something is wrong. Stop and analyze it. Try to figure out what's causing the problem.

If the problem is something a horse does periodically and at about the same time each practice session, maybe you need to understand the limitations on that horse. Maybe he just needs a breather or to score some cattle to relax and reassure him that everything is okay. Maybe he just needs a change in the routine to revitalize him.

If the problem reaches a point where it becomes dangerous—the horse tries to rear, run into the side of the chute, or go over the fence—stop. You need to evaluate things immediately. A horse can do many different things that tell you something is wrong. You need to pay attention to them. Stop and analyze the problem before you make another run.

When I have a problem, I first see what kind of response I get by using my bridle and feet to direct the horse. If I get no response at all, I know the horse is mentally gone; he's out of it. Then, I'm really careful.

The horse doesn't think rationally at that point. He doesn't respond because he's totally absorbed in what's going on with himself, and it's all related to the box, the steer, or his required performance. You can get into a dangerous situation here, and the horse might hurt you.

When a horse has totally lost it in the box, I might get off and tie him up. Or if I don't really know the horse, I might take him to the round pen and work him there. I'll crowd him a little to see if he locks up, gets mad, or loses it again. But I'm not on him then, and I'm not trying to hurt the horse. From the ground, I'll try to see if I can get him through a mad spell and show him that we can work together.

It takes time and effort to learn where a horse is mentally and how much he can take. But I want to know if the problem is only a little tantrum, or a full-blown rebellion.

If a horse in the box hasn't lost it mentally and you feel some response when you cue him, that tells you the horse is still listening and tuned in to you. When a horse still respects your hand on the rein and pressure from your feet and legs, you should be able to work with him and maneuver him back into position. When

*When a horse scores well, it means the rider is calling the shots—not the horse.*

you do, take some time and let the horse stand there. Reward him for what he has given you and allow him to relax.

Find a place in the box where the horse can get along with you. That's the only way to get longevity out of your rope horse. Otherwise, you risk lowering his tolerance and decreasing the value of his performance. Compare that with maintaining what he gives now or increasing his level of performance with proper handling.

In some instances, when an old horse really knows and understands what he's supposed to do—or not do—in the box, leg or rein cues might straighten him right up. A good horseman understands that and knows how much pressure a horse can handle and if the corrections do any good or not. Correcting a horse is a trial-and-error thing you learn with experience, and each horse is different.

## Scoring

Scoring is the most obvious way for either a header or a heeler to work in the practice pen to help settle a horse in the box. When your rope horse scores well, he can stand quietly when a steer is turned out of the chute. That means

you're calling the shots, not the horse.

When he starts to move around too much in the box, tries to leave too early, or pops up in the front end anticipating the run, it's time to score him. How I correct the horse depends on where he positions his head or where he's trying to go with his body.

I try and relax the horse in the box and then study how the scoring affects him. Then I begin to develop a pattern when I'm scoring, so the horse learns that every time we go in the box it's the same routine. There's a pattern being set, and the routine lets the horse know what's happening, which allows him to be comfortable there.

There's another approach I sometimes use on a horse who's uncomfortable in the box. For example, when I'm riding a horse in the arena and he does something wrong, I correct him right then and there. The correction tells a horse that the spot in the arena where he made the mistake isn't a good place to be. Then I immediately provide him with a good place—the box. I walk him into it and try to relax him, rub him, and show him that the box is a good place to be.

If a problem in the box is engraved pretty heavily on a horse's mind, then I might have to find a way to work with him in the box by allowing him to be a little bit less than correct in some way. For him to be comfortable, I might have to let him do some little thing to relieve his stress; I give a little to get what I need. For example, I might have to set the horse in a less desirable position in the box, but if he will handle more quietly that way, I can live with it.

For example, I had a good heel horse who always wanted to hold his head way over to the left, almost as if he wasn't even paying attention to the steer. When I first got him, he was really nervous in the box and didn't want to stand. It wasn't a good situation.

So I tried to show him where I needed him to be and also to make the box comfortable for him. But for him to become comfortable and relaxed, I had to give something in return—a release of sorts—and allow him to hold his head way over to the side. We finally found a way he could relax in the box. The position wasn't what I really wanted, but at least he wasn't trying to throw his hind end out of position, rear, or jump out of the box like he had before. I could tolerate what he needed to be comfortable, and we still got a good start out of the box.

After that, he scored perfectly—if he could stand his way in the place I wanted him to be. After I took him through a routine to get there, he would stand forever. However, because his head was to the side, I couldn't really see the steer to break with him and could be a little late out of the box. So instead of watching the steer, I watched my header. When he started to nod, I started my horse.

That's one way of scoring a difficult horse. But if I had settled only for exactly what I wanted, I would have never gotten any use from that horse's performance ability.

At first, I scored that horse a lot, again trying to relax him in the box. He champed the bit, pranced, and even quivered in the box. I rubbed him to soothe him and rode him in and out of the box repeatedly. To be successful, I had to act relaxed myself. I did anything in and around the box to break up his old routine and teach him that it was no big deal to ride into a box. Once he learned he didn't have to run hard after every trip to the box, I actually scored the steers. We found a routine we could both live with by finding a way to make the box comfortable for the horse.

A horse won't score very well if you run him on steer after steer after steer. The horse begins to think he's supposed to jump out harder every time or he gets stronger every trip, more on the muscle. You have to consider that while maintaining your rope horse's performance.

## Position on the Steer

When I start a run and I'm hazing the steer into position for the header, I position myself a little wide off the steer so he can see me and I can turn him if I need to. Then I follow that same pattern and stay to the outside until after the header has roped, and the steer is about three-quarters of the way through the turn. Then I move into position to heel the steer, putting the hind end of the steer so it just clears my horse's nose. This all is to the right, with the steer's left leg lined up just outside the right front leg of my horse.

When a horse breaks from the box, I want him to get out really hard and fast. I like a horse who can and will follow the steer to the left, if you need him to, or to the right. The horse should be so responsive to my hand that, if I need to move him sideways, I can—without breaking his stride.

A heeler's first responsibility is to hold the steer on course and keep him from going to the right. So when you heel, you must act as a hazer and make that steer go where you want. You must be quick out of the box to do that.

Some steers are harder to hold in position; they want to edge closer, almost against you. So you might have to move up to the steer's shoulder, or sometimes even right at his head, just to hold him in position. An old roping steer seldom is scared of you; he's been doing this for a long time. When you have to move in closer to the steer to hold him, you give up your good outside position, but you must first hold the steer so the header can get his shot. When having to ride close to a steer to hold him as he makes his turn, you usually have to check your horse and make a sharper corner. This makes it a little harder to set your timing and the angle of the swing for the delivery of your loop.

I usually hold my hazing position until the header has caught and the steer's head

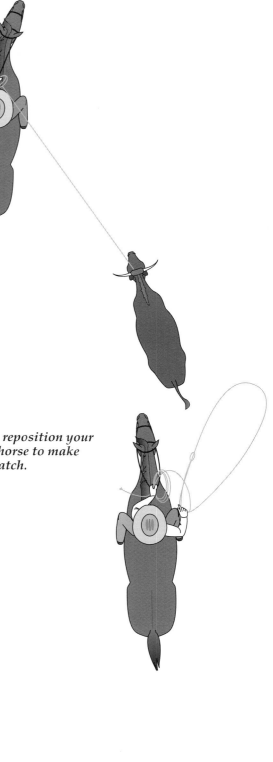

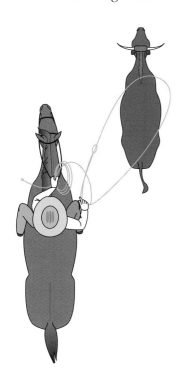

*First position your horse to the side to haze the steer for the header.*

*Then reposition your heel horse to make the catch.*

*Track a steer and learn how to best position your horse for throwing a heel loop.*

*When I haze the steer into position for the header, I stay far enough away from the steer that he can see me and I can turn him if necessary.*

*I continue to haze the steer until the header has roped.*

has started to come around. Then when my partner makes his move turning the steer, I check my horse up and pivot to the inside to get on the left side of the steer, letting the hind end of the steer move out in front of me, which gives me an open shot. This is a hard move for horse and roper because of the severity of the turn.

For example, say the steer makes a sharp turn and his speed dies, instead of him flowing freely through the corner. That means the heeler has to make another sharp corner. So the horse makes more of a pivot, going across the corner in one stride instead of two.

You have to be careful at that point and be patient. If the header doesn't turn and really move out, you'll be too close to the steer. Then you have to let him move forward and restart your horse because you almost come to a stop when making the pivot.

Try to make the transition smooth and easy for your horse when you rein him across. This is where the dry work and your warm-up pay off. When you ask your horse to give his head or move away from your leg, he knows what to do to make the kind of turn you need.

However, if the steer is easy to hold going down the arena, and you can get a good outside position, 8 to 10 feet to the right of the steer, you can make more of a gradual turn on your entry to the corner and better stay in rhythm

*A sequence of two.*
*1/ When Jake has made his head catch, I bring up my loop and begin to reposition myself to catch the heels.*

*2/ As Jake begins to move the steer through the turn, I drop back from the hazing position at the side, to move my horse off the left hip of the steer.*

with the steer. This gives you an easier shot and keeps everything moving forward until delivery.

If I draw a steer I know is going to drag or set back on the rope, then I position myself more directly behind him, to better drive him forward. Usually a steer won't stop if you're directly behind him. The most important thing is to position yourself to keep everything moving forward smoothly.

In the practice pen, when a horse is slow in taking his position on a steer, I might try to hustle the horse up, or I might run a slower steer to make it easier for the horse. What I do depends on where the horse is physically. Is he too old to run, or just being lazy and not putting out the effort? Is he too fat and out of shape to run?

People often try to rope with out-of-shape horses; that's a pretty widespread problem. Many people practice rope only on the weekends and aren't really heavy into competition. The people who compete all the time realize the importance of having a horse in shape, so they ride their horses during the week to keep them fit.

*Use every opportunity in the practice pen to teach your horse about position and rate.*

# Rating a Steer

It's important to have a horse who can rate a steer well. Your horse has to be quick enough to hold the steer in position for the header, and he also has to make the transition from hazing to cowing. Either way, he must match his speed with the steer's and hold the position.

I have a gelding who gets stronger, more on the muscle, the more he's used in the practice pen, and he doesn't rate as well. But with a mare I ride, when I quit asking her to go faster, she maintains her position in relation to the steer. Even when I make the turn and ask her to close the distance to the steer, her natural tendency is to hang back and maintain that certain distance from the steer.

It's hard to find a horse with the right attitude when it comes to rating well. Some start cheating and cut off too soon in the corner. A lot of horses like to run down the arena, but when you turn them, they can be hard to direct. Some horses simply try to run off.

When you realize that your heel horse doesn't stay in good position and rate well behind a steer, go to the practice pen and track a lot of steers or even a burro. There, you pretty much let the horse go until he gets too close on the steer and finds out that's not a good place to be.

Practice tracking without your rope so you can fully concentrate on controlling the horse. Turn him loose, but when he moves out of bounds, correct him. Whenever he's not in the right spot, stop and move him to wherever he should be. Then set things up and start tracking again. For him to learn, you must turn him loose and trust him to do it right. If he messes up, correct him and do it over until he responds well. When he does respond, reward him for it by working on something else, or stop and relax for a while.

# Swinging the Rope

During a run I start out with quite a bit of lead between the coils in my left hand and the loop in my right. Then I continue to feed even more rope into my loop as I bring it up into position to throw.

That's mainly because I ride with my rein-hand in such close contact with my horse's mouth. Even though I like my roping rein set long, during a run, my left hand is in a low, stationary position because I take up short on the rein when I rope. And, because of that, I must have a longer span on the lead between my hands to bring my rope into position to swing.

First and foremost, when you swing your rope, you want the horse moving forward with each swing you take. His forward motion and the timing of your swing are hooked to the timing of the steer's motion. The header controls the steer's head, and as the steer comes around the corner, his body changes position. The steer starts striding out, with his legs moving up and down.

As you come into position to heel, you also try to adjust the rhythm of your swing to the steer's rhythm as he moves forward. Your swing should come over the top of the steer at the height of his jump every time. His jump and your swing are synchronized. Move forward and position your horse correctly in relation to the steer and, at the same time, coordinate your swing with his jump.

You match your swing with each jump until you know that on the steer's next forward stride you'll be able to place your loop. As you bring the loop around the back side of the rotation for the last time, the steer's feet hit the ground. Then as your loop starts forward, bring the bottom of the loop down and into position just as the steer's feet leave the ground to come up. Your loop meets his feet in the air. When your loop arrives, he's at the height of his jump, and you put the loop right where you want it.

## Handling the Slack

Knowing how to handle your slack correctly is important because it helps ensure that your loop stays on the steer's feet.

After you deliver a loop, you should still have your right hand on your slack. Roll your hand to grab the slack with your knuckles up. Then, all you do is lift the slack about shoulder high to keep the loop on the steer's feet. Many people don't realize that pulling the slack on a heel loop is that simple.

As the steer continues to move forward and your horse begins to stop, the loop tightens on the steer's feet. The loop usually stays on the feet because of the way you handled the slack, lifting on it. Let the horse and the steer pull the slack out; it's a safety factor for you.

When you grab the slack, you should still have three coils in your left hand. When you lift up the slack, be careful that you don't pull any of those coils out of your other hand. That can get you in trouble, creating too much slack for you to safely handle between your hands.

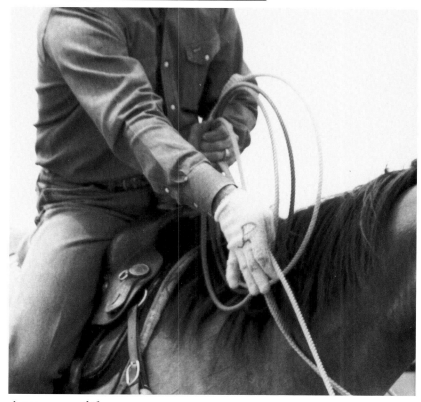

*A sequence of three.*
*1/ After delivering the loop, your right hand should still be on the slack.*

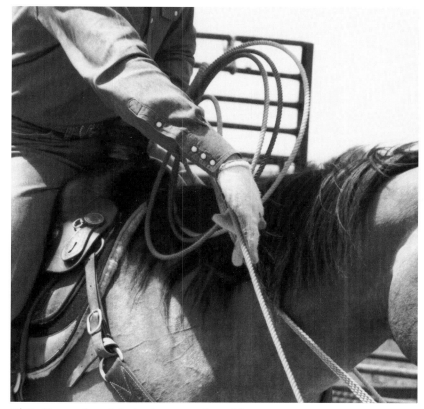

*2/ Roll your hand, bringing your knuckles up.*

## Taking A Dally

Before you take a dally, think about what has happened so far. You began to deliver your loop at the same time your horse was starting to drop his hind end and check his speed. When the bottom of your loop hit the target, everything came to a stop. The horse's forward momentum should stop right with the impact of the bottom of the rope.

Then you lifted the slack about shoulder high or as far as the amount of rope between your hands allowed. The horse stopped, and the steer's hind feet were in the loop. As the steer continued forward, the loop began to close on his feet. Then you take a dally around the horn. You must determine the right time to do it.

What tells me it's time to go to the horn is my feel for the timing of the run, the distance to the steer, and how tight my rope is. Probably, more than anything, I dally off the rhythm of the run. In team roping, the rhythm is set by the stride of your horse and the stride of the steer. As the steer comes around the corner and hops, you rotate your rope and hit a rhythm. That's when the timing, the rhythm of the run, is set.

The main considerations when you dally are rhythm and timing—and controlling the amount of rope you have between your hands. If you go to the horn with the right amount of lead, you're pretty safe because that piece of rope will be fairly controlled. Having that control is what helps keep your hand clear of the dally.

The important thing when you dally is to go slow and make the correct moves. Most people panic when it's time to dally. When a novice roper catches and his horse stops, the novice is apprehensive about dallying anyway. He's heard he can get hurt doing it. He also thinks that wrapping his rope on the horn fast will take care of the problem. But when you start speeding up and failing to do things correctly, step-by-step, you get into trouble. Keep things under control. You do that by following a procedure.

It's a good idea to practice step-by-step on the roping dummy, dallying counterclockwise with your thumb up. You can go slowly, deliver the rope, pause, and pay

*3/ Then lift your slack about shoulder high to keep the loop on the steer's feet.*

As you lift the slack, you should have about a foot or foot and a half of lead between your hands. Lift your right hand only as high as that amount of slack allows you. From that position, start to the horn to make your dally.

*A sequence of four.*
*1/ If you drop a coil, don't immediately go to the horn; you'll have too much lead between your hands.*

*2/ Instead, either pick up the coil or let the whole coil slide until you have the correct amount of lead.*

3/ *Use your wrist and hand to feel for the horn as you start your wrap.*

4/ *When you dally, don't see the rope with your eyes, feel it with your hand. Keep your eyes forward.*

*Don't have too long a lead between your hands. It can cause problems when you go to the horn. To practice dealing with this problem safely, have another person hold the end of your rope while you practice dropping a coil and letting it slide before you dally.*

attention to where your hand is. You should lift up the slack, and you can even dally if you've roped the dummy from your horse. Take the time to learn the procedure.

Once you're horseback and in the practice pen, so much about the dally depends on the length of your lead. For example, imagine that I have roped a steer. I've delivered my loop and have three coils in my left hand. I roll my right hand over and lift the rope. My horse is stopping, the steer is leaving me, and the rope starts to tighten. At that point, I have to either dally—right then—or use a coil.

If I can dally, that's fine. But if things are happening too fast and I don't immediately go for the horn, I have to drop a coil

from my left hand and let it slide. When I let the coil go, I don't bring my hand down to the horn and dally right then.

This is so important: I let the coil slide through my right hand, which controls the amount of lead between my hands. I don't want the length of that whole coil between my hands, which is why I let it slide. Then, when I make my wrap, I take it from the same point, so to speak, on the next coil, which means I still have the correct amount of lead between my hands.

So if you can't go to the horn when you first catch, drop a coil. But wait to dally until the full coil slides through your right hand and you reach the same spot on the next coil. Control the length of the lead between your hands.

Here's the best way I've found to practice that without getting into trouble. Get on your horse and have someone else hold the loop end of the rope. Then you go through the motions. At first, lift the slack and go to the horn on the first coil. When you're comfortable with that, you can practice with speed and try to get the dally.

Then, using the next coil down, practice the maneuver. Drop a coil from your left hand and let it slide through your hand, with the other person pulling on the end, until you're at about the same point on the next coil. That allows you to have a safe amount of lead when you go to the horn.

When you move your hand down to the horn to dally, the length of rope between your hands is ideally a foot to a foot and a half. Pay attention to that. Have someone pull the end of your rope, just like a steer moving away from you, and practice letting that second coil go. Do it right and do it over and over again.

Use anything you can to practice going to the horn correctly. You might even get a couple of calves or goats to heel. Just be sure whatever you use is light enough that—if you make a mistake—its weight won't cut off your fingers. If you get a hand tangled in the rope with a calf on the other end, the weight of a calf may pull the rope snug enough to skin up your hand, but it shouldn't totally wreck your hand. Do not exceed 250 pounds of calf.

As a kid, somehow I was able to get through thousands and thousands of loops on both the dummy and roping steers. I don't really remember how I learned correct procedures for staying safe on the horn. But I do remember learning to handle my rope and know where my rope was at all times.

I developed a feel for a rope, not by looking at the rope with my eyes, but by feeling the rope in my hands. Become proficient in that feel. Handle your rope over and over again. It's surprising how many people have fingers broken, rope-burned, or cut off simply because they have no feel for the rope and aren't really aware of it.

## Stopping the Steer

Once you deliver your loop, your header must face his horse with the steer between you. Each header has his point of view about when to face. I'm the heeler; I just rope the steer, stop him, and hope the header has turned around and backed up once I've brought the steer to a stop.

In an ideal situation, after I rope and dally, my horse actually stops the steer. As the header turns toward the steer, he faces both me and the steer. His timing, when he faces, is based on my throw. He might start his horse's hip around when he sees my loop hit or when my slack comes up.

When the heeler ropes the steer and the header goes to face, ideally the head horse never quits pulling on the steer during his pivot.

Some people have the perception that the heeler stops everything, and then the head horse turns back. If that was the case, instead of stopping 500 pounds of steer, the heeler would have to stop the steer's 500 pounds plus 1,200 pounds of head horse. That's a lot of moving weight—and a big jerk.

But that isn't exactly how things happen. If the header faces the way he should, it means a quicker time and is a lot easier on the steer and the heeler. When the head horse faces properly, he's already

*Your heel horse should stop when you throw your loop.*

looking at the heeler and is backing up when the steer comes to a stop.

I think this type of face evolved from ropers trying to make faster and faster runs, probably at rodeos, rather than at 10-head average ropings. A few tenths of a second at a rodeo means the difference between first place and not winning anything. Team ropers figured out that it's faster in the face to move the head horse's back end around, using the front end as the axis for the turn, rather than the rear end.

When the turn revolves off the rear end, the maneuver throws slack back into the head rope and really jerks the heeler if the header times it wrong. In the face, pivoting a horse on the hindquarters takes longer and is harder on everyone. So the headers found a different maneuver to increase their chances of winning by making it faster and easier to face.

## Stopping Your Heel Horse

Your horse should stop off your throw. At first, if you never catch, your horse does not know the jerk is coming. Later, when you catch only occasionally, your horse knows the jerk is coming, but he starts setting up for the stop. More than anything, horses become apprehensive about the jerk, rather than failing to stop at all.

Too, people who have never roped much can take the stop out of a horse altogether. Sometimes a novice roper keeps kicking the horse, throws his rope, and rides forward; he never does stop, let alone at the right time. He doesn't give the horse a cue or show him where to stop.

Or when he throws, sometimes a novice roper lets his horse continue dribbling forward without stopping, picks up his loop, and rides to the end of the arena. Again, he never stops the horse, and that's the pattern for performance that he builds. The horse thinks he's supposed to do that. When you throw, stop your horse, and build a correct pattern in him.

Ideally, your horse should come to a complete stop when the bottom of the loop hits the ground or when the steer's feet travel through it. The horse should shut down before you go for the slack. I want my horse to begin stopping as I make my delivery. He should be straight in his stop, using his rear end, and he'll probably slide a few feet. Then, when the rope hits the ground or starts to travel underneath the steer's feet, my horse comes to a complete stop.

# Practice and the Heel Horse

When you go to the practice pen, you practice either for yourself or your horse, to prepare for the competition. If you have the rare horse who works perfectly most of the time, he doesn't need many runs. So you worry only about yourself and make the practice runs to better prepare yourself for what you want to do.

How you prepare yourself usually depends on the type of competition you enter. If you must rope fast at a rodeo, practice your positioning and your approach to the steer to set up for a fast shot. Then you're familiar with the maneuvers you need in that competition. If you're headed to an average roping, you practice a more calculated, consistent style because the money is paid to those who rope consistently for many runs, rather than fast day money or rodeo runs.

Practice sometimes for the horse, too, depending on what he needs. Does he need to track some cattle to keep him honest and give you a good throw? Or do you need to work on his stop for more control? Maybe he needs scoring because he's becoming a little apprehensive in the box. If your old horse becomes nervous when the chute-gate bangs, relax him in the box and score some. You may need to

score a new horse to learn more about him—where he likes to stand and what makes him comfortable or uncomfortable in the box.

The difficult thing about having a good rope horse is maintaining him. The biggest source of trouble with a horse is making successive hard, fast runs. If overdone, they ruin a horse. It's one thing to rope hard when you go for the money; that's how the game is played. But the practice pen is where you go to maintain your good horse.

With your good, fast "money" horse, sometimes you must work with him in practice to keep him honest and doing his job correctly, without taking shortcuts. That doesn't mean you rope and turn the steer or heel one every trip. Instead, you use some runs to do the maintenance work.

When I run a practice steer and somebody heads for me, I usually don't dally on every run. That depends on the horse I'm riding, the type of cattle we're roping, and what we're trying to accomplish with the practice.

I don't want my good horse to take any unnecessary jerks, but he knows what he's supposed to do. So I can take him through a run and save the practice cattle. On the other hand, a green horse might need to learn how to handle the jerks a little better. Or we might be breaking in fresh cattle, getting them shaped up and ready for roping. Then I would pick up my dally.

In the practice pen there are ways to minimize stress on the steers. If the heeler wants to dally, he tells the header, who undallies when he sees the heeler rope the heels. As the heeler, you can stop the steer, but without any undue stress on him. Or you can rope, dally, and set your horse in the ground, but then undally as the rope comes tight. This minimizes the pull on the steer.

On one of my horses, the more runs I make, the harder he goes at it and the stronger he gets in everything he does. I don't normally practice a lot with him. If I do and he tends to get too strong in his approach and not really listen to me, I change tactics.

I may let him break out of the box, run about three strides, and just when he feels like he's really getting on the muscle, I check him with my bridle rein. I want him to back off right then, come to a complete stop. He must respond. If he doesn't, then I get more severe with him the next time, and so forth, until he does respond. Usually, the first run, I'm pretty definite about asking the horse to stop. I get his attention. A horse figures things out pretty quickly. The next run, when I pick up on the reins, the horse usually will bury himself in the ground stopping.

In the practice pen I sometimes go a bit beyond what I need and overdo things a little because I want the outcome, the horse's response, to be really sharp when I'm competing. In a competitive run, I might not pull my horse to a stop, but I do want him to respond and slow his speed when I check him. And he must do that even though I might ask him to work fast and hard again once the steer turns.

Sometimes you have to be firm with a really strong rope horse who begins anticipating too much. As I said, this particular horse is not the ideal practice horse, but he is a great rodeo horse because he gives 110 percent, all-out. However, when I'm rodeoing, I usually make only one or two runs a day, so he's perfect for the job and easy to maintain.

But with too many runs, he starts working too hard and too fast, anticipating too much. For example, if I make 10 practice runs on him, the first few will be good, but the last 7 or so won't be any fun at all. I must stop him and remind him to respond to me. Being in the practice pen allows me the privilege. Each horse has a little different problem spot; that's his.

Sometimes heel horses start turning too early on the corner and have a tendency to

fall across and into position. In this case, you might make the horse go on past the steer, holding up his shoulder so that he can't drop into the corner too soon. Or you might pull the horse up and then out, away from the steer, just to remind him that he has to stay with your hand until you release him. Only then can he come across.

When you want to practice, but your horse doesn't really need it, you might want to keep a practice horse. Because I rope a lot, I usually keep a practice horse solely for that purpose.

The good competitive horse's outlet from the stress of competition is the practice horse who takes the daily grind for him. But you also must let the practice horse have an outlet from the stress of making those successive runs.

When you make a lot of runs on any horse, you soon learn where that horse's need for a release from the stress comes into play. Either he prances back up the arena or acts up in the box. Whatever it is, it helps relieve his tension that has built during the runs. Working with a practice horse in that respect is similar to working with one in the box. You both may have to give a little to find something you can both live with while you do the job.

One thing I always do at the end of a run helps prepare my horse for the next run. When the run is over and I undally, I let my horse stand for a moment's pause, just to settle him. It's my way of telling him, "It's time to relax; roping that steer wasn't a big deal." Then I walk him off.

I like horses who walk one step at a time from the arena, with their heads

*Some rope horses tend to get too strong in their approach to the steer. When that happens, I let the horse break from the box, but check him about three strides later.*

down after the run. But a lot of horses never quit moving; they prance sideways. To me, that's not as enjoyable as one who's relaxed.

A horse should do his job and not be nervous about it. I think most rope horses learn nervousness and radical movements because of the things we allow them to do during the runs—without taking the time to teach them to relax in their work.

## Making Your Header's Practice Better

Jake and I have reached the point in our roping where we almost read each other's mind because we have practiced and competed so much together. When you're working with a new partner, remember that everybody has a pattern in everything they do—even in the way they do things in the roping pen. When you partner up with somebody to rope, it should take you only a couple of days to figure out that person's pattern.

That's the real advantage in practicing with the same header all the time. You have the opportunity to become more and more familiar with his pattern and way of doing things, just as he does with you. Consequently, each can learn how to compensate for the other whenever a problem develops. Each person habitually uses the things he does well as a roper so that both become more consistent in their performance as a team.

When you practice, you learn what your partner likes and dislikes in every aspect of the run. Take, for example, when you leave the box and haze a steer. You learn how that particular header likes the steer to run down the arena, whether he wants you to haze a lot or let the steer go more toward the right fence.

Sometimes the conditions under which a header ropes best can be directly attributed to the particular horse he's riding

that day. Maybe the horse won't work as well when a steer goes to the right, or perhaps the steer needs to be more to the right to give the header the best throw on that particular horse. Maybe the horse can't run hard at all, so you must try hard to push the steer to the header. When it comes to the horse your partner is riding, knowing little things like that make a difference in your run.

How the header handles a steer is another thing you become familiar with over time. With time and experience, each header develops a pattern on how he makes the corner and the angle he uses in turning the steer. You must learn his style. Adjust your riding and approach to the corner and to the steer in relation to how that particular header leaves the corner. What you do is based on what your header does. The better you know your partner, the more that allows you to position yourself best to throw a good loop.

Much of a heeler's maneuvering to hold good position has to do with angles and changes in speed, so you must have an idea of where your header will go when he turns the steer. You evaluate his pattern each trip in the practice pen to determine how you will ride in many given situations. The more you rope with the same header, the more things you learn about him that you can put into your computer bank. Knowing those little things gives you a better idea of what might take place during a run, and that gives you a better chance to catch the steer.

So there are advantages to roping with the same person all the time, but it's up to you to use them. You can best help your team by going to the practice pen and becoming aware of how your partner approaches his roping. As different types of runs take shape, you learn the advantages and disadvantages of each situation as it relates to your partner and his horse.

# 15 PLAYING BY THE RULES

## Jake: The Rules

ONCE, a student of mine, who was a wrestling coach, gave me a book and said, "I want you to have this because a lot of things in this book apply to your roping." When we talk about playing by the rules, I always remember reading this in that book:

"What is the description of a champion? A true champion is one who competes according to the rules, one who enjoys the heat of the battle, and one who holds his head up regardless of the final outcome."

That says it all.

## Faults and Disqualifications

There are not many rules that you have to abide by in team roping, but you do need to be familiar with the rules wherever you compete. Sometimes the little things make the difference. In the United States Team Roping Championships or Professional Rodeo Cowboys Association, for example, not following the dress code can get you disqualified. What isn't acceptable is usually pretty standard—no T-shirts, for instance, and no caps. You wear a cowboy hat and boots.

As for the actual roping rules, there are three legal head catches—around both horns, around the neck, and half a head, which constitutes one horn and the nose. Anything else is an illegal catch. A crossfire, called by the flagger when a steer isn't in forward tow, can also disqualify a team.

When you break the barrier coming out of the box and don't give the steer his full head-start, that's a 10-second penalty, rather than a disqualification. When a

*To win, you have to play by the rules. That's true no matter where you compete—at a weekend jackpot, a PRCA-sanctioned rodeo, or at the USTRC National Finals, where this photo was taken.*

Photo by Brenda Allen

heeler catches only one foot, there is a 5-second penalty added to the team's time, but it isn't a disqualification. Those rules run pretty consistent from the local jackpots right through to the top ropings. Sometimes, however, the rules do vary in other respects, such as the dress code or the way the monies are paid. It always pays to check and find out.

# The Cross-Fire

A cross-fire occurs when the heeler already has thrown or is starting to throw his rope before the steer has been turned off in a different direction by the header. The steer must be in tow and moving forward for a legal heel catch. The header sets and turns the steer, but until he is lined out and moving forward again, a heel catch is illegal. So a heeler always must be conscious of that.

The steer dictates the forward motion a lot of the time. Some steers, it seems, keep turning forever and are never really considered in forward tow. When a steer, for example, leads almost too easily, but keeps turning, that's an easy shot for the heeler to make. But a flagger might look at that situation and rule that technically the steer wasn't in tow.

It's a judgment call on the flagger's part. When you are trying to make a fast run, nobody likes to take a chance on throwing a heel loop on the corner and being flagged out. But, for example, you might need a 4-second run and draw a steer that runs harder and, consequently, probably will go farther down the pen. You know that even if the heeler ropes him fast, you are going to be 5 seconds on the run. What do you, as the header, do then?

I would rather take a chance on maybe making the 4-second run and not being flagged out than make 5-second run and not win anything. The heeler obviously takes a chance when he ropes a steer like that. Maybe he takes a cross-fire shot and risks the flagger's call. It's a calculated risk, and the bulk of the decision when a cross-fire is possible is pretty much the heeler's. All I can do as a header is get the steer in tow and moving in the other direction as soon as possible.

# Novice Competitors

Most people want to compete after they've been to a few local practice ropings. But before you do compete, go to as many practice ropings as you possibly can and to as many different arenas as possible. Also, watch ropings and see what it takes to win. If you can't do it in the practice pen, there's a good chance that you're not going to do it at a roping.

When you aren't as familiar with the pen or the other ropers, sometimes you have a tendency to be a little timid in the new situation. Not only that, your horse might react differently to various arena conditions. So season yourself at many arenas; each has a different atmosphere—different size, different length box, and different type cattle.

Prepare yourself for roping competition the same way you season a green horse. He might work perfectly at home, but the first time he's away from the house and in a different situation, he becomes a yo-yo in his performance level. So you haul him until he performs consistently wherever you are. Becoming a competitive roper is much the same thing. You need lots of experience.

When you start hauling, don't load yourself with too heavy a competition. Go to small jackpots at first. I cringe when I see people who have just barely begun roping pay $150 to enter a competition when they don't have a chance to win. I think, "Man, why don't you give me that $150 and come to my house and practice?"

Start at small, inexpensive ropings, where you can make quite a few runs and gain experience. At the practice ropings and small jackpots, you also learn how to control your emotions and your adrenaline so you don't pressure up during competition. You need to do that because your horse will react to the competitive situation a lot like you do.

There are only three legal head catches—around both horns, around the neck, and half a head.

The header must have the steer turned and in forward tow before a legal heel loop can be thrown. Otherwise, the heel loop is considered a cross-fire.

When a heel loop is considered a cross-fire, the team is flagged out and no time is recorded.

*At times, winning the PRCA championship title depended on how well we roped during the National Finals Rodeo. That's when all the hours of consistent practice paid off for us.*

PRCA photo by Dan Hubbell

**When a handicap system is used, ropers are rated from 1 to 9, based on their level of ability. Generally, less skilled ropers are classified as #1, #2, or #3 competitors; average ropers receive a #4, #5, or #6 rating; and top hands are considered #7, #8, or #9 ropers.**

# Handicapping and Team Roping

There are plenty of area practice ropings and jackpot ropings open to anybody, all around the country, where a new roper can gain experience. In recent years the biggest thing in team roping has been the USTRC, where a handicap system has been devised to evaluate each roper's skill. Numbers representing each roper's skill level are used to help level the playing field for competitors with different levels of expertise.

The USTRC, I think, has been a tremendously great concept for roping, a shot in the arm for the sport and the industry. The organization has revived roping by bringing many novice ropers into the sport and providing open ropers at the top end with more money in more jackpots. In other respects, the USTRC helps all of us because it helps the horse industry.

Before the USTRC, a novice either roped against the best or didn't compete. That's like me playing basketball for a living and having to play Michael Jordan every day—and paying to do it. It might be fun a couple of times a year, but I wouldn't want to be beaten every day by the best in the business.

In the past a lot of team ropers felt that way. They had other jobs, and roping was their hobby, but they had to compete against the guys who roped for a living. Now the hobby ropers put up the same money and compete against ropers of their own caliber. They aren't giving away their money anymore. So the USTRC has put a whole new light on roping, and I am thankful for it.

# The Competitive Header

When you begin competing, so much depends on the type roping you do—if you're rodeo roping for fast time or going to an average roping where consistency plays more of a role.

Too, when you compete a lot, your program often starts to fall apart because you sometimes take shortcuts. If you're hauling to a lot of rodeos or ropings, you're not able to practice as much either.

In team roping competition, it's all percentages. If I can throw and catch 80-100 percent of the time, it allows my heeler to rope with good, high consistency. But when a header ropes at only 50 percent, the heeler starts to lose focus and concentration. That pulls down the partner's numbers too.

*At the National Finals Rodeo, where this photo was taken, a team needs a 4-second run to be competitive. To make that fast a run, a roper sometimes must reach with his loop or use a shortcut that he might not otherwise take.*
Photo by Brenda Allen

Some headers are great ropers when they're close to steers and can take that easy shot. Then there are guys who rope better when they reach, but can't rope up close to a steer. The top ropers can do both.

Consistency is the name of the game—to win, to keep your confidence, and to keep your horse working well. With consistency, everything seems to flow naturally during your run. But, for instance, if your horse ducks, the handle is bad. So your heeler must take chances, and then his horse might start cutting the corner. Everything in the program begins to crumble.

Preparing to compete depends, to a great extent, on the type cattle you rope and where you're roping. The Bob Feist Invitational, for example, has a longer score; you run farther down the arena with fresher cattle. Obviously, I wouldn't practice by jumping right out of the box and making my horse turn off. If I did, when I got to the Bob Feist, my horse wouldn't work right for that type set-up, and I'd give my partner a terrible handle. Instead, I would practice on fresher cattle that run hard, and let the steer get quite a distance ahead of me. I'd also make sure my horse stayed true in his position and free-running to the steer.

In this type competition, I really want my horse to use his hind end and slow the steer down, so my heeler can get a good, quick shot. At home I might not even turn the steer in the practice pen, but do what we call steer stopping. I simply stop my horse after I've roped and dallied, but don't turn off. That lets my horse know that, when I take hold of him, he really

needs to use his back end and slow things down in a hurry. That plays to my favor with the fresher cattle, and not many horses can do that well.

## Rodeo Roping

For the National Finals Rodeo, where I need a 4-second run, I won't practice by letting the cattle get way out, running my horse the distance, and then asking him to drag his back end. Instead, I score the steer at about the same spot at home where he will most likely be in the Finals.

At a rodeo, when you rope only for the fast time, you don't have the luxury of getting close to the steer every trip. You have to reach a little more in your delivery. That's when I start off with a little bigger loop and use a little more spoke. And I usually drop a coil to cover the distance. I basically throw the same kind of loop, but the loop is a little bigger because I'm not as close to the steer.

When I reach a long way to rope a steer at a rodeo, I am not as concerned about getting the rope tight on the steer's horns as I might be at an average roping. My horse usually feels it when I reach, so he anticipates, and I might have a hard time getting back around the saddle horn with my rope. When I reach, I want to have enough slack between the steer and me so that when my horse drops in the turn, I can still get to the horn and dally.

*Watch the flagger and be sure he has dropped the flag before you undally and ride up to give slack to the steer.*
**Photo by Brenda Allen**

When I'm trying to win a go-round, I don't want my rodeo horse to use his hind end to set the steer; that would be too slow. My rodeo horse makes the lateral move on his own. When I reach, he will usually anticipate the throw, so I have to be on my toes.

Maintaining a good rodeo horse is where discipline in the practice pen comes in. At a rodeo you don't have the time or luxury to correct him; time is money, and the clock is ticking.

I have found that—no matter how you tune your horse in the practice pen—he works a little tighter at the rodeos, more tense and quicker to anticipate. That affects everything in your run. It's a terrible feeling when your horse anticipates, and you must compensate by reaching. But I've always had the attitude that you do what it takes to win.

## Average Ropings

At an average roping, where I'm more concerned with catching and handling every steer consistently, I won't be reaching. I can shorten my spoke a bit because my range, the distance I need to reach, will be shorter. Too, using a shorter spoke helps makes it easier to be sure that I get all the slack out.

Because I need to catch several head consistently, I take a little more time to rope and slow down the steer. I take longer in my handle, again to break down the steer's momentum. When I bring his head around, I slow him and hold his head. I want to make a smooth lateral

move and then pull him along nice and slow. Basically, I take more time to set up things for my heeler.

You get the consistency to win an average roping by having a good flow to each run. A one-footer, for instance, will put you out of the money, so you don't risk it. Instead, you slow things down and make everything really smooth. Compare that approach with rodeo roping and going too fast, which means the heeler often has to chase the steer.

## The Box and Competition

When I back in the box to compete, I always make sure that my heeler is ready. A common problem occurs when a roper backs in the box, looks at the partner, and then gets his rope and reins ready. A horse can only stand in the box so long. He gets more hyper by the minute and, at this point, the roper hasn't even gotten his game-face on and isn't concentrating at all.

I glance to make sure my partner is in the box, and I don't look over there anymore. If he has a problem, he must tell me and break my concentration. Otherwise, I don't worry about him; I have enough to worry about. And I want to spend the least amount of time possible in the box.

I want my horse sitting on ready, but I feel he can maintain his concentration for only a couple of minutes while I'm in there preparing myself. I want to get in the box, get things ready as quickly as possible, and leave as quickly as possible. However, I want to make sure everything is right, too, for me to start my run.

One thing I do in competition helps cut down on the noise factor for my horse. I put earplugs in his ears. That cuts down

on the noise of the chute opening and also helps a young horse who isn't used to noisy crowds.

Another problem I often see in the box occurs when a roper calls for his steer, but the steer's head is turned back. That's natural; the cattle always want to turn back toward the herd. But the position of the steer's head is important.

Don't ever call for a steer when his head is turned back. As soon as the gates open, your horse jumps forward because he hears the bang of the gate, and you, of course, take hold of him. But the steer hesitates to straighten out his head before he takes off. When that happens, the timing is bad, and usually you get out late. Or your horse takes off and runs through the barrier; then you beat the steer out of the chute, and it costs you a penalty.

Focus on your steer. Always make sure he is standing at the front of the chute and looking directly forward. Sometimes right when you nod, a steer turns his head back anyway, which will mess you up.

I never call for a steer when he's laying down on his front end, on his knees. At jackpots, they'll sometimes say, "Oh, that's just the way he starts." But I'm not taking a chance on one like that. You know that it takes that steer an instant longer to get up and go, so your natural reaction is to stay in the box a little longer—but that son-of-a-gun takes off anyway.

## Horse Problems

After you have competed a while, you'll probably notice a couple of problems developing with your head horse. He won't score as well, or he starts ducking off when you throw your rope. Those two places are where a head horse will come unraveled. That's because, when you continually try to make fast times, you are reaching all the time, taking chances.

With a solid younger horse, maybe 8 or 9 years old, you can maybe go to 10 or 15 rodeos, or maybe even the whole summer, without ever going to the practice pen. You might not have to free him up or score any cattle. You might see problems coming, but they just haven't gotten that bad yet, and you're busy and on the road.

However, if you're riding an older, smarter horse, you might make one or two rodeos and then need to practice. Maybe during your last run you felt the horse was too quick; you barely got your loop on the horns and got your dally, but you could feel the horse wanting to duck off. You still made a good run and you still won something, but you can see a problem developing. Once things begin to deteriorate, you almost have a domino effect; everything begins to go downhill.

## Solutions on the Road

Scoring well and making sure that a horse is running free are usually what you concentrate on when you start reaching and trying to make fast, competitive runs. The horse begins to anticipate too much.

If I had a chance to practice and score two or three steers and rope one before each rodeo, my horse would work great. If I did, I would also like to have my heeler right there, because those seasoned, smart horses can sense when the pressure is there—and when it isn't.

Any heel catch behind the shoulders is legal as long as the rope goes up the steer's heels.

When you're traveling and competing and need to tune a horse, being a veteran roper pays off because you probably have met somebody in that area along the way. He might have practice cattle and won't mind you roping a few steers to tune your horse.

Here's another thing that sometimes helps when I'm at a rodeo and don't have the opportunity to go to the practice pen: I might slip into the arena during the bull-dogging or calf roping. When somebody doesn't show and they turn out a steer, I hustle my horse up behind him. It may not cure the problem with my horse, but it will help. Sometimes you might get reprimanded, but at least you can make a quick fix, and you won't get penalized. When you're on the road, you must take advantage of every opportunity.

Too, if they run slack all day at a rodeo, they're often short of help to run the cattle out of the arena. I might get in the arena then and run some steers out of the pen to free up my horse. It won't be too obvious, but I will build some life into my horse if I have to bump him with my spurs. It wakes him up, and then I can re-create that energy when I make my next competitive run because a horse usually remembers what his last run was all about.

## Clay: The Rules

Team roping rules are pretty simple, really. The header comes from behind a barrier, which allows the steer a head-start. There is a time penalty if the header breaks the barrier.

Sometimes the heeler comes from behind a barrier, too, depending on the rules at a particular roping. In that case, the heeler can break a barrier the same as a header, and it's a 10-second penalty. It pays to know the rules wherever you rope.

Heading, you have only three legal head catches; anything else is a no-time. A team can be flagged out, or disqualified, on a cross-fire, when the heeler ropes before the steer is in forward motion after the turn. If the heeler catches one of the steer's hind feet, there is only a time penalty.

Both header and heeler must be dallied, ropes tight and facing the steer, in order to get a flag on the time. The fastest time wins. That's simple enough.

## The Cross-Fire

A cross-fire refers to delivering the heel loop before the steer has changed direction. The call is made by the flagger, based on his judgment. It's at the heeler's discretion to pick the time when he thinks the steer is legally lined out in tow and not in transition, still making the turn.

Usually for a really consistent roper, the cross-fire rule never even comes into play. That's because a consistent heeler generally delivers his loop on the second, third, or fourth jump the steer takes away from the turn. And, by the time a heeler crosses over into position to throw, the steer is usually lined out anyway.

Remember, you throw a heel loop by timing it with the steer's action; your delivery works off his jump forward. Usually when the header turns off a steer, his back end swings around and then the steer's body becomes straight. The next hop he takes then, moving forward and away from the heeler, is a legal shot.

But a lot of the time that next hop is not a really clean jump because the steer's body is still in the transition of the turn. He might fish-tail a little bit at that point or take a quick, short jump, but not a good rhythmic jump.

Probably the second or third jump provides the most opportune time for a heeler to throw. In the course of the run, the heeler sees the first jump as the steer comes out of the turn and begins moving forward. That first jump gives the heeler a reading on what to expect when the steer hops the second and third times. Sometimes you think you can throw on the first jump, but you might be a little out of position to take the best shot. That can mess up your loop, and it happens because you don't get a read on the steer—he's still in the turn sometimes.

If you took an average of the top 50 heelers in the business, the second or third jump is probably when most of them throw. And they understand cattle well enough to read the situation and are good-enough horsemen to get positioned well on the steer during the transition of the turn.

If somebody ropes real consistently and with good position on the steer, usually 99.9 percent of the time he won't be affected by the cross-fire rule. It's seldom a problem to most good heelers because they stay true to the pattern; they follow through on the basics each time they rope.

# Competitive Savvy

When you compete, be aware of what is going on in the arena. Know where the flagger is throughout your run. Look at him and make sure he has dropped the flag before you undally and ride your horse up to give slack to the steer.

As far as safety for heelers is concerned, here's something important to do. Be aware of the head horse and the header as you pull your slack and go to the horn. Know what they're doing. Although you're focusing on the steer, peripherally you must keep an eye on the header's position. If he isn't coming around to face the steer by the time you start down to the horn with your rope, watch out. Don't dally if he is still driving away from you, with the steer in tow.

If you dally and the header continues forward, the rope will slide through your hand and burn it. And the jerk on the horn with the steer still moving forward will hit your horse really hard. Worse yet, you might cut off a finger or really get in a wreck.

Being aware of the header's position is important for any roper at any level of expertise, not only the beginner. Many times I have roped a steer and started down to the horn with my rope, then looked up to see the other guy still blazing away from me. Fortunately, my experience and awareness of what could happen alleviated the chance of real trouble. To be safe when team roping, you must be aware enough to take in the whole picture during the entire run.

# Speed and Position

When people begin competing, sometimes they become so focused on getting faster that problems creep in. They lose sight of good technique.

More than anything, speed in team roping comes from the horse's position—relative to the steer. When you and your header find and maintain good position throughout the run, you aren't wasting time. A fast time when you're heeling revolves around your ability to position your horse well when the header turns the steer back. Where you position your

horse depends on how much risk you are willing to take.

When you compete, you have consistency and risk to consider. Consistency travels down the scale as the risk increases. You can ride way out, away from the steer, and be in position to get a throw at the steer when he first comes around, but that's the only throw you'll get. In that case, there is an increased risk to completing a successful run. Compare that with waiting to throw on the steer's second or third jump, which offers you more opportunities to catch more consistently.

So you must evaluate how much risk you are willing to take. And, yes, there are times when the roping at a rodeo is so tough that your only shot with a loop and chance to win any money involves taking a risk. Even then, when you evaluate the amount of risk in your game plan, it comes right back to where you ride your horse into position to take the shot.

Once you actually rope the steer, the only place where you can really speed up and handle the rope any faster is in how you pick up your slack or come back to the horn. During the time that lapses between those two maneuvers, you and your horse actually are coming to a stop because you have already thrown your loop.

Again, however, you must consider the risk in trying to be faster in handling the rope. When you deliver the loop and the steer steps into it, you can shorten up on your rope by sliding your hand down it. This makes a shorter span of distance to cover before the rope pulls tight, which means you can come right to the horn to dally. But there is an element of risk because you are sliding your hand down the rope—not lifting the slack and holding it up. You are just hoping, at that point, that the loop stays on the steer's feet. You weigh the risk and take the chance.

The mechanics of roping, however, remain much the same in competition as they are in practice. The swing has to line up with the angle of your position and in relation to the steer. You do all those things, and you still have to rope the steer in good time.

However, the biggest problem when people rope is laziness—lazy riding and roping. Ropers take throws they aren't in

*Receiving world championship buckles at the Finals—there's no feeling quite like it.*

PRCA photo by Dan Hubbell

control of. They deliver loops whenever the horses or the situations dictate instead of controlling the time of delivery for the best shot.

The roper doesn't actively ride his horse into position; the run just sort of happens, and the roper is simply a passenger. The horse comes into the game wherever he wants, and when the roper reaches a steer, he throws. He didn't plan to be there. It's like being in the back seat of a car; you go wherever the driver takes you. Or, you can get behind the wheel and go where you want to go.

# Analysis, Focus, and Imagery

If you want to compete well, you must have a strong desire to know every part of the game and focus on each. You look at why certain things happen in competition and study those situations. You must figure out and know what you did wrong. Then you know where the correction is needed, or what must be different for your next run to be successful.

You constantly analyze everything when you compete because that makes you more familiar with what must take place—the moves you need—to make a successful run.

Making the right moves pertains to both your riding and the mechanics of your roping. Everything revolves around these two areas. Depending on the problem, your swing, delivery, or timing might need work, or you might need to maneuver your horse differently.

There are many little intricate details in this sport, and you can get pretty scientific about roping, which a lot of people do. But some people don't concern themselves with any of those things, and many people are so gifted physically that they get away with that approach to a certain extent. But they never really know or understand how they do things in the roping pen.

Roping is no different than any other sport; certain things can help a competitor reach his full potential. They give you a better chance for a better performance. What you want out of roping will affect what you put into it—how much attention you pay to things that can help you reach maximum performance.

To relate focus and concentration to your roping, think about your heeling. Put a good run in your mind and mentally perform it over and over again. Do it to the best of your ability, as close to perfect as you can. By actively focusing on your roping this way, you train your brain to tell your body what to do.

It's mental imagery, and you practice it for a good response when you need it. You practice so that your body can do the correct things without you thinking about them. That's important because everything happens so fast in the roping pen.

Sometimes to train your brain and engrave that muscle memory for a given situation, you may have to localize and really focus on a particular part of your run repeatedly. It's a conscious act of thought then, but later, when you back in the box and as the run takes place, everything you do becomes an automatic reaction because it's so well-placed in your mind.

When you break down a good run, there are so many individual things involved; you can't think of them all during a 10-second run. But all these intricate parts that take place during one run—through practice—can become reactions.

Often it takes real concentrated effort to alter or change some aspect of your roping. Train yourself to focus and concentrate so that when it's necessary, you can force out every thought except that which pertains to the maneuver you want to perfect. Do this when you rope the dummy and in the practice pen. The more you can do this, the more effective your practice will be and the better you can compete.

Some people don't have a true grasp of how much ability they have. I realized at a really young age that I had concentration and the ability to focus. For some reason I could understand and comprehend that—mentally—there was a different level where I could go to focus on one particular thing. Usually, as soon as I understood a maneuver involved in roping, I could perform it because mentally I had a grasp of it.

A lot of people don't think that kind of focus is something they have, or they don't really understand how to use their concentration. It takes time to develop, but anyone can do it with practice.

I remember my early competition days when I felt the pressure of a situation. I knew I had to get through the run mentally as much as I had to get through it physically. So I would get away from everybody, sit, and control my thoughts—force out all the junk interfering with me making a good run.

That's what people have problems with—the junk, and that's why they ask me how I mentally deal with competition. They let other thoughts interfere—the saddle that's being given away, the money for first, the buddies on the fence, or their partners. Twenty thoughts pertain to the situation but have no business being considered in the actual physical run. These thoughts are just distractions forcing themselves on you. You must force them out of your mind and replace them with thoughts of what you must do to complete your run.

Sometimes that has to be very literal practice. It can't be, "Well, I'm going out and doing my best." What does it take to be the best? Focus on the mechanical moves you need during your run. What specifically must you do with your horse? Tell yourself, "I may need to push my left hand over more." Your mental practice must be very literal and deal with the mechanics necessary to complete a good run. You must visualize the physical things step-by-step as you perform the function.

Roping, however, becomes the whole game, not just a head game when you compete. But if you can't control your thoughts, then you can't control your body. If your brain doesn't tell your body what to do—the right way—your body can't perform. Some people's thoughts turn them into locked-up, tense competitors; they can't loosen up and perform and can't physically do the job.

But if you can relax and turn your brain loose, your body will perform. That happens when you occupy your brain space with the right things, rather than the wrong things. Only then can you turn your body loose to react to all the things you have trained it to do. It's built into your subconscious.

211

# 16 COMPETITIVE TEAMWORK

## Jake: Partners and Pressure

HAVING A really competitive roping team depends on the people involved. Two individuals who rope great might not be compatible at all as far as their roping styles are concerned. Both Clay and I have proved that; seldom have we split up and been successful with other partners.

I think that has more to do with our roping styles than anything, because I've had other great partners, such as Allen Bach. He's won the world title, and he's very competitive, but together we're just a team like anyone else.

Until Clay and I started roping together, I never had a real bond with a partner that made me think I had the advantage over everyone else. With Clay, I always knew that—no matter what—if I turned the steer, I was going to win. That's having a lot of confidence in your partner, and that works both ways.

However, you must have a strong personality to deal with a really good partner. In the roping pen, when you work on the

*A combination of many things makes a good team. With practice, we've become pretty good at team work, both in and out of the competitive arena.*

212

*When you're as intense and focused as we are, it sometimes takes a few minutes after a run to get out of the competitive mode.*

other side of Clay, for example, you can become a little tentative. He can be an intimidating guy to his partners because 90 to 100 percent of his catches are by two feet and for the money. That really puts pressure on his header. But, again, that pressure can work both ways and affect him too.

When a header becomes tentative, he often lets the steer get a little farther down the arena before he leaves the box. When a header does that, he knows he won't break the barrier; he knows if he takes a chance that he might break out. Too, when he's in too big a hurry, a header might not handle the steer well to give the heeler a solid shot. That's a lot of responsibility on the header—and pressure too.

Then, for example, a header can miss a steer altogether. And he might miss two in a row; maybe he's drawing bad cattle at the time. Now he worries: "Well, is my partner going to quit me?" A header begins to lose confidence then. But he can make one good run and gain his confidence back. Competition is always a seesaw deal.

Clay and I work well together and complement each other in our roping styles. He's about the only heeler I ever roped with who, no matter what the situation or how I handled the steer, came up with a way to catch. Very few ropers can do that. Although lots of heelers can catch two feet, Clay has that little extra something. I don't know if it's his concentration, his self-discipline, or his style of heeling, but Clay can pull a rabbit out of a hat in a bad situation every single time.

But he is human. When he does miss— once in a great while—everybody just gasps: "What happened? He doesn't do that." Nonetheless, it's a big responsibility to turn steers for him. Lots of guys rope lots of cattle, but Clay by far is the best.

Clay is so disciplined in his heeling and so smart that he simply won't take a bad shot. He might take a hard shot, but he always is riding for position when he does, just to make the difficult throw a little easier. Clay won't beat himself even when the chips are down, but he'll force another roper into making a mistake. Usually that happens because the pressure Clay puts on his competitors is so intense; the other ropers beat themselves.

To this day, I have a hard time just roping and not being the best. I don't want to stay even with the competition when I rope. I want to pull away from the crowd.

*It's hard when you travel a lot to find a balance between rodeo and your family life and make it all work financially too. Rodeo is an up-and-down sport no matter how well you rope.*

That's one reason, during those so-so years at the National Finals, Clay and I could come from behind.

I didn't like that feeling though—pulling the rabbit out of the hat during Finals week. It always worked for us, but how many times can you do that? I wanted to have the title locked in ahead of time, which would have taken the pressure off, but we put that pressure on ourselves. Two years at the Finals, all we had to do was catch the last steer to be world champions—and right then you think of so many things that can go wrong.

## Attitude and Sportsmanship

When it comes to sportsmanship, I won't cheat to win. But if there is some place I can gain an advantage, I'll take it as long as I'm not bending and breaking the rules. I won't try to intimidate anybody either, or make them mad enough to mess up their performance. The bottom line: My close friends, team ropers I really respect, and I all believe in God; that plays a big role in our roping and how we approach competition.

However, when I compete, I do go into my own zone; I'm that focused. Consequently, I steer away from people as much as possible because I don't want distractions when I'm about to compete. I won't be rude, but because I am so intense, I can become a little perturbed by interruptions. It's also hard for me right after competition, especially when I mess up. But 10 or 15 minutes later, after I've had time to get over my little temper tantrum, I'm out of my competitive mode.

I am a true competitor; I want to win—always. If you're that way, remember that you must also balance that with other things in your life. Don't win a roping at the cost of all else. Clay and I both have struggled in the past to find that balance— financially, competitively, and with our families.

Rodeo is a great life for a single man. When an entire family rodeos, it can be good, too, but the financial situation might suffer as a result. However, if only one family member rodeos, sometimes the family suffers. So that's been the hardest thing about rodeoing and roping—finding a balance.

For years, Clay and I did what nobody else would do. We hauled a lot and had roping schools, too, which is how you burn out. Your roping suffers; you don't get to practice as much or rarely prepare your horses for competition. Your family suffers the most because you're gone so much. But rodeo is an up-and-down sport; no matter how well you rope, your emotions and money are involved. I had to rope well—I have five kids. That's a lot of responsibility, so I worked hard and hustled.

As a result, I have won as much as anybody, but I don't feel I'm any different than any other roper. Roping is something at which I've excelled, but it's kind of like a kid's game to me, and I'm having fun with it. I sure don't want people hanging around because I'm a great roper. I want people to hang around Jake Barnes because he's a good guy, a good human being.

If you stop and think about this game, it's really pretty simple. I rope steers—and that's supposed to be something? If you want to make a hero out of somebody, look at Mother Teresa.

# Handling the Hauling

Learning how to keep yourself and your horse healthy on the road is important. Maintenance and nutrition are as important for a horse as they are for a human being. After all, the better you feel and the more rest you get, the better you perform.

Clay and I both have been fortunate with our horses. I think I've had one truly great horse. He was 14 when I got him, and he lasted until he was 19. At the time, I thought I did a good job of maintaining him, but looking back, there were times I could have done better; I realize now what a great horse I had.

However, when I was younger, I always tried to put my horse first. Caring for my horse was a psychological deal back then too. I had to take care of him; that horse made my living.

There has been one rule of thumb I try to follow when I haul horses. Every 4 or 5 hours, I unload my horse, give him chance to drink water, stretch out, and move around for a few minutes. Sometimes, however, I have been in such a hurry trying to make the next rodeo that I've hauled longer without a stop.

My horse's diet is mostly good hay—alfalfa if I can get it—and I usually grain him with whole oats. Normally, I feed the same amount every day and keep a salt and mineral block out. Clay and I keep a salt and mineral block in the trailer whenever we're hauling. On the road I've never had any trouble getting a horse to drink water he's unaccustomed to.

I do think it's important to turn out a horse as much as possible because it's natural for him. He'll graze almost all day when he's turned out. However, when you keep a horse penned all the time, you basically give him only the feed needed to maintain him. I do think a horse needs something to occupy his time. That's where the pasture turn-out comes in, or giving a penned horse good grass hay to occupy his time. Many horses pick up bad habits—walking the fence or cribbing—because they are bored. When a horse is given something to occupy his time, those habits might never get started.

When traveling, Clay and I always try to have a pen available for the horses at each stop so they can roll and lay down. Some people are so lazy when they travel with horses. Tired after pulling to an event, some competitors just tie a horse to the trailer and leave him there.

215

*Good maintenance and nutrition are as important for the horse as they are for a human. The better you and your horse feel, the better you perform.*

Too, whenever Clay and I know we have a couple of days' layover, we find a pasture, turn out the horses, and let them graze for a couple of days. That always helps them freshen up.

As I said, neither of us have had many health problems with our horses, and as far as health care is concerned, I haven't been that conscientious about it at all. I don't make a schedule for deworming, for example. If anything, I deworm a little more often, rather than not enough.

Nor have I given many vitamins to horses. I think a good diet and exercise go a long way toward keeping a horse healthy, along with taking advantage of the breaks from traveling. Even then, however, Clay and I don't grind on our horses with a lot of practice unless a horse really needs a tuneup.

When roping and rodeoing, there is a lot of hurry-up-and-wait, so I take advantage of the downtime and work on horsemanship. I do dry work to keep my horse responding well. However, when I'm home between trips, my horse has a rest period more than anything.

About all I do then is exercise him.

I've had very few foot problems on a very few horses, and those were older ones who already had the problems before I got them. I don't know a lot about shoeing. When traveling, I ask around in a community to learn about the shoers there—then all I hope is that the shoer gets my horse's feet level. Of course, I would prefer having my own shoer work on my horses, but that isn't always possible.

There's no set schedule for having my horse shod, I just pay attention to his feet. Shoeing a horse is like clipping my fingernails; I clip them when I notice they need it. When my horse's feet begin to get a little long, I have him shod. I don't believe in timetable shoeing, for example, at 4 weeks, whether he needs it or not. One thing I try to do regularly, however, is use hoof dressing to keep the foot soft so the hoof doesn't get hard and crack.

Even more important, I clean out my horse's feet quite often, especially before loading a horse in the trailer. It's so important then to make sure a horse's feet aren't packed with mud or rocks. He has to stand on those feet for the next 300 to 400 miles.

If someone has reached the point of roping competitively, I assume he has a handle on basic feeding and health care

*Shared goals and similar attitudes contribute to a comfortable partnership. That's important because when one partner has a problem during a run, how the other partner handles it affects the team's confidence at the next event.*

for horses. Sometimes, when I see people at our clinics, I'm not so sure, but generally most people have a lot of consideration for their horses. Seldom do I see an underfed roping horse. If anything, people care for their horses too well, and in many cases, the horse is more like a dog to them. People who enjoy their horses that much tend to take good care of them.

However, you must remember that when a rope horse is overweight, he can't give 100 percent in competition. If anything, I prefer to have my horse a little on the lean side, rather than too heavy. Horses are like people to me; when they're in shape, they're probably on the lean side naturally.

## Clay: Partners and Pressure

A combination of many things makes a competitive team—the shared goals, similar attitudes about sportsmanship, and the way the partners handle the head-game in competitive roping. With practice, Jake and I have become pretty good at every part of

it, both in and out of the competitive arena.

We both always focused on getting to the top—not settling for less than putting our best effort toward the cause. Fortunately, we are both physically gifted with the ability to accomplish our goals. More important, we also have the ability to analyze and break down situations in the roping pen, so we can focus on becoming better ropers. And both of us can compete under stressful, pressurized situations. Being successful has also required that we spend long hours together in practice, even living near one another, and that both of us have good horses to ride.

All those things have helped us achieve what we wanted. It's not that we are the best at any one part of the roping picture, but Jake and I both are pretty good in every aspect of roping. Altogether, being pretty good at many things has made our roping a step above everyone else teamed up at the time.

217

Early on, Jake and I realized that accomplishing our goals would require an all-out effort. We both had the same understanding: If we tried harder than anyone else at every part of the game, that would give us an edge. Having the edge meant we had a better chance to succeed than any other team, and a better chance meant we could and would win more. By winning more, we could have another championship. So competing became a step-by-step process, and we kept stepping up the stairs. By putting out the effort, we had a chance to do well.

So much practice, really learning and mastering the basics, helped us not to choke in competition. It's only by doing the right things so often in the practice pen that you ingrain the basics deeply into your style of roping. You must root yourself in the basic mechanical moves of roping—sound moves that are correct.

Then in competition, when you must catch the steer by making sure all the correct steps take place, you can do it. You almost ensure that you catch—unless something really freaky happens. The competitive arena is where all you've worked for in the practice pen pays off.

Because he has practiced so much and so correctly, Jake has an ability and is disciplined enough during competition, more so than anyone else in the game, to score right and make sure that the right steps take place each run. He always rides for position, going to the right spot on his steer. A lot of the time, that makes the big difference in him catching or not.

But no matter the sport—golf, baseball, or basketball—the athlete who is most fundamentally sound in the physical maneuvers and can perform those functions well is the best. That's just the way it is, and it requires hard work and effort if you want a chance to succeed. Jake's made the effort; he's the best at performing the maneuvers required of a header.

I grew up in an era when the ropers considered the "baddest" dudes of the land were those who caught every steer at a 10-head roping. Consequently, I didn't grow up learning to rope fast. Instead, I grew up learning the basic maneuvers needed to catch the steer. A good, basic foundation was rooted in my system. Then, later on, I learned how to rodeo-rope and speed up the basics. But I always had that foundation to fall back on when I ran into a problem.

Sometimes I still go back to the drawing board, back over my mental list of the things that must happen for me to heel well. I can do that because I know and understand the basics—the correct position, the timing and rhythm, and what makes the perfect loop. I study those things in order to catch the steer when I need to. In many cases, you don't necessarily have to be a fast roper; winning sometimes just comes down to catching the steer.

# Attitude and Sportsmanship

Sportsmanship, to me, seems to fall into the category of how you should conduct yourself during your life in general. However, particularly in competitive roping, sportsmanship is important because it can be an asset or detriment to your team. Which it is depends on the way you act toward your partner, for instance, when he misses a steer or messes up during an event.

If you give your partner the impression that you're totally disgusted with what happens during one run, you make him feel apprehensive about the next run. This is not in your best interests because you need your partner to enter the competitive arena next time with the most confidence possible. You always do what you can to give your partner the edge, the best opportunity to do his job.

As for one roper's attitude toward another—the competition—that depends on an individual's upbringing. Some ropers become cynical about competition at times; others are jealous-hearted in regard to those who do well. We see that displayed all the time in many sporting events.

*A competitive horse must haul well. That includes, for example, his willingness to eat in a different place from day to day or accept a change in the taste of the water from one place to the next.*

Personally, I don't like to show any ill feelings, animosity, or envious feelings toward anyone. However, sometimes competition can make you feel that way; after all, you do compete against another individual. But when the wrong kind of thoughts and feelings come to my mind, I try to stop them because they won't do my roping any good. Instead, I like to replace those thoughts with ones more beneficial to me in the competitive situation—what that steer will do, how I need to handle my rope, or what I need to do with my horse.

## Handling the Hauling

Because I'm from the West, where we feed primarily alfalfa hay, I feed very little grain to my horses. The alfalfa seems to work fine to keep a horse's energy level where I want it.

Probably, if anything, I see too many horses who feel too good. I try to maintain my horses at a certain level of energy. I know immediately if my horse is getting too much protein, for example. An excess of energy from his feed makes him high, and he doesn't perform as well

in the arena. Or when I tie him, he paws or looks around and whinnies, or he prances around. A horse should be healthy and feel good, but he shouldn't be beside himself with energy. However, Jake and I see many people do just that at the clinics.

Occasionally we do see some underfed horses, who haven't been dewormed properly. The haircoat looks dead, and the horse might be skinny and out of shape.

With your horse, you must reach a spot between the two extremes. If you can tolerate your horse being at the highest level of energy, that's fine. But I don't tolerate an unmannerly horse, who's so high and high-strung that he can't stand still or is looking for something to bite or kick.

I deworm my horses regularly, and sometimes I use vitamins, biotin, or bran, more as precautions against the problems a horse can develop from road-related

*Taking care of your rope horse's feet is important, no matter if you're at home or on the road.*

Although I seldom have used leg wraps when traveling with horses, I've been fortunate to haul horses who didn't have any lameness problems to speak of. Although the wraps probably are beneficial, in 20 years of going up and down the road, very seldom have I put a protective hauling boot on a horse.

However, I am careful about how I haul a horse and about the horse next to him in the trailer because I don't want a horse's legs bumped and bruised. Although I use standard mats in the trailer, I do keep my trailer deeply bedded in sawdust or shavings. I've also been fortunate to haul horses who didn't fight being in the trailer or act vicious toward other horses. Either of those things can result in leg problems. Nonetheless, I always keep an eye on a horse's legs, to make sure he hasn't been kicked or isn't swelling anywhere.

I usually pull the horses out of a trailer about every 6 hours to walk them and give them a break. Although I have gone longer periods and have stopped in shorter times, I've never run into any particular problems one way or the other. A horse can stay in the trailer longer than most of us think—6, 7, or 8 hours. I think about the horse-hauling vans running down the road from coast to coast and how long those horses stay in a trailer sometimes. However, how long a horse is comfortable in a trailer depends so much on whether the horse can urinate going down the road. If the trailer stall is big enough to allow him to stretch out, that's fine. If not, you must unload him. The break from the trailer is good for him anyway.

All my horses have hauled well. However, if a horse doesn't haul pretty well, won't drink or eat on the road, or thinks the trailer is a bad place to be, I can't use him in my business anyway. A competitive horse, who is hauled a lot, must be fairly hardy. I think a certain amount of that is learned as a horse becomes seasoned to the hauling. Often the more he's hauled, the more a horse learns to relax in the trailer. The problem horses are the high-strung ones, who fidget in the trailer all the time.

When it comes to shoeing, I like a shoe that gives some traction and grip, a nar-

stress. The supplements seem to help keep a horse's blood count and energy level up and keep his digestive tract clean, which decreases the chances of him having a problem.

When I'm on the road, keeping a horse exercised and feeling good is the priority, because my horse is a tool I use to make my living. So the better I care for him, the better chance I have of him performing to my expectations.

*The arena surface can affect your run; how much it does depends on your horse. Some horses handle different types of ground better. Other horses, like my buckskin, become so focused on doing the job that they go all out no matter the conditions.*

rower, rimmed shoe. I don't like a wide-rim shoe because it loses traction when I'm roping. I don't get real tricky or creative with my shoeing. When I have a horse shod, I want him level, and I want the shoer to leave him as wide behind as he can to maintain the heel width and promote growth. That way I don't wind up with contracted heels. I don't have much problem with a horse losing a shoe unless the ground is slick or bad. Sometimes a horse just happens to catch the shoe wrong and pull it off.

I do pay attention to the arena dirt, and most horses seem to pay attention to it. The way a horse works is so often dictated by the ground to a certain extent. Extremely hard ground, for example, makes a horse feel a little different in the way he travels than he does on a better type surface. Extremely deep dirt has another feel altogether because a horse must labor to get through it. I like a firm arena surface, with about 2½ to 3 inches of cushion on it. A horse can press down into that, have traction, but still be on a good firm surface.

Handling the dirt depends on the horse. Some horses take better care of themselves in different arena situations than others.

But sometimes you have a horse who really goes all out. You must be more cautious with him because he's not considering the surface he's on at the time. He's strictly keyed into running and doing his job. If he gets into a situation where the ground won't take the move he's trying to make, you could go down.

For example, I have to be a little careful on my buckskin horse sometimes because he does everything so hard and moves really strong. All of a sudden he buries up and turns to position himself on the steer. If the ground is deep or slick, where he shouldn't really make that kind of move, I try to ease him around the turn and take hold of him to make sure he doesn't make a really hard, strong move. Otherwise, he'll slip. So you must always take the dirt into consideration, based on the horse you are riding.

# A PERSPECTIVE

## Jake: Change

THE UNITED States Team Roping Championships coming along has been one of the biggest changes in team roping in recent years. However, more and more I see people treating their roping more as a business, a true profession. You can make a good living at roping nowadays. There are so many good, major jackpots now, too—the Bob Feist, the George Strait, the Windy Ryon, along with the USTRC open ropings.

Too, I think there are more real teams now. There used to be good headers and good heelers, but not really good teams until Clay and I got together. Now, however, we often see good headers and good heelers pair up as a team. I think that's why it is harder for any one team to dominate roping now. These guys work as a team and try to get better. More of the good top hands on both ends, heading and heeling, rope together now.

As for the future, I look for team roping to get better. However, I think the sport needs to be modified in some ways, with more management. I don't think that the full potential of our athletes, the ropers, is being used. Sometimes it seems as if we run around like chickens with their heads cut off. Right now, we're making the motor vehicle, trailer, gas, and tire companies a good living. I think ropers need to focus on more major events and less traveling, with competition somewhat like Professional Bull Riders in the picture. I hope and pray that someday roping gets to that point. On the one hand, I have a family; I want to stay home and watch my children grow up. But on the other hand, I don't feel that I'm at the end of my career, either. I still feel that I have a lot left.

The associations aren't managing me right as an athlete, and I'm not going to wear myself out for nothing. Don't get me wrong, I am really grateful for what I have done in the sport. I have to take advantage of that right now. And I sure don't want things to get to a point where I can't compete anymore or do roping schools; I'd end up having to get a job somewhere working for 5 bucks an hour.

The roping school industry is good, and there is more profit margin in it. So that's what I look for now. I love to be out there, beating up the road and trying to win a world championship, but your expenses eat up a lot of the profit.

Everybody thinks the National Finals Rodeo is such a big deal, and, yes, it does pay good. You can win $40,000 or $50,000 there. In previous years, I've held the records. I got the most money won at the finals, $45,000, and I've also won the most money at the end of a season, which was $99,000 then. But I can go to the USTRC finals in Guthrie and win $30,000 in one day. It takes 10 days in Las Vegas to win $40,000.

Our sport needs some fine-tuning, but I believe a lot of things are going to be a lot better. I want to see some changes not only for my sake, but also for young kids like mine. Like I've said, rodeo is a tough lifestyle—and it has been a great one for me. However, I'm one of the few who has been successful at it, and I still feel like I won the lottery. So I won't encourage my kid to go out there and work it. I feel that if he works to become the best at his sport, then he ought to be able to retire on it. I'm not able to do that, and I'm pretty conservative with my money. So I think we need some management where these young guys know there is a future for them. We need to put a pot of gold at the end of the rainbow for them. That's why you seldom see a lot of great ropers. Think what a team roping there would be if the National Finals paid $100,000. There would be incentive to work at being the best.

## Clay: Change

There are so many more team ropers now. The sport kind of exploded a few years ago. Since then, the information available about roping, plus the schools and videotapes, have really come into play and helped the sport. Kids, for example, can watch a roping videotape over and over again. They really can see how team roping works, how to handle a rope, the horse, and cattle. Then they figure out how to do the roping themselves. All across the country, thousands of young people have learned to rope and do a really good job of it. The ropings are a lot tougher nowadays.

Now, too, you have the masses of people who rope just as a hobby, and the USTRC has created an opportunity for them to compete at their own level. But, as far as

the big difference in roping, I would say that more people have figured out how to rope well. Everyone is learning how to get better, and that has made the ropings quite a bit tougher—no matter where you go or at what level you compete.

Too, roping clinics and schools are so popular. Early on, Leo and Jerold Camarillo did some, and Walt Woodard has been doing them forever. Allan Bach has put on roping schools for a long time. Now it seems like everyone who has a school does really well with it. The people are coming to learn.

When I started roping, the event organizers hadn't figured out how to let everybody rope and have a fair chance in the competition. Even I went through a period then where I wasn't good enough to go into the PRCA, but I was better than everyone else at many of the ropings. I was trying to make a living by going to jackpots and amateur rodeos, but I reached a point in the late '70s when the organizers sometimes wouldn't let me rope. I had to move into PRCA competition. Back then, you either had to make it or quit.

Denny Gentry came along with the USTRC and revived the sport of jackpot roping. There had always been team roping at rodeos and amateur rodeos, but weekly jackpots, where you could make good money, the weekly things, were basically nonexistent. Now anyone at any level of skill can make money roping.

The *Western Horseman*, established in 1936, is the world's leading horse publication.
For subscription information: 800-877-5278. To order other *Western Horseman* books: 800-874-6774.
*Western Horseman*, Box 7980, Colorado Springs, CO 80933-7980. Web-site: www.westernhorseman.com.

# Books Published by Western Horseman Inc.

**BACON & BEANS** by Stella Hughes
144 pages and 200-plus recipes for delicious western chow.

**BARREL RACING** by Sharon Camarillo
144 pages and 200 photographs. Tells how to train and compete successfully.

**CALF ROPING** by Roy Cooper
144 pages and 280 photographs covering roping and tying.

**CUTTING** by Leon Harrel
144 pages and 200 photographs. Complete guide on this popular sport.

**FIRST HORSE** by Fran Devereux Smith
176 pages, 160 black-and-white photos, about 40 illustrations. Step-by-step information for the first-time horse owner and/or novice rider.

**HEALTH PROBLEMS** by Robert M. Miller, D.V.M.
144 pages on management, illness and injuries, lameness, mares and foals, and more.

**HORSEMAN'S SCRAPBOOK** by Randy Steffen
144 pages and 250 illustrations. A collection of handy hints.

**IMPRINT TRAINING** by Robert M. Miller, D.V.M.
144 pages and 250 photographs. Learn to "program" newborn foals.

**LEGENDS** by Diane C. Simmons
168 pages and 214 photographs. Barbra B, Bert, Chicaro Bill, Cowboy P-12, Depth Charge (TB), Doc Bar, Go Man Go, Hard Twist, Hollywood Gold, Joe Hancock, Joe Reed P-3, Joe Reed II, King P-234, King Fritz, Leo, Peppy, Plaudit, Poco Bueno, Poco Tivio, Queenie, Quick M Silver, Shue Fly, Star Duster, Three Bars (TB), Top Deck (TB), and Wimpy P-1.

**LEGENDS 2** by Jim Goodhue, Frank Holmes, Phil Livingston, Diane C. Simmons
192 pages and 224 photographs. Clabber, Driftwood, Easy Jet, Grey Badger II, Jessie James, Jet Deck, Joe Bailey P-4 (Gonzales), Joe Bailey (Weatherford), King's Pistol, Lena's Bar, Lightning Bar, Lucky Blanton, Midnight, Midnight Jr, Moon Deck, My Texas Dandy, Oklahoma Star, Oklahoma Star Jr., Peter McCue, Rocket Bar (TB), Skipper W, Sugar Bars, and Traveler.

**LEGENDS 3** by Jim Goodhue, Frank Holmes, Diane Ciarloni, Kim Guenther, Larry Thornton, Betsy Lynch
208 pages and 196 photographs. Flying Bob, Hollywood Jac 86, Jackstraw (TB), Maddon's Bright Eyes, Mr Gun Smoke, Old Sorrel, Piggin String (TB), Poco Lena, Poco Pine, Poco Dell, Question Mark, Quo Vadis, Royal King, Showdown, Steel Dust, and Two Eyed Jack.

**PROBLEM-SOLVING** by Marty Marten
248 pages and over 250 photos and illustrations. How to develop a willing partnership between horse and human to handle trailer-loading, hard-to-catch, barn-sour, spooking, water-crossing, herd-bound, and pull-back problems.

**NATURAL HORSE-MAN-SHIP** by Pat Parelli
224 pages and 275 photographs. Parelli's six keys to a natural horse-human relationship.

**REINING, Completely Revised** by Al Dunning
216 pages and over 300 photographs showing how to train horses for this exciting event.

**ROOFS AND RAILS** by Gavin Ehringer
144 pages, 128 black-and-white photographs plus drawings, charts, and floor plans. How to plan and build your ideal horse facility.

**STARTING COLTS** by Mike Kevil
168 pages and 400 photographs. Step-by-step process in starting colts.

**THE HANK WIESCAMP STORY** by Frank Holmes
208 pages and over 260 photographs. The biography of the legendary breeder of Quarter Horses, Appaloosas, and Paints.

**TEAM PENNING** by Phil Livingston
144 pages and 200 photographs. How to compete in this popular family sport.

**TEAM ROPING WITH JAKE AND CLAY**
by Fran Devereux Smith
224 pages and over 200 photographs and illustrations. Learn about fast times from champions Jake Barnes and Clay O'Brien Cooper. Solid information about handling a rope, roping dummies, and heading and heeling for practice and in competition. Also sound advice about rope horses, roping steers, gear, and horsemanship.

**WELL-SHOD** by Don Baskins
160 pages, 300 black-and-white photos and illustrations. A horseshoeing guide for owners and farriers. The easy-to-read text, illustrations, and photos show step-by-step how to trim and shoe a horse for a variety of uses. Special attention is paid to corrective shoeing techniques for horses with various foot and leg problems.

**WESTERN HORSEMANSHIP** by Richard Shrake
144 pages and 150 photographs. Complete guide to riding western horses.

**WESTERN TRAINING** by Jack Brainard
With Peter Phinny. 136 pages. Stresses the foundation for western training.